C000043731

Praise for *Modern Witchcraft with T...*

"A brilliant and accessible book for the modern witch who v... their relationship with the theoi, daimones, and heroes of A... ...book is extremely well researched, drawing on and referencing historical primary sources without trying to be a historical reconstruction of times past...The book will prove to you through direct experience that the gods of Greece aren't merely dust-covered archaic statues of stories lost to the mists of time, but rather that they are still as alive, powerful, and thriving as they were in ancient and classical times."

—Mat Auryn, bestselling author of *Psychic Witch* and *Mastering Magick*

"This book gives you a solid basis and a wonderfully researched view on incorporating Greek god workings into your magical practices...It was a bewitching and captivating read!"

—Jen Sankey, author of the forthcoming *Enchanted Forest Felines*
and *Stardust Wanderer* tarot decks

"An excellent resource for Witches, Wiccans, and Pagans looking for information about the Greek deities beyond the twelve Olympians. Through history, mythology, and knowledge from modern devotees, Jason and Astrea look beyond the traditional image of the Greek gods and goddesses formed through myth to present a fuller picture of how the ancients understood them and how we can work with them today."

—Gwyn, blogger and host of *3 Pagans and a Cat* podcast

"The research that went into this work is evident from the very beginning. Jason Mankey and Astrea Taylor take turns diving into many aspects of working with a beloved pantheon. They disseminate this information in an accessible and enlightening manner, which leads a practitioner forward in their education of the Greek gods...This is a text that any practitioner will benefit from revisiting time and again."

—Vincent Higginbotham, author of *How Witchcraft Saved My Life*
and *Thrifty Witchery*

"An indispensable work for anyone looking to practice with these deities."

—Lilith Dorsey, author of *Water Magic*

"This book is a necessity for those interested in the lore of the Greek pantheon, as well as how contemporary pagans work with these gods and beings. The writing is lively and joyful. Buy this book. Read this book. Refer to this book often."

—Melissa F. Lavin, PhD, associate professor of sociology,
State University of New York at Oneonta

"Rigorously researched and sumptuous in detail, *Modern Witchcraft with the Greek Gods* offers fresh insights with each reading. Mankey and Taylor have meticulously crafted an authoritative text tempered with an abiding love and deep respect for their subject that shimmers on each page."

—Martha Kirby Capo, author of *Thrifty Witchery*

"Rather than a ham-handed appropriation, this is a thoughtful approach that feels like it takes the wishes of the gods themselves into consideration...*Modern Witchcraft with the Greek Gods* is a book that is destined to fall open to favorite pages, to become worn with use and stained from spell-craft."

—Terence P Ward, temple priest in the Hellenic reconstructionist group
Temenos Oikidios, and author of *Empty Cauldrons*

MODERN
WITCHCRAFT
WITH THE
GREEK
GODS

ABOUT THE AUTHORS

Jason Mankey is a third-degree Gardnerian High Priest and helps run two Witchcraft covens in the San Francisco Bay Area with his wife, Ari. He is a popular speaker at Pagan and Witchcraft events across North America and Great Britain and has been recognized by his peers as an authority on the Horned God, Wiccan history, and occult influences in rock and roll. You can follow him on Instagram and Twitter @panmankey. Jason is the author of several books, including *The Witch's Book of Spellcraft, The Horned God of the Witches,* and *Transformative Witchcraft.* Author photo by Tymn Urban.

Astrea Taylor is an eclectic pagan witch with over two and a half decades of experience in the witching world. She's the author of *Air Magic* and *Intuitive Witchcraft: How to Use Intuition to Elevate Your Craft.* She has a bachelor's degree in science from Antioch College and a master's degree in environmental sciences from Wright State University, which inform her scientific takes on spirituality. In her spare time, she presents workshops and rituals online and at festivals across the country, and occasionally she blogs as *Starlight Witch* on Patheos Pagan. Find her on Instagram @astrea taylor, on Facebook at *Astrea Taylor, Author,* and on Twitter @AstreaWrites. Author photo by Cody Rowlands.

HISTORY, INSIGHTS &
MAGICKAL PRACTICE

MODERN
WITCHCRAFT
WITH THE
GREEK
GODS

JASON MANKEY

ASTREA TAYLOR

Llewellyn Publications
Woodbury, Minnesota

First Edition
First Printing, 2022

Cover design by Shannon McKuhen
Interior art by the Llewellyn Art Department

Llewellyn Publications is a registered trademark of Llewellyn Worldwide Ltd.

Library of Congress Cataloging-in-Publication Data (Pending)
ISBN: 978-0-7387-6876-2

Llewellyn Publications
A Division of Llewellyn Worldwide Ltd.
2143 Wooddale Drive
Woodbury, MN 55125-2989
www.llewellyn.com

Printed in the United States of America

OTHER BOOKS BY JASON MANKEY

The Witch's Book of Spellcraft
(cowritten with Matt Cavalli, Amanda Lynn & Ari Mankey, Llewellyn, 2022)

The Horned God of the Witches
(Llewellyn, 2021)

Llewellyn's Little Book of Yule
(Llewellyn, 2020)

Witch's Wheel of the Year
(Llewellyn, 2019)

Transformative Witchcraft
(Llewellyn, 2019)

The Witch's Altar
(cowritten with Laura Tempest Zakroff, Llewellyn, 2018)

The Witch's Book of Shadows
(Llewellyn, 2017)

The Witch's Athame
(Llewellyn, 2016)

OTHER BOOKS BY ASTREA TAYLOR

Air Magic
(Llewellyn, 2021)

Intuitive Witchcraft
(Llewellyn, 2020)

Belle Dame Sans Merci
(2017)

House of Transformation
(2015)

I remember entering into the Greek myths as if I had returned to my true homeland.
—Margot Adler, *Drawing Down the Moon*

Gods and goddesses never really die, they just go underground.
—Christine Downing, *The Goddess: Mythological Images of the Feminine*

*We dedicate this book to the gods of the Greeks,
who have captured our hearts, minds, and spirits.*

CONTENTS

Guest Passages

DISCLAIMER & NOTICES

Witchcraft and magick are not always safe practices. It's important to use caution when dealing with fire and candles, and never leave a burning candle unattended. Trance mindsets are great in the right situations, but not while operating heavy machinery or using sharp objects. Please ensure that whatever you burn isn't harmful to you or your animals. Research herbal contraindications with any medicines or other herbs you're taking. Be cautious when using essential oils: don't ingest them and don't use them undiluted on your skin. If you're not sure if you're allergic to an herb, do a skin test before using it as intended. If irritation or an allergic reaction occurs, stop using it. Consult a doctor, therapist, or another health care provider if you have any concerns. While magick is quite useful, specific results are never guaranteed due to the multitude of unique circumstances we all have, including the will of the gods and the amount of work we put into our goals in the magickal and mundane worlds.

Whenever possible, we retained the guest passage authors' original content, but some homogenization occurred. Spellings and capitalizations were modified to be consistent with those used in the majority of this book.

Introduction: The Allure of the Greek Gods

by Astrea Taylor

Why would a modern Witch choose to work with the Greek gods? After all, there are so many other gods and pantheons out there. Some of them have better reputations. You may have ancestral connections with other deities, or they could be closer to your current home.

If you've ever been called by a Greek deity, you know there's a powerful allure. There's something about them that draws you in and relates to you on a very personal level. I believe this is because the Greek gods are still very much alive today and they're all around us.

Speaking from personal experience, the Greek gods changed the course of my life forever. At the early age of eight, I had an ecstatic experience while reading about the Greek gods. I picked up my mother's copy of *Mythology* by Edith Hamilton and started reading. I remember that I could see through the dining room window that dusk was coloring the skies indigo. A swooning sensation overcame me and filled my body with bliss as I read about Artemis, a goddess who raced through the wild woods, her pack of deer running alongside her. Electricity shot up every nerve in my body, and my mind felt as if it were glowing. This pleasant surge expanded until it extended outside of my body as well. Artemis felt so familiar to me, as if I had known her my entire life. I could almost feel my feet pounding over the rocky forest soil and a bow in my hand as we hunted together.

I had never experienced anything like those feelings before. They were bigger than I was, and bigger than everything I knew. My rational mind didn't understand the feelings, but a deep part of me knew the gods had stirred something within me that was primal and true. That's the moment I knew I was a Pagan—in this life, and perhaps in a past life as well. Over the next few nights, I repeated the same conditions to try to bring about those feelings again. I took the book to the dining room window at dusk, and I read about other gods and goddesses. It worked, though it wasn't as strong as the first time, and some deities had better effects than others. Looking back, I must have read the book thirty times— the more I learned, the more I wanted to learn.

My experience with the Greek gods was strikingly similar to how ancient people described a union with them, but it's not entirely unique. Many people say that they were called to them when they were young, and they felt similar awakening or ecstatic sensations. The Greek gods were known for their attractiveness, for producing ecstasy, and for initiating and maintaining a soul-level connection with people all over the world.

Years later, when I identified as a Witch, my love for the Greek gods seemed incongruous at first, mostly due to the sterilized versions of pagan history that are commonly circulated (including in Hamilton's *Mythology*). However, when I looked deeper into the ancient Greek culture, it was clear that magick was very much a part of their lives.

Ancient Witchcraft, Magick, and Power

Witchcraft and magickal concepts proliferated in the ancient world, especially in connection with pagan deities. Historians believe the vast majority of ancient Greeks used magickal practices with deity reverence in order to enhance their everyday lives.[1] This combination is made clear in the great reverence for Hekate, an older goddess of magick, liminality, and Witchcraft. When the old gods fought against the new ones, she allied with Zeus, the head of the new order of gods. After the old gods were defeated, the new gods all honored Hekate greatly, especially Zeus. He allowed her to retain her powers and rulership. In other words, the Greeks shifted into a new era of power and hierarchy while retaining Witchcraft and magick. It was unthinkable to win the war without the goddess of magick, and it was just as impossible to conceive of a future without her.

Magickal practices were pervasive in the ancient Greek world. The entire Greek region of Thessaly was associated with Witchcraft and Hekate. Plato, the Athenian philosopher (c. mid-400s BCE), believed in the magickal abilities of the witches and magicians.[2] Magick remained a ubiquitous force even in Roman times, when Pliny the Elder, the Roman states-

---

1. Fuller, "From Daimon to Demon," 7.

2. Luck, *Arcana Mundi*, 43, 150.

man and philosopher (c. 75 CE), was constantly afraid of being bound by a spell.[3] Magick was so popular that even the Olympian gods used it against each other.

However, some people (including some Hellenic Reconstructionists) believe there's no place for magick or Witchcraft with the Greek gods. They say it's excessively prideful to take matters into one's own hands, and magick is an act of defiance against the gods. Although Greek myths document the gods punishing people for being excessively prideful, it was never for Witchcraft or magick. One of the best-known ancient Greek stories of pride and punishment was the story of Icarus. His father created wax wings for him, which allowed him to fly through the air just like a god, or so he thought. As Icarus started to fly toward the sun, the heat melted his wings, causing him to fall into the sea and perish. His wings weren't magickal, though—they were a technological invention. The fault lay in his thinking that he was immortal and as powerful as a god, a belief that most Witches do not adhere to. Likewise, in Greek myth and fiction, there's no evidence of excessive pride on the part of Witches and magicians such as Circe, Calypso, Perseus, Aeetes, Medea, Agamede, and Simaetha. Numerous Greek historical records indicate that magick was considered commonplace. The only punishments associated with it were for the deadly magick of poison that led to murder.[4]

People have used the gods in their magick for millennia. The Greek Magical Papyri, or *Papyri Graecae Magicae (PGM)*, is a collection of several grimoires with spells, rituals, and curses that date from about 400 BCE to 200 CE. The *PGM* is still used by many witches and magicians today and is considered an important part of the Western Magickal Tradition that gave birth to the many strains of Modern Witchcraft. One researcher estimated that a whopping 85 percent of the spells in the *PGM* call upon at least one deity.[5] There isn't evidence of anyone who was punished or struck down by the Greek gods for calling upon them in a spell or ritual. If anything, magick was probably seen as one of the best ways to interact with the gods in order to make one's wishes known.

These days, a multitude of our current magickal practices come from ancient Greek magick, or they're very similar to it.[6] This includes the use of spells, rituals, cleansing, incense, music, an altered state of mind, magick circles, and incantations. There are records of the ancient Greeks working with celestial energies, herbs and correspondences,

---

3. Graf, *Magic in the Ancient World*, 1.

4. Collins, "Theoris of Lemnos and the Criminalization of Magic in Fourth-Century Athens," 477.

5. Björkland, "Invocation and Offerings as Structural Elements in the Love Spells in *Papyri Graecae Magicae*," 29–47.

6. Faraone and Obbink, *Magika Hiera*, 250.

cardinal directions, elements, wands, and chalices. They venerated their ancestors and their mighty dead, and some worked with spirits of the deceased in their magick, as well as *daimons*, intermediaries between people and the gods. They practiced divination so well that a prophecy often informed entire armies about the best courses of action. The Greeks practiced magick for love, health, blessings, protection, and healing. However, just as common were curses, bindings, and what we would call hexes. Ancient Greek practitioners made potions, amulets, weavings, and human figurines. With so many similarities to today's magickal practices, it's possible the Greek gods may already be present, whether we call upon them or not.

Most historians agree that ancient Greece shaped the world that followed, and some of the best parts of our society may have come from the Greeks. It's our opinion that the Greek gods were behind these improvements, and they continued to evolve alongside humanity into the modern era. Because the gods have changed again and again over time and location, it's clear to us that their magickal workings don't have to be relegated to the past, either. The Greek gods can be adapted to modern practices, just as they have for several millennia.

I experienced those early years of wonder and awe at the Greek gods a long time ago. Since then, my practice has evolved. In many ways, I grew up with them. Artemis guided my youth and my teenage years. I believe she shielded me from dangerous situations many times. When I immersed myself in my studies at college, Athena approached me. When I bought a house, Hestia warmed her way into my heart. Pan and Dionysus appeared at various points in my life to help me release limited mindsets and experience something greater. When I was ready to choose love over anxiety, Aphrodite sent waves of love into my heart. Over the decades, I've called upon the Greek gods in magick, from small spells to large rituals that aided me on my spiritual path and transformed my life.

So why might a modern Witch want to work with the Greek gods? Perhaps the greatest reason is that they're still here. They show up when we call upon them in rituals and spells. They want to interact with us, lend their power, and live on through our modern practices. With all the support and power they have to offer, the better question might be: why *wouldn't* someone want to work with them?

How to Read, Enjoy, and Use this Book

The majority of this book is about the Olympians and their more influential peers, which are covered in the first two sections of this book. Each god or goddess has a history section that summarizes their origins, their most important myths, how they were honored by the

Greeks, their evolutions beyond Greece, and their veneration in the modern era. These sections are summaries—they're quite limited compared to the amount of material that is available about them. Think of the history sections as starting points. If you feel called to do more research on them, we encourage you to do so. Entire books have been written about many of the gods and goddesses, and the bibliography contains the ones we recommend the most.

In addition to a historical section, each entry on the Olympians and other major deities also has a section with magickal activities, including spells, incantations, recipes, and/or rituals. We believe the variety of offerings reflects the numerous ways modern Witches interact with the gods and goddesses. Some prefer to invoke them in spells, which are more immediate than a ritual. Other Witches are more partial to calling upon them in ritual, which can be a more immersive experience. No matter which magickal methods you prefer, we believe that most people who read this book will find something that resonates with them and draws them closer to the mysteries of the gods.

Before invoking the gods for magick, we recommend that you do a bit of devotion to get to know them. When in doubt, treat them as you would a new friend. Just as you wouldn't expect someone you just met to do favors for you, the wise practitioner doesn't expect a strong relationship with the gods without becoming familiar with their energies first.

Each entry on the primary deities also includes insights from a modern practitioner.[7] We asked our friends who have worked extensively with a Greek deity to share their personal experiences. Sometimes more than one personal reflection is shared to provide a variety of perspectives.

We chose these personal insights to provide a more in-depth understanding of each god or goddess from a current perspective. Some contain personal *gnosis*, or wisdom gleaned from doing magickal work and learning what the god wants for them. Personal gnosis often gets a bad reputation these days, but the ancient Greeks practiced it as well with the knowledge that it was one person's interpretation. We hope these insights will assist you in understanding the gods and goddesses and possibly working with them on your own.

After the sections on the Olympians and other major deities, there is a section on other popular deities who generally called ancient Greece home. These gods were important in the ancient world and are also favored by modern Witches. This section features the general myth and history of each deity, and some entries have a modern reflection and/or a ritual as well.

---

7. The two exceptions are Ares and Hephaestus—more on that in those individual sections.

The last section of this book consists of entries of lesser-known Greek gods, suitably called "Other Notable Deities." We included as many deities as possible in an attempt to show the diversity of the ancient gods and the possibilities of whom you could work with in your magickal practice. However, these entries are short—it would be nearly impossible to incorporate all the Greek gods and goddesses into this book, as there were thousands of deities. We included those most often called upon in modern Witch circles. This section includes the primordial forces, the Titans, and some other Greek (and a few Roman) deities often honored by Witches.

A few Roman gods are mentioned in the last section of the book, and some of their holidays appear in Appendix I: Calendar of Ancient Holidays & Celebrations. Although this isn't a book about the gods of Rome, we included short entries of those deities and holidays that weren't mentioned in the earlier history sections for a few reasons. The first is that there simply isn't a lot of information about the Greek holiday calendar, and it's entirely probable that not all the Greek holidays have been preserved over time. The wealth of information about the Roman holidays is fascinating and provides a clue to how the Greeks might have lived. Second, it's important to note how influential the Roman gods were on the Western world. Their reach extended to the north and far beyond that of Greece. While the Roman colonization of these lands was not condonable, they left spiritual and religious remnants at these locations that deeply affected the people who lived in those regions. Due to this connection, centuries later, the Roman gods pervaded the myths and literature far more than the Greek ones did. Lastly, these deities and holidays were included because some of them are relevant to some modern Witches. The deities are called upon in ritual, and the holidays are celebrated, sometimes along with the other holidays that comprise the Wheel of the Year.

The final two appendixes describe the classical spell structure and the Greek-style ritual structure. These are general outlines for honoring the Greek gods in ways similar to what was practiced in ancient Greece. We recommend that you modify them for whatever purposes you wish. How you work your magick is entirely up to you, but we thought it would be useful to include them.

Jason Mankey and I are both devotees of the Greek gods, and have been for quite some time. We each have a rich solitary practice, but our backgrounds are quite different. Jason is a third-degree Gardnerian High Priest who runs a traditional coven and an eclectic Wiccan coven with his wife, Ari. I am an intuitive Witch and eclectic Pagan who leads moon circle rituals and assists a few other nontraditional groups. You may see these differences reflected in our passages, but we feel they add to the varied nature of how modern people relate to the Greek gods. For simplicity's sake and for reference, we noted who was writing each passage in the book.

We hope you enjoy reading about the Greek gods, their evolutions, and the perspectives of modern Pagans and Witches in this book. We encourage you to approach whichever deities appeal to you and integrate them into your magickal practices as you see fit.

A Few Notes about This Book

This book was written to be a guide for the modern Witch who wants to work with the Greek gods. It contains some historical information, cultural context, modern interpretations, and suggested magickal practices. Researching this book has been a tremendous joy. It's clear that the Greek gods have been around since the beginning of time in one form or another, and they're still here. However, some complicated matters came up while researching this book.

This is not a book for Hellenic (Greek) Reconstructionists. While attempting to recreate the past in the modern era is a wonderful experience for some people, and we have great respect for the past, the Greek gods have been worshipped in a variety of ways and in numerous places. That history goes far beyond ancient Athens and Sparta into the Roman Empire, nineteenth-century English poets, and the current era. The Greek gods are well traveled, and this book reflects that. So in these pages, we don't try to recreate the past, but rather we place the gods in the present.

Another issue that arose was the need to relay a bit about historical Greek culture and how the Greeks viewed the deities to put them more in context. Although it's hard to summarize Greek spiritual life in a few sentences, the ancient Greeks generally lived in a world immersed in spirits and gods who were present in every activity and location. *Religion* was not a word that existed at the time, but the presence of the gods pervaded their lives and provided a constant spiritual connection. The Greeks believed in many powerful gods who were neither good nor evil but who had their own self-interests, strengths, weaknesses, and sets of morals, which were sometimes in conflict with those of each other and humanity.

Belief in the gods was not a concerning matter to most Greeks—the gods simply were, and the observance of them was more an attitude about life or a way of life. The gods interacted in meaningful ways with people in their daily lives, rituals, and festivals. Celebrations and group rituals encouraged community engagement and an experience of something greater than oneself. These interactions often affirmed the roles in Greek culture, making the gods a kind of community enforcer. However, the gods weren't viewed the same way by all Greek people, and they weren't all honored in any given city. Greek cities were eclectic in nature, with citizens preferring some deities over others and some-times even changing whom they counted among the twelve Olympians.

Some of the gods were often seen as two sides of the same coin, which is why, for example, Zeus can both give and destroy. Active devotion with offerings was considered the best way to gain the gods' favor, and people made offerings to multiple gods several times a day. They could be invoked aloud or in writing due to the belief that the gods didn't always understand humans and couldn't read minds. Some people believed it was important to discuss your history with the gods because they were so timeless that they sometimes needed reminding of who their supplicants were.

THE ROLE OF THE GODS IN THE LIVES OF THE ANCIENT GREEKS

If you lived in ancient Greece in the country, your day might start with you noticing the presence of Hestia, the hearth (goddess), and depending on your role, you might add more oil to her flame. As you got dressed, you'd give thanks to Athena for helping make such a finely woven garment. Passing through the door to your home, you'd say a prayer to Hekate and Zeus. Then you'd walk to the edge of the property and pause at a *herm*, a tall stone pillar guarded by Hermes. You might hope Hermes would deliver news from a loved one who had recently gone to the temple of Asclepius seeking healing of a wound. You'd see that Helios, the sun, hadn't driven his cart too far across the skies yet, and the red blush of Eos, dawn, was still present in the sky. You'd look out at your crops and praise Gaia and Demeter for the height of the corn before saying a prayer for Zeus in his role as the thunder-bringer to provide much-needed rain and fertility for the crops.

You might see your neighbor's children playing like Artemis and Apollo, and have fond memories of your youth. Thoughts might turn to whether the people in your household would have any more children, as was the societal expecta-tion. You might hope for a blessing from Hera, goddess of marriage, and Arte-mis, goddess of childbirth, before Ares incited another war.

A warm wind might blow by, and you'd thank Zephyr, god of the west wind, and interpret it as a sign from Zeus that all was well. You'd think of the next festival with relish—it was always just a few weeks away. You'd hope that the dramatic plays happening soon would bring the gods to life again, and the traveling poets who sang of the great heroes and gods would be there too.

This degree of divine saturation of all aspects of life might seem extreme, but it's important to note that the ancient Greeks had a much different mindset. They saw the world as the ever-unfolding presence of the gods and the Fates. To them, life was full of moments and images that revealed those divine connections.[8]

꙰꙰꙰꙰꙰꙰꙰

The next issue that deserves attention is the difference between myth and cultural/religious practices, which were often quite different. These days, many people take myth literally, but the Greeks didn't believe myth was the ultimate truth—rather, myths were seen as folkloric stories or were used in dramatic parts of rituals.[9] Myths of the gods were not the same across Greece. In some regions, independent versions evolved. For some of the gods, this evolution was used to add narratives to new political developments. Some scholars believe the stories about Zeus's sexual notoriety came about after a city with different ruling gods was conquered. The Greek conquerors changed the vanquished god's name to Zeus, and Zeus even took on some of the old god's myths. The city goddess retained her name and powers, but her partner became Zeus. By recreating the myths of a defeated city, the Olympian hierarchy was reinforced. It promoted the Olympian order and rules (from Zeus) and affirmed the patrilineal aspects that the Greeks found important.

Another important issue to touch upon is the syncretization of the gods: in other words, combining gods from different cultures with no distinction. In the ancient world, syncretism was extremely common. The Greek philosopher Herodotus used the concept of syncretization in the fifth century BCE to explain the existence of other religions and justify the power of the Greek gods. He noted correlations between Egyptian and Greek gods and added other deities' names to the Greek gods' names, seemingly as epithets, such as Zeus Amon.

Alexander the Great, the Greek-Macedonian king, syncretized freely as well. In his campaign in the fourth century BCE, he ordered the construction of numerous syncretic temples throughout the Mediterranean, Southern Europe, the Middle East, Africa, and India. He blended the Greek deities with numerous local gods, which demonstrates the Greek belief in the flexibility of the gods to adapt to new places and take on new names and aspects. This demonstrates that the gods' power did not wane or cease once they left Greece—if anything, it grew. The Romans syncretized by allowing the Greek gods to

---

8. Foucault, *The History of Sexuality, Vol. 2: The Use of Pleasure*, 78–79.

9. Burkert, *Greek Religion*, 8–9.

inspire the Roman religion, and then by syncretizing Roman gods with the Celtic and Germanic deities in the lands they colonized. Early Christians and Hellenic Jews also syncretized their beliefs with the Greek gods, especially the mystery religion aspects so common in the ancient Greek world.[10]

While historical syncretization was rampant, we want to make it clear that this book does not syncretize Greek gods with non-Greek deities, spirits, or saints. For example, we would not consider the Egyptian god Amon's myth or qualities in the passage about Zeus. Our view is that the gods from non-Greek cultures are distinctly different because the cultures they arose from are not the same. However, we do mention historical syncretism to show how the Greek deities evolved over time.

The definitions of magick and Witchcraft can be hazy, especially when applied to events, stories, and beliefs from thousands of years ago. Even today, the words *Witchcraft* and *magick* mean different things to each practitioner. Most people agree that Witchcraft and magick are more than devotion, invocation, incense, and offerings. Ancient Greek paganism is most known for this kind of interaction with the gods, but the Greeks also engaged in magickal activities. In the magickal activity portions of this book, we take some inspiration from the past, but we also use modern ideas to fully round out the possibilities and give the reader more options.

Another issue we encountered while writing this book was limited information for some deities, such as Hestia. Most of the ancient records were written by wealthy men who lived in two of the largest cities, Athens and Sparta. These people wrote the majority of the poems, myths, philosophy, art, and commentary. While these are good primary sources for some aspects, these writers didn't take into account the lives and perspectives of people who were poor or working-class, women, slaves, and people who lived in the country. To bridge this gap, we used secondary sources (interpretations of primary sources) as well as perspectives from sociologists, historians, anthropologists, and philosophers who made educated guesses about archaeology, art, secondary records, and extrapolations. These give additional insight into ancient Greek culture and its spiritual practices.

The last factor to mention is that ancient Greek culture was not a utopia for all of its people. As is true today, the upper class enjoyed far more benefits than the middle and lower classes. Some areas of Greece were misogynous, with firm gender role expectations. The Greeks colonized and conquered cities throughout the Mediterranean region, Europe, the Middle East, Africa, and India, and sometimes people from those lands were

10. Faraone and Obbink, *Magika Hiera*, 250–51.

captured and enslaved to work for the state or the wealthy. Other abhorrences included rape, infanticide, and, rarely, human sacrifice.

One could look at the worst parts of ancient Greece and want to dismiss it all; however, its situation was not unique. Several other cultures from the ancient world were similar both before and after the Greek region rose to prominence. Moreover, many of the same problems still exist in the world today in one way or another. Some of these issues were only recently overturned or enacted in the United States, including the abolition of most forms of slavery in 1865, the right of women to vote in 1920, and the Voting Rights Act of 1965. Even with these progressive measures, institutional inequality still exists, and slave labor still produces many commonly used goods.

The goal of this book is not to romanticize ancient Greek culture or discuss its complicated faults. We believe it's important to acknowledge these shortcomings but not use them in our practices in the modern era. We can take part in the evolutionary aspect of the gods without condoning the practices of ancient people.

Even though there certainly were bad aspects of ancient Greek culture, there were also many inspiring things about it too. Their community rituals were full of revelry, dancing, music, and feasts. The mysteries gave people spiritual depth. Personal magick was common to most people. Art and design developed into meaningful works that fostered a greater love of the gods. Many of the gods were celebrated for their complex gender roles and identities, and ancient Greek games encouraged athletic competition, beauty, and skill.

Even amid plagues, wars, droughts, and other challenges and limitations, the ancient Greeks found a way to live immensely spiritual lives and celebrate the gods who inspired them in every moment. Everything I've learned from researching this book boils down to that point. No matter what era we live in, we can cultivate magickal lives that satisfy our souls to their very core. We sincerely hope this book assists you in that worthy endeavor.

A Brief History of the Greek Gods
by Jason Mankey

In 2014, my wife, Ari, and I visited the United Kingdom for the first time. One of those days entailed waking up at 3:00 a.m. and hiking through still-slumbering London to catch a tour bus headed for Stonehenge and the English city of Bath. Welcoming the sun while standing among the stones at Stonehenge is an experience we will never forget. There's certainly energy at England's best-known Neolithic site, but as modern Witches, it didn't feel familiar to us.

After stopping for breakfast, we arrived in Bath, site of the most famous Roman baths outside of Rome, which were built there in the first century CE. Our tour guide told us we'd have only two hours in Bath, which he assured us was plenty of time to visit the ancient baths and the museum that houses the artifacts from Aquae Sulis, the Roman town that grew up around the baths. Aquae Sulis gets its name from Sulis, the local Celtic goddess of healing and sacred waters who was honored at the hot spring that the Romans built their baths upon. Aquae Sulis literally means "waters of Sulis."

Sulis might not be a goddess you've heard of, and her name was certainly new to us, but the Romans equated her with their Minerva, who was known as Athena in Greece. The temple built at Aquae Sulis was dedicated to Sulis-Minerva, as the Romans viewed both goddesses as the same being. The Roman baths are impressive, but they pale in comparison to the artifacts inside the museum. While the energy of Stonehenge had felt unfamiliar to us, the energy at Bath was familiar. Minerva is a goddess who's well known to the two of us—a statue of her watches over our living room—but she wasn't the only familiar face in the remains of Aquae Sulis.

Standing alongside a variety of Celtic deities whose names have been lost to history were gods we call to by name in our home. There was winged Mercury, the Greek Hermes, standing proudly with his caduceus (serpent-entwined staff), clearly recognizable to those who know the myths of the ancient Greeks. Next to him and holding a club the size of a small person was Hercules, or Heracles in Greek, a deity as familiar to us as the sun in the sky. The most powerful moment for us at Bath was seeing an image of Bacchus, known as Dionysus to the Greeks, beckoning his followers to come to him with his ivy-covered thyrsus (staff or wand).

The finer details on these carvings faded long ago, victims of time and Christian vandalism, but the iconography denoting the gods of Olympus is unmistakable to those who honor them. Unlike at Stonehenge, where we had simply stood and marveled, at Bath we had the urge to kneel on the ground and worship. All around us were gods we honored on a near-daily basis. The people at Aquae Sulis worshipped the same gods we worship today. It was a powerful moment, and our tour guide was wrong—we most certainly required more than two hours in Bath. This was an issue we wouldn't rectify until we made a second trip to Bath two years later.

Even in the ancient world the Greek gods were never confined to just Greece, and today their images adorn buildings on continents that their first worshippers didn't even know existed. The names of the gods of Olympus have been on the lips of human beings for over 3,500 years, something that's unlikely to change soon, or maybe even ever. While the popularity of Zeus and his extended family has waxed and waned over the centuries, it has remained ever-present.

When most of us think about the Greek gods, we think of mythology, especially the stories of the gods and their earthly offspring, as told in anthologies such as *Bulfinch's Mythology*. Thomas Bulfinch (1796–1867) and the storytellers who came after him make the attributes of the Greek gods appear clear and unambiguous. Aphrodite was just the goddess of love and beauty, for instance, with no mention of her waving a spear on the back of Ares's chariot or appearing with battle armor on the ring of Julius Caesar.[11] In reality, the Greek gods were complicated, and their attributes often varied from place to place.

The Greek gods also adopted various guises as they traveled across the ancient world. Local deities became equated with figures such as Zeus and Hermes, and later, the Romans adopted the myths of the Greeks and applied them to their native deities. Despite them traveling throughout Europe, Asia, and Africa, much about the gods remained Greek. Though not all of the gods who called Mount Olympus home were born in Greece, their

---

11. Hughes, *Venus & Aphrodite: History of a Goddess*, 113.

followers came of age there, and to this day it's hard to imagine figures such as Artemis and Poseidon without seeing them in a way similar to how those in Athens saw them 2,600 years ago.

This book is designed for Witches who want to know more about the deities of Olympus in both the Classical period and today. While it has a lot of history in it, it's not an academic work and does not claim to be the final word on the Greek gods. It's also not a book on Greek devotional polytheism or an attempt to recreate the religion of the Greeks from the year 400 BCE. This book is for people looking to connect with the deities we cherish in the here and now. However, knowing where the Olympians came from and how their worship spread from the Mediterranean Sea to the shores of the Indian Ocean, to the British Isles, and then across the Atlantic Ocean, is an illuminating journey.

In recent years, some individuals have attempted to place the Greek gods in a gilded cage and restrict their worship on the basis of ethnicity. The Greek gods have never been limited in such a way. While we have respect for those trying to revive the religious traditions of classical Greece, the Greek gods have traveled far and wide over the last 3,500 years and have never been limited to just one geographic locale. In fact, some of the Greek gods have origins that lie far from the Greek mainland.

Ancient Origins Through the Mycenaean Period

There are many ways to tell the story of how the gods of the Greeks spread across the earth. But instead of beginning our tale in the usual spot, Greece, we've chosen to start in the heart of Eurasia, in the present-day country of Ukraine (and surrounding environs). There, starting about 6,000 years ago, a group of people we today call Indo-Europeans began spreading out across Europe and Asia. The Indo-Europeans were not a racial group, but rather a cultural group. They lived primarily as herders of cattle, which necessitated their need to travel.

The Indo-Europeans are of primary importance because they spread their language and culture from the Indian Ocean to the Atlantic Ocean and most points in between. The language this book was written in, English, has Indo-European roots, as do Armenian, Phrygian, Greek, Gallic, Italian, Balkan, and German.[12] Not only do these languages all share a linguistic heritage, but the original deities of these cultures are also related due to the Indo-European influence. The mightiest of the Greek gods, Zeus, was born on the steppes of Ukraine.

---

12. West, *Indo-European Poetry and Myth*, 6.

The earliest version of Zeus bears little resemblance to the god we know today. We probably wouldn't have even recognized him six thousand years ago. He certainly wouldn't have been dressed in a Greek toga, but even then he was a sky god and the bringer of thunder and lightning. If that sounds similar to the god Thor, there's a good reason for this. Thor was born on those same Ukrainian prairies as Zeus. As the Indo-Europeans spread across the continent, they shared their sky god with the people they met, and either this proto-Zeus was absorbed into existing pantheons or it replaced other local deities.

Not all of the Greek gods come from the Indo-Europeans. When the Indo-Europeans first arrived in Greece, they found a land and dozens of islands that were already inhabited. The Indo-European gods found their footing in the rocky cliffs of Greece and were soon worshipped next to the deities who already inhabited that land. When did this occur exactly? No one is completely sure, and there's debate over whether the Indo-Europeans acted as invaders or simply assimilated to the land we know today as Greece.

Indo-European deities were generally goddesses and gods of things that can be seen. More abstract ideas do not seem to be a part of their pantheon, as reconstructed by linguists. The sky and the storms that roll through it are easily seen and experienced. The sun and moon are other examples of clearly visible things that were honored as deities. As herders who relied on easily accessible sources of fresh water, the Indo-Europeans honored river deities. The ground they walked on and relied upon for nearly everything was another form of deity, generally worshipped as an earth mother.

If you survey many of the cultures influenced by the Indo-Europeans, you will see several similar types of gods. The Celts, Norse, and Greeks all have deities representative of the forces honored by the Indo Europeans. Some of these deities would end up as secondary figures in their respective pantheons, but they would live on in myth and in smaller dedicated groups. The Indo-Europeans who lived a nomadic lifestyle were very much in tune with the rising and setting of the sun. It was such a specific event to them that they honored a deity of the dawn. In the Greek pantheon, this once-major figure was reduced to a minor one: Eos, goddess of the dawn. (Eos means dawn, and it's also the source of the Saxon goddess that the Christian holiday of Easter was named after, Eostre.)

How many of the major Greek gods have origins in Indo-European culture? It's possible that Zeus might be the only one to have such a truly ancient pedigree, but there are hints that at least some of the other Olympians absorbed or retained some of the Indo-European influence. In Homer's *Iliad* (written down somewhere between 700 and 800 BCE), the goddess Hera is consistently referred to as "cow faced."[13] For some of us today,

---

13. West, *Indo-European Poetry and Myth*, 185.

"cow faced" is an insult, but for a people who relied on cattle for their very survival, this was probably a compliment.

One of the few consistent myths that has been teased from what remains of the Indo-Europeans is the idea of union between land and sky. In the *Iliad*, the coupling of Hera and Zeus brings new growth to the earth in a way that would have been understood by the Indo-Europeans:

> So speaking, the son of Cronus, caught his wife in his arms. There
> underneath them the divine earth broke into young, fresh
> grass, and into dewy clover, crocus and hyacinth
> so thick and soft it held the hard ground deep away from them.
> There they lay down together and drew about them a golden
> wonderful cloud, and from it the glimmering dew descended.[14]

Hera was not Zeus's only partner. The union of sky god and a mother goddess was also articulated in some of his other couplings. The coupling of Zeus and Demeter, who has the word *mother* in her very name,[15] was also accorded a special place among many Greeks. The poet Hesiod (who lived between 750 and 650 BCE) wrote of their union:

> Pray to Zeus of the Earth and pure Demeter
> for Demeter's holy grain to ripen heavy,
> at the beginning of ploughing.[16]

The end result of Zeus and Demeter's union was not limited to crops—it also produced the goddess Persephone, she of the spring and, later, the dead. The Thracian goddess Semele is better known today as the mortal woman who was the mother of the god Dionysus, but she, too, was once a mother goddess, and the Thracians were also influenced by the Indo-Europeans.[17] Both Persephone and Dionysus were deities of growth and vegetation, the end result of the joining of sky and earth.

While Zeus and possibly other deities have their origins far from the Mediterranean Sea, the Greek gods are still essentially Greek. They came of age on the islands and mountains of Greece, but before the names of Poseidon, Artemis, and Athena were spoken upon the lips of the Greeks, it's worth taking a moment to briefly explore the first great culture that we might consider Greek: the Minoans.

---

14. Homer, *The Iliad of Homer*, translated by Richard Lattimore, 303. The line spacing here is identical to the original.

15. West, *Indo-European Poetry and Myth*, 176.

16. West, *Indo-European Poetry and Myth*, 182.

17. West, *Indo-European Poetry and Myth*, 175.

The Minoan civilization is named after the legendary King Minos and thrived for nearly 1,500 years, lasting from 2700 BCE to 1100 BCE (give or take a hundred years on either side, depending on whom you ask).[18] The heart of the Minoan civilization was Crete, the largest of the Greek islands located about a hundred miles from the mainland. At the height their influence, the Minoans established colonies on other islands and most certainly came into contact with people on the Greek mainland (along with people who lived much farther away, such as the Egyptians).

Today, the Minoans are probably best known for the frescoes that decorated the palace at Knossos, which was first excavated by the Englishman Sir Arthur Evans (1843–1907) at the close of the nineteenth century. Evans, who was wrong about a great many things about Knossos, believed that the palace he was excavating had been built by Minos himself (hence the name Minoan for the civilization, coined by Evans). Crete, and the city of Knossos specifically, play a large role in Greek mythology. This island was the home of not just the Minotaur, but also the inventor Daedalus and his son Icarus, who flew too close to the sun and drowned in the sea.

Despite the presence of the Minoans in Greek mythology, the Greek gods did not reside in Knossos at the height of their civilization. On a visit to Knossos (and the accompanying museum in Heraklion), I saw the religious implements and art of the Minoans up close. There were beautiful frescoes featuring dolphins, distinguished ladies, and acrobats leaping over a bull, but no trace of Zeus or Aphrodite.

Other archaeological remains shed some insight on Minoan religion. Goddess figures holding snakes (often called the Minoan snake goddess) hint at snake veneration in ancient Crete. The double-sided ax known as a labrys, worn by many women today as a symbol of empowerment, was sacred to the goddesses at Knossos whose names have been lost to history. Rhytons (ceremonial drinking vessels) in the form of a bull's head suggest that bulls were an important part of religious life at Knossos. None of these things have much to do with the gods of Olympus, though Crete's bull worship might have given birth to legends of the Minotaur, and gods such as Zeus and Poseidon were known to take the form of a bull when visiting Earth.

Even if the great gods weren't born in Crete, the ancient Greeks seemed to realize that there was something important about the ancient Minoan civilization. In later centuries, it would be said that Zeus himself was born on Crete. Psychro Cave in eastern Crete is where Zeus was allegedly born, and it's a popular tourist destination today. It's impressive enough that you do wonder if Zeus could have possibly been born there.

---

18. Tzorakis, *Knossos: A New Guide to the Palace of Knossos*, 16.

For many Modern Witches, the influences of the Minoan civilization figure prominently in their Craft. The Minoan snake goddess often appears in Witch circles, and statues of her adorn many of our altars. Today, the labrys is a symbol of female self-empowerment and represents strength. In the bull-headed rhyton of the Minoans, many Witches see a reflection of the Horned God. The Minoans might not have worshipped the gods of Olympus, but the first great civilization of the Mediterranean is still honored by many Witches.

The Minoan civilization began to decline in approximately 1600 BCE (there's a lot of debate over the date) with the eruption of the volcano on the nearby island of Thera (also called Santorini). The explosion at Thera was one of the largest volcanic explosions in history, wiping out much of the island. Today, visitors to Thera literally stay on the caldera of the great volcano that erupted 3,600 years ago, as much of it is beneath the waves of the Mediterranean Sea.

The eruption on Thera most likely hurt agriculture on Crete and throughout the Mediterranean, weakening the once-great empire. The Minoan civilization was conquered a few hundred years later by invaders from mainland Greece who had been busy building their own great civilization. These people were the Mycenaeans, and it's with them that we first truly encounter the gods of Olympus.

The Mycenaean period was short compared to the long reign of the Minoans, and the two periods of time overlap. Mycenaean culture began on Greece's mainland in the Peloponnese (a peninsula located in southern Greece) and lasted about five hundred years, from 1600 to 1100 BCE. The Mycenaeans lived in city-states ruled by kings and left behind extensively fortified palaces. The stones used to create these palaces were so immense that later Greeks believed they had been built by Cyclopes. Many of the events in Greek mythology were thought to have occurred during the Mycenaean period. Actual historical happenings, such as the Trojan War, took place during this time as well.

Both the Mycenaeans and the Minoans were seafaring peoples, and not surprisingly, their cultures overlapped for a period of time. Eventually, though, the more warlike Mycenaean culture became the dominant power on Crete. There's some disagreement over whether Mycenaean elements were simply absorbed into Minoan culture slowly over time or there was an all-out battle between the two civilizations. The end result of the cultural exchange between the Minoans and the Mycenaeans was Linear B, the first Greek form of writing, which was inspired by the script of the Minoans, Linear A.

Thanks to the Linear B tablets, we know that the Mycenaeans honored Zeus, Poseidon, Hera, Dionysus, Artemis, Athena, and most likely Ares and Hermes.[19] That means

---

19. Burkert, *Greek Religion*, 43–45.

eight of the twelve major Olympians were worshipped during the Mycenaean period. But the worship of the Greek gods during that time would have been much different from what came afterward. Apollo's absence from the pantheon is the most glaring omission, but also missing are Aphrodite and Demeter. It would be several more centuries before all twelve deities of Olympus met upon that mountaintop.

Unfortunately, while Linear B mentions the names of the gods, it doesn't have much to say about them. Most of what is recorded in Linear B is simply lists of goods, and when the gods are mentioned, it's generally in relation to what had been sacrificed to them. There are no bits of poetry or liturgy, and the Linear B tablets are silent on matters of mythology. The few tidbits in them that suggest something to do with Mycenaean religion differ depending on the region. On Crete, for instance, mostly priestesses are listed as presiding over sacrifices and worship of the gods, while on mainland Greece, male priests are a much more frequent occurrence.[20]

Greek mythology tends to romanticize the Mycenaean period as a true golden era for both Greek culture and the gods. Some of that romanticization might have been because that period was a cultural highlight that was quickly lost. Unlike the civilization of the Minoans, Mycenaean culture dominated for a period of only about four hundred years. The Mycenaean period came to an abrupt end around 1100 BCE, and for a period of about four hundred years, Greece was plunged into its own version of the Dark Ages. Literacy was forgotten, and the great palaces of the Mycenaean period were consumed by fire (most likely by foreign invaders).[21]

The Dark Ages were undoubtedly a difficult period for both the Greeks and their gods, but a foundation would be set for a second flowering of Greek culture. The island of Cyprus became a home to many Greeks, as well as a major exporter of religious ideas. Both Apollo and Aphrodite would enter Greece proper through Cyprus, and the age of the Olympians would truly begin.

Keeping track of Greek history and the rise of the Greek gods can be challenging. To make things a little bit easier, we've come up with this handy timeline outlining many of the most important events involving the gods in ancient Greece, the Roman Empire, and even the modern world. There is a great deal of disagreement in scholarly circles when it comes to dating the beginnings and endings of both civilizations and eras, so do not look upon this timeline as the last word on the subject. This timeline was created with the input of the many books included in our bibliography.

---

20. Burkert, *Greek Religion*, 45.

21. Burkert, *Greek Religion*, 43, 47.

TIMELINE OF THE GREEK GODS

4000 BCE	Indo-Europeans leave the steppes of Eurasia, spreading out across Europe and Asia.
3300–1200 BCE	**Bronze Age.** The first metal tools are forged (out of bronze).
2700–1100 BCE	**Minoan civilization.**
1600 BCE	Minoan civilization begins to decline, and the volcano on Thera erupts.
1600–1100 BCE	**Mycenaean period.** Most stories from Greek mythology are set during the Mycenaean period.
1200–700 BCE	**Iron Age.** Iron and steel tools begin to gradually replace those of bronze.
1260–1180 BCE	The Trojan War. No one knows the exact dates of the Trojan War, but it most likely occurred between these dates.
1100–750 BCE	**Greek Dark Ages.** The great palaces of the Mycenaean period are abandoned, and literacy is lost.
850–800 BCE	The modern Greek alphabet is developed.
800–700 BCE	Homer's *Iliad* and *Odyssey* are written down.
776 BCE	First Olympic Games.
753 BCE	Rome is allegedly founded.
730–700 BCE	Hesiod composes the *Theogony*.
700–480 BCE	**Archaic period.** Temples and other worship centers are built, and the look of the gods is established.
508 BCE	The first democracy in Athens is developed.
490 BCE	First Persian War. The Spartans win the battle of Marathon, as told in the 2006 movie *300*.
480 BCE	Second Persian War.
480–323 BCE	**Classical period.** This is the era most of us think of when we imagine ancient Greece. It is Athens in all its glory and is when monuments such as the Parthenon were built.
470–322 BCE	The philosophers Socrates, Plato, and Aristotle teach in Athens.

Timeline of the Greek Gods *(continued)*

432 BCE	Completion of the Parthenon in Athens.
431 BCE	The beginning of the Peloponnesian Wars between the Greek city-states of Athens and Spartans. The Spartans would eventually conquer Athens in 404 BCE.
356 BCE	Alexander the Great is born. He dies in 323.
330–323 BCE	**Hellenistic period.** Greek culture is dominant throughout the Mediterranean.
200 BCE–400 CE	The Greek Magical Papyri (*Papyri Graecae Magicae*, or *PGM*) are written and shared widely throughout the Mediterranean.
146 BCE	Greece becomes a protectorate of the Roman Empire, which essentially brings it into the Empire. A marble temple of Jupiter is built in Rome.
100 BCE	Birth of Julius Caesar.
58–51 BCE	Caesar conquers Gaul (which includes modern-day France) and begins expeditions into Britain.
27 BCE	The Pantheon—from the Greek *pantheion*, "[a temple] of all the gods"—is first built in Rome. It would be rebuilt several times over the next few centuries.
19 BCE	(Caesar) Augustus officially becomes the first emperor of the Roman Empire.
0–300 CE	The Orphic hymns are written sometime between these dates.
60–70 CE	Roman baths (in Bath, England) are built.
79 CE	Eruption of Mount Vesuvius, burying the Roman towns of Pompeii and Herculaneum in ash.
285 CE	Emperor Diocletian splits the Roman Empire in two, creating an Eastern Empire and a Western Empire.
312 CE	Co-emperor Constantine defeats his rival Maxentius at the Milvian Bridge, allegedly under a Christian sign. The year 312 is often listed as the year Constantine converted to Christianity.
313 CE	The Edict of Milan is issued, officially recognizing Christianity as a religion in the Roman Empire.

Timeline of the Greek Gods

380 CE	Eastern Roman Emperor Theodosius I proclaims Christianity the official religion of the Roman Empire.
390 CE	Christian zealots destroy the Library of Alexandria.
392 CE	Theodosius outlaws paganism and pagan rituals.
415 CE	**The death of Hypatia.** Hypatia, a pagan teacher in Alexandria, Egypt, is tortured and murdered by a mob of Christians. Her death is often seen as the end of the Classical period.
476 CE	The Eastern Roman Empire is conquered by the Germans.
608 CE	The Roman Pantheon is converted into a Christian church.
901–1000 CE	The *Picatrix* is written. The Middle East, and not Europe, ultimately preserved the works and mythology of the Greeks and Romans.
1256 CE	The *Picatrix* is translated into Spanish.
1300–1600 CE	**The Italian Renaissance.** The gods of antiquity would feature prominently in art and literature during this period.
1374 CE	Petrarch's epic poem *Africa* sparks renewed interest in the Olympians.
1486–1750 CE	European Witch Trials. Magick was still popular during this period of time, but ignorance even more so.
1792 CE	Thomas Taylor's translation of the Orphic hymns is published.
1806 CE	William Wordsworth's poem "Composed by the Side of Grasmere Lake" is published, starting over a century of Pan being England's most popular literary topic.
1867 CE	*Bulfinch's Mythology* is published.
1942 CE	Edith Hamilton introduces the Greek gods to a new generation in *Mythology: Timeless Tales of Gods and Heroes*.
1955 CE	Poet Robert Graves's *The Greek Myths* suggests that Demeter, Persephone, and Hekate personify the maiden-mother-crone archetypes.
2005 CE	Percy Jackson, son of Poseidon, makes his debut in Rick Riordan's *The Lightning Thief*.

THE OLYMPIANS CONQUER NEARLY ALL

Most scholars date the Greek emergence from the Dark Ages to around 700 BCE. Greek colonies were established in Italy and Sicily during the 700s, and the modern Greek alphabet was developed. Perhaps most importantly for us, the epic poems attributed to Homer were in (oral) circulation during this period, and were likely written down by the year 700 BCE.[22] Democracy had not yet sprung up in Athens, but the Greek city-state was on its way to being established.

The period from 700 to 480 BCE is known as the Archaic period and is most important as the era of the poets Hesiod and Homer. Before Homer and Hesiod, Greek mythology was a jumble of local cults and mythologies. Differences in how the same god was viewed from place to place would continue long after the Archaic period, but Homer and Hesiod created a unified Greek mythology and religious cult.

There is no one authoritative text when it comes to the gods of Olympus, but the works of Homer and Hesiod come close. The Greek historian Herodotus (c. 484–c. 425 BCE) wrote that Hesiod and Homer "first revealed to the Greeks how the gods were born, what they were called, ... and how they looked."[23] These two poets took the various gods of ancient Greece and established their places on Mount Olympus and gave them a story that would make sense to the outside observer. There are still contradictions, of course—for example, while Athena reigned supreme in Athens, her brother Ares held sway in more warlike Sparta—but most Greeks could at least agree that Homer and Hesiod wrote of the same gods, and that those gods were likely whispering in their ears as they wrote.

Homer is the best known of the two poets today, and his *Iliad* and *Odyssey* are required reading in many high school literature classes and the subject of numerous adaptations. The *Iliad* is set during just a few weeks of the Trojan War and focuses primarily on the rage of the Greek warrior Achilles. The story of the ending of the Trojan War, along with the journeys of its protagonist, Odysseus, would be told in the *Odyssey*. The story of the famous Trojan Horse occurs in this tale. While Homer's stories focus on specific characters, the gods make frequent appearances, and during these appearances Homer shares their motivations and history.

Hesiod's most famous work is the *Theogony*, which provides a genealogy of the Olympians along with bits of mythology and other insights. The story of how Zeus conquered his father, Cronos, and claimed his throne is told in the works of Hesiod. The two poets

---

22. Burkert, *Greek Religion,* 121.

23. Graziosi, *The Gods of Olympus,* 29.

don't always agree on the specifics of the gods. In Homer's *Iliad*, Aphrodite is the daughter of Zeus, while in Hesiod's *Theogony*, she rises from the foam of the sea. But the two poets did generally agree on the character of the gods. Hesiod and Homer set the stage for everything that would come after them.

Not only were the most familiar stories of the gods set down in writing during the Archaic period, but the look of the gods was established as well. This was the era of the first great Greek sculptures, cast in both marble and bronze. The ancient Greeks praised the beauty (and sacredness) of the human body, and this found its ultimate expression in sculpture. Before statues of the gods adorned the temples of Greece, the gods were represented by more mundane items, such as pieces of wood.[24]

The Archaic period was also marked by the extensive building of temples and other worship centers. While the great Parthenon in Athens would be built during the Classical period (480–323 BCE), the Acropolis was home to temples long before Athena's most famous shrine was built. It's impossible to imagine ancient Greece without temples and statues appearing marble-white, but in actuality the Greeks painted their statues and temples. Time and vandalism have taken such gifts away from us, but the Greek world was far more vibrant-looking than it's generally given credit for.

The Archaic period also saw Greek traders establish outposts and trading stations throughout the Mediterranean. Homer himself wrote in the *Iliad* that the gods had traveled to both Africa and Europe, and there is material evidence that they did so during the Archaic period.[25] Where the Greeks went, so did their gods. The exchange went both ways, and periodically foreign gods would find themselves welcome on the shores of ancient Greece. The Egyptian goddess Isis found herself at the center of her own festival in the Greek town of Tithorea.[26]

The Classical period was not a tranquil time for the city-states of Greece. It was marked by frequent wars with the Persian Empire as well as battles among the Greeks themselves. When we think of Greece during this period, we tend to focus on the city-state of Athens, home of the great philosophers Socrates (c. 470–399 BCE), Plato (428/427 or 424/423–348/347 BCE), and Aristotle (384–322 BCE). Philosophy and scientific theory weren't the only thing the ancient Athenians pioneered; Athenian experiments with democracy would

24. Graziosi, *The Gods of Olympus*, 49.

25. Graziosi, *The Gods of Olympus*, 5.

26. Burkert, *Greek Religion*, 120.

resonate over the centuries and even inspire the United States of America's Founding Fathers.[27]

Much of what we know about the Greek gods as worshipped in ancient Greece comes to us from the Classical period. This was when Greek culture could be said to have been at its height. It was the era of plays in honor of Dionysus and democracy in Athens. When modern-day individuals attempt to recreate the "original" worship of the Greek gods, it's the Classical period they most look to emulate. Much of that is because the Classical period would also be the last time the gods of Olympus were worshipped primarily by Greeks.

Few individuals did more to change the entire world than the man we today call Alexander the Great (356–323 BCE). Alexander's father, Philip II of Macedon (359–336 BCE), conquered most of Greece, but his son would go on to conquer Egypt and Persia, and in the process spread Hellenic (Greek) culture and its gods across the Mediterranean to the borders of India. Alexander is also the perfect individual to illustrate the power that syncretization had on the deities of Olympus and those they came into contact with.

Shortly after taking control of Egypt in 331 BCE, Alexander left the city he founded, Alexandria, and headed west. His destination was the oasis of Siwa, home to the oracle of the Egyptian god Amon (known to the Greeks as Ammon). As the newly installed pharaoh of Egypt, Alexander was now seen as a god to the Egyptians, and his visit to Siwa was designed to bolster his connections to the Egyptian pantheon. Alexander was successful in his mission. Amon's oracle was favorable to the conqueror, with the oracle proclaiming Alexander the son of Ammon and Zeus.

Alexander was not the first individual to conflate the gods Zeus and Amon. Greeks who had settled in Northern Africa long before Alexander's arrival had long thought of Ammon as just another name for Zeus.[28] In the wake of Alexander's endorsement from Amon's oracle, statues merging the physical characteristics of Amon and Zeus became popular in both Egypt and Greece, and later the Roman Empire, where the dual god was known as Jupiter Ammon.

Alexander's brief life (he died at age thirty-three) would have tremendous repercussions. Going forward, the Greek gods would exist in a world where they were often conflated with Egyptian and Persian deities. Alexander's death marked the beginning of the Hellenistic period (323–30 BCE), an era when Greek culture and language would be the

---

27. Greek democracy, like early American democracy, was limited to male landholders, and both societies were built on the backs of slaves.

28. Graziosi, *The Gods of Olympus*, 97–99.

predominant one in the Western world. Alexander's empire did not last much longer than his life span and was quickly divided and warred over by his generals and their descendants. The Hellenistic period was not ruled by one empire; it was united by a shared culture, and that culture was Greek.

That culture would majorly influence the next great empire, the Romans, a people who had adopted the gods of Olympus centuries before Alexander. The Romans had their own gods, of course, but those gods lacked the personality, mythology, and approachability of the Olympians. Roman gods were primarily utilitarian; they were about function over style. The original Jupiter, before absorbing the attributes of Zeus, was honored because he maintained the Roman Republic. The early Romans had no need for stories showcasing a god's philandering ways, at least until they couldn't resist such tales.[29]

It's hard to pinpoint exactly when the Roman gods became one with the gods of Olympus. It's probably something that was worked out over several centuries, since the first Greeks settled in Italy at the end of the Greek Dark Ages. Ten of the twelve major Olympians were conflated with Roman deities:

- Zeus-Jupiter
- Hera-Juno
- Aphrodite-Venus
- Hephaestus-Vulcan
- Ares-Mars
- Demeter-Ceres
- Artemis-Diana
- Hades-Pluto
- Poseidon-Neptune
- Athena-Minerva

The Romans, who were originally not much of a drinking culture, did not have a clear equivalent for Dionysus. The Romans had a god of grapes, Liber, but Liber lacked the power to bestow drunkenness or divine madness.[30] Instead of transferring the mythology of Dionysus to Liber, the Romans decided to import Dionysus and call him by an alternative Greek name: Bacchus.[31]

---

29. Graziosi, *The Gods of Olympus*, 129.

30. Gately, *Drink: A Cultural History of Alcohol*, 28.

31. Graziosi, *The Gods of Olympus*, 133.

The other inhabitant of Olympus without a Roman counterpart was Apollo, and instead of renaming him, the Romans simply imported the god whole cloth. Apollo is simply Apollo, whether in Athens or Rome. The victory of the Greek gods was complete.

Or was it? While today we often think of the Roman and Greek versions of the deities listed above as being essentially the same, there were differences sometimes. Genealogies were often amended, and gods with lower profiles in Greece sometimes had larger ones in Rome. Ares, for instance, was not particularly popular in his homeland but was central to the Roman pantheon.[32] As the gods traveled, whether to Rome or to Memphis in Egypt, their worship went through subtle changes, and along the way they found themselves sharing space and being worshipped with gods from pantheons far from Greece.

The Roman Empire took the gods of Olympus even further afield. The images of Hermes at Bath are Roman ones. The Roman Empire made the gods of Olympus more popular than ever, and later would bring about their decline.

Ancient Rome was not some sort of pagan paradise. Rome was often at war, the Roman economy was built on slavery, and women had few rights. Life was cheap, hard, and often short. But the Romans were generally tolerant of religions outside of classical paganism and were especially welcoming of deities from foreign pantheons. This acceptance is easily seen in Roman art.

A monument found in Reims, France, dating back to the year 100 CE depicts the antlered Gallic god Cernunnos flanked by Apollo on his left and Mercury (Hermes) on his right. There's no conflict between these three figures; in a polytheistic society blending Gauls and Romans, it probably just made sense to people that their various deities would all be depicted together.[33] In Bath, carved into one of the stones that was most likely part of the temple there, Mercury stands next to the Gallic-Celtic goddess of abundance Rosmerta as if it's a natural thing for two very different deities to be doing.[34]

Over one hundred years before the stela at Reims and the carving at Bath were created, Julius Caesar (100–44 BCE) had already brought the gods of the Celtic Gauls into the Olympian pantheon. Writing around the year 50 CE, Caesar equates the various gods of the Gauls to those of the Romans. Caesar's conflation of the two pantheons is incomplete, and sometimes the deities in his pairings don't seem to have that much in common, but

---

32. Graziosi, *The Gods of Olympus*, 133.

33. Jason spends a lot of time writing about the Reims stela in his book *The Horned God of the Witches* (on pages 85–87), published by Llewellyn in 2021.

34. From the display at the Roman baths in Bath.

it's yet another example of how easily the Romans could absorb the beliefs of others into their understanding of the Roman gods.[35]

There were a few religions that the Romans did have trouble absorbing, though not for lack of trying. Stories of Christian persecution at the hands of the Romans are often over-blown, and in most cases could have easily been avoided by Christians if they had bothered to pay their taxes and make the proper sacrifices in honor of the Roman emperor. But the glories of martyrdom drove Christians to be rather unaccommodating of the rules of Rome, and the Romans often retaliated by escalating hostilities. In 303 the Roman Emperor Diocletian (243/245–311 CE) formally outlawed Christianity.

The man credited with being the first "Christian emperor," Constantine I (also called Constantine the Great, c. 272–337 CE) had visions not just of Christian symbols but also of the Greek Apollo.[36] It's true that Constantine granted special status to Christians dur-ing his reign as the sole emperor of the Roman Empire (324–337 CE), but he also built pagan temples during the construction of his city, Constantinople, and was not baptized until he was on his deathbed. Constantine didn't outlaw paganism or make Christianity the only legal religion in the Empire, but he set the table for such actions, and in 380 CE the Emperor Theodosius (346–395 CE) proclaimed Christianity the official religion of the Roman Empire.[37]

Making Christianity the official religion didn't suddenly mean that worship of the Olympians immediately ended. But over the ensuing decades and centuries, formal wor-ship of the gods in public settings ceased, and the gods who had first watched over the ancient Greeks and later the Romans were now suddenly seen as demonic entities. The golden age of the Olympians had ended, but they would rise again.

THE SURVIVAL AND TRIUMPH OF THE OLYMPIANS

In 2018 my wife and I visited Greece to see the place where so many of the deities we cher-ish were born. That journey took us through half a dozen museums, many of them full of statues from Greece's Archaic period through its time as part of the Roman Empire. Although several of the statues we saw were whole and, other than not being painted, must have looked similar to how they did in antiquity, the majority of the statues we viewed had been vandalized.

---

35. Graziosi, *The Gods of Olympus*, 139.

36. Kirsch, *God Against the Gods*, 140.

37. Kirsch, *God Against the Gods*, 274.

After the Christianization of the Roman Empire, the gods of Olympus still held a degree of fascination for their former worshippers; but instead of viewing the statues of antiquity as simply empty vessels, Christians were actively afraid of them. Believing the statues to still contain power, Christians aggressively vandalized the treasures of the ancient pagan world. It's painful to look upon the beautiful face of Aphrodite and then glance downward and see that her nipples and vagina have been removed from her body.

Surprisingly, the arms and heads of pagan statues were especially problematic to Christians. Believing the statues to harbor demons, Christians would remove the arms and heads from statues before disposing of timeless works of art in garbage dumps. Separating a statue from its arms and head was thought to vanquish the power of the demon, suggesting that Christians believed the gods of Olympus still maintained a great deal of power—because if they didn't retain much of their former glory, why go through all the trouble of decapitating them?

As the Roman Empire declined in the West, the power of Christianity continued to grow. But the gods of Olympus were still a part of society, though often in more subtle ways. The Greeks had named the planets in the sky after their gods, and eventually the Romans did too. Mercury, Venus, Mars, Jupiter, and Saturn (a Titan and the father of Zeus/Jupiter) were all named after Olympian deities or figures related to them. We've continued this practice as new planets have been discovered, with Uranus, Neptune, and Pluto all getting a planet or celestial body named after them. The constellations in the sky also retained the names of figures from Greek mythology. (Orion's Belt was never replaced by Noah's Ark.)

The days of the week are mostly named for the Olympians. Martedì, mercoledì, giovedì, and venerdì (Tuesday through Friday in Italian) are named after Mars, Mercury, Jupiter, and Venus, respectively. In English, Tuesday through Thursday are named after the Norse gods Tyr, Odin, and Thor, while the goddess Frig claims Friday. The Roman equivalents of those gods, in order, were Mars, Hermes, Zeus, and Venus. Friday is named after Frig because she was the Norse goddess who was thought to match up best with Venus. In Italian, Saturday took the name *sabato* in honor of the Christian sabbath, but in English it's still Saturn's Day. The Olympians may no longer have been worshipped, but their names were still being spoken.

Despite how modern Christians often feel about topics such as astrology and magick, both practices were downright common during the Middle Ages and into the early modern period. One of the most impactful works involving magick and astrology is a magickal text known as the *Picatrix*, which has a long and tangled history. It was first written in

Arabic during the tenth century CE before arriving in Europe a couple of centuries later, where it circulated widely after being translated into Spanish and later several other European languages.[38]

The *Picatrix* was concerned primarily with utilizing the power of spirits for personal gain, spirits connected directly to the planets along with the sun and moon. One scholar described the instructions and exhortations involving the planets in the *Picatrix* as being equivalent to prayer, and they certainly do sound that way.[39] It's important to note that even though most of the people who used the *Picatrix* were probably Christians, the invocations to the planets in the book certainly sound like worship.

Though the *Picatrix* was written in Arabic in the Middle East, much of the information in it comes directly from Greek religion. The prayers to the planets in the *Picatrix* contain terms directly from Greek religious practices.[40] In a prayer to Saturn (Kronos), the petitioner sounds much like a worshipper might have over a thousand years ago, long before the book was written:

> O Master of sublime name and great power, supreme Master; O Master Saturn: Thou the Cold, the Sterile, the Mournful, the Pernicious; Thou whose life is sincere and whose word sure; Thou, the Sage and Solitary, the Impenetrable; Thou, whose promises are kept; ... Though, the old and cunning, master of all artifice, deceitful, wise, and judicious; Though who bringest prosperity or ruin, and makest men to be happy or unhappy! I conjure Thee, O Supreme Father, by Thy great benevolence and Thy generous bounty, to do for me what I ask.[41]

The *Picatrix* required more than just words for its magick to work; it also required the likeness of the gods to whom its prayers were being directed. Luckily for the users of the *Picatrix*, the grimoire also included descriptions of the various gods who showed up in its pages. A description of Jupiter, for instance, dates back to the writings of the second-century writer Pausanias (110–180 CE). There are several other descriptions of deities such as Venus and Mars that also date back to the classical pagan past.[42] But the *Picatrix*, written

---

38. Seznec, *The Survival of the Pagan Gods*, 53.

39. Seznec, *The Survival of the Pagan Gods*, 53–54.

40. Seznec, *The Survival of the Pagan Gods*, 54.

41. Seznec, *The Survival of the Pagan Gods*, 54.

42. Seznec, *The Survival of the Pagan Gods*, 54–55.

down long after the Olympians were at their apogee, also contains some descriptions of the gods that are more Babylonian in nature.[43]

These clear descriptions of the gods of Olympus are in sharp contrast to how many of the gods were depicted in Europe during the Middle Ages. The names of the gods might have still been on everyone's lips, but not everyone remembered what they looked like. Mars might be depicted as a knight fighting in the Crusades, and one of the oddest images of all shows Jupiter as a pleasantly plump Christian monk, complete with a goblet and a crucifix.[44]

Due to the destruction and desecration of pagan statues, art, and worship spaces, there were few places to view the gods of Olympus as they had appeared in antiquity, so people depicted them in contemporary ways. If Jupiter is the king of the gods, why not depict him as a traditional European king? Mars as a warrior-knight in chain mail makes much more sense in this context. But the gods of Olympus most likely wanted to be thought of in their classical forms, and the period known as the Italian Renaissance would provide that opportunity.

The return of the Greek and Roman gods to their classical forms is due largely to the Italian writer Francesco Petrarca (1304–1374), more commonly known in English as Petrarch. His never-quite-finished epic poem *Africa* was written to tell the tale of the Second Punic War and its hero, Scipio, who defeated the Carthaginian general Hannibal. Since Petrarch's poem was set in the time of classical Rome, he included descriptions of the Roman gods as they had appeared during that time frame. Though the poem was never fully completed, it circulated widely after his death and led to the Olympians triumphant return to art and literature in their classical forms.[45]

Inspired by Petrarch's descriptions, images based on those from classical antiquity began to reemerge in Italy around the start of the fifteenth century. The gods not only adorned fine art but also were painted on furniture and lauded in poetry and prose. To the uncritical eye, it probably felt like many in Italy were actively worshipping the Olympians once more, though worship in the conventional sense seems unlikely.[46] What's important is that the gods had reclaimed their traditional looks, and people were again interested in reading their stories and creating new ones.

---

43. Seznec, *The Survival of the Pagan Gods*, 160.

44. Seznec, *The Survival of the Pagan Gods*, 161.

45. Graziosi, *The Gods of Olympus*, 202–3.

46. For additional conjecture on whether the Olympians were again being worshipped in the Italian Renaissance as they were in classical antiquity, see Seznac's *The Survival of the Pagan Gods* and Godwin's *The Pagan Dream of the Renaissance*.

There's probably another reason for the return of the Olympians to prominence other than Petrarch's poetry, and that is the fact that the gods allow people to easily express ideas and truths about themselves. A painting of Bacchus is an easy way to illustrate joy and drunkenness, and Venus is a symbol of beauty. Christianity simply doesn't offer this sort of shorthand. There's simply nothing comparable to Cupid in the Bible.

As we've seen, the gods didn't quite disappear with the Christianization of Europe, and they didn't disappear after the period we call the Renaissance either. Since the 1400s, they've been an inescapable part of both art and literature. In the English-speaking world, there have been several different books that have reawakened interest in the Greek gods (see the timeline table earlier in this chapter). One of the most significant was the translation of the Orphic hymns into English by Thomas Taylor (1758–1835) in 1792.

The Orphic hymns are a series of devotional poems that most likely represent the text used in an all-night ritual by an Orphic cult near the region of Anatolia (in present-day Turkey).[47] Because the Orphics were a mystery cult, we don't know much about them, but they seemed to be concerned primarily with the survival of the soul after death. Exactly when the Orphic hymns were written is an open question, with most scholars dating their composition between 0 and 300 CE.[48]

Despite Dionysus being the primary deity of the Orphics, Taylor's translation of the hymns most likely contributed to the reemergence of the god Pan in the English imagination. At the start of the nineteenth century, Pan rose up and acquired a space in the collective imagination that was much larger than the one he had occupied in ancient Athens.[49] Today we are seeing something similar with the goddess Hekate, who has quickly become one of the most popular goddesses in Modern Witchcraft.

The 1899 book *Aradia, or the Gospel of the Witches*, written (or transcribed, depending on your view) by American Charles Godfrey Leland (1824–1903), allegedly contains some of the mythology, magickal practices, and rites of a group of Italian Witches. Not surprisingly, Diana features prominently in the work, illustrating the continued importance of the Olympians.

Today, the Olympians remain ever present, and most people in the English-speaking world are more likely to use their original Greek names, too! (Even though many of us pronounce their names incorrectly, they are gods, so they know when we're talking to them.) Long after we are all gone, it seems likely that people will still be speaking about Artemis, Apollo, Aphrodite, and Hera and that the gods of the Greeks will continue to look down upon us from metaphorical Mount Olympus.

---

47. Dunn, *The Orphic Hymns*, 1–3.

48. Dunn, *The Orphic Hymns*, 1.

49. Jason writes a lot about the god Pan and his prominence in English literature in his book *The Horned God of the Witches*, published by Llewellyn in 2021.

THE
OLYMPIANS

ZEUS
by Jason Mankey

Zeus is the one Greek god whose origins can be found in his name. The Greek *Zeus* comes directly from the Indo-European word *diyéus*, which translates to "day/bright sky."[50] Diyéus is also preserved in the name of Zeus's Roman counterpart, Jupiter, who was also known as Diespiter.[51] Despite the ubiquity of sky gods (of which Zeus is one) in various world mythologies, only among the Greeks and Romans did the god of the sky become the most powerful force in the world.[52]

Though Zeus's origins are unquestionably Indo-European, Zeus is the unifying force and presence in Greek mythology; everything is connected to him. The primordial powers of the earth (Gaia) and sea (Ouranos) are his grandparents, and the Titans who preceded him live at his discretion. Even more importantly, the eleven Olympians below him are either his siblings (Hera, Poseidon, and Demeter) or his children (Ares, Hermes, Athena, Apollo, Artemis, and Dionysus). In many retellings of Greek myth, both Aphrodite and Hephaestus lack a direct connection to Zeus, but in other versions both are said to be the children of Zeus (Hephaestus being the son of Zeus and Hera, and Aphrodite being the daughter of Zeus and Dione, at least according to Homer). Even Hekate, generally thought to be a Titan, has Zeus as a father, at least according to some chroniclers.[53]

Only one of Zeus's Olympian children is legitimate (Ares, whose mother is Hera), while the rest of his Olympian offspring are the result of a series of affairs with other goddesses

---

50. West, *Indo-European Poetry and Myth*, 168.

51. Burkert, *Greek Religion*, 123.

52. West, *Indo-European Poetry and Myth*, 169.

53. Dowden, *Zeus*, 42–43.

and, in the case of Dionysus, a mortal. This has led many of us to think of Zeus as a philanderer, but there are important reasons for Zeus's children to have several different mothers. As the Greek pantheon as we know it today was solidifying during the Mycenaean period, Zeus was most likely inserted into various myths, replacing now-unknown fathers. It was important for the Olympians to be united by the bonds of family, and Zeus's affairs away from Hera allowed that to happen. It also served to preserve the worship of local goddesses, though their roles were often marginalized a result.

Zeus's prodigious appetite for sex was not limited to divine entities, and his couplings with various mortal women produced a plethora of Greek heroes. Though few of these individuals reached the status of a full-fledged god (like both Dionysus and Heracles), their amazing achievements echoed the power and knowledge of their father. Extraordinary human beings could also be the children of Zeus. In Egypt, Alexander the Great was hailed as the son of Zeus-Ammon when Zeus became one with the Egyptian sky god Amon.[54]

Anywhere the Greeks traveled, they were likely to link local deities and heroes to Zeus. Zeus is not just the father of the gods; he is humanity's father and their lord and king. Many of our ideas about ancient Greek society are colored by the emergence of (limited) democracy in Athens, but many other Greek city-states had kings, and earlier Greek history is full of kings and absolute rulers. Even Athens in the age of democracy had its despots. Those who had the last word in society looked to Zeus to legitimize their power. Hesiod would proclaim the divine right of kings long before any pope, writing that "kings are from Zeus."[55]

The image of Zeus as a crusty and wizened old ruler on high is a common one among Witches, but to the Greeks, Zeus was something completely different. Despite frequent portrayals as an older (and still powerful) gray-haired gentleman, Zeus was often depicted in art as a man in the prime of his life. The Artemision Bronze statue from about 460 BCE (and recovered in the Mediterranean Sea in 1926) depicts Zeus as an individual at the height of his power.[56]

---

54. Dowden, *Zeus*, 43. There are competing ways to spell Ammon. We've chosen *Ammon* in the text because it's how Dowden spells the name of the god. The most popular spelling online is currently Amun, though Amon is also common.

55. Dowden, *Zeus*, 72.

56. Seltman, *The Twelve Olympians*, 16. It's worth noting that there is a minority of scholars who believe the Artemision Bronze is a representation of Poseidon and not Zeus. The statue is missing the item being held in the subject's hand, which would solve the mystery decisively (either a lightning bolt or a trident). A trident, though, would have obscured the subject's face, which makes it much more likely that the figure is Zeus.

Statues of Apollo, always in the blush of youth, might be more aesthetically pleasing, but Zeus in art was unquestionably the most powerful and vital deity in the Greek pantheon.

Depicting Zeus as a powerful, full-grown adult was a way to honor him and show respect for his power. The true form of Zeus was unknowable, and to look upon it deadly, and in myth Zeus arrives on Earth in a variety of guises. Most often Zeus appears to his lovers as an animal, the best-known forms in mythology being those of a swan, a bull, and a cow. Zeus was also capable of taking human form, appearing to Alcmene (the mother of Heracles) as her husband, Amphitryon.[57] In one of his most outlandish exploits, Zeus assumed the form of his daughter Artemis to seduce the nymph Callisto (sometimes spelled Kallisto). Outside of flesh (and fur), Zeus was also known to take the form of a golden rain.

Zeus feels no need to don a disguise while abducting the youth Ganymede, though later versions of the tale sometimes have Zeus appearing as an eagle. Zeus brings Ganymede (thought to be the most beautiful young man on Earth at the time of his abduction from Troy) to Olympus and makes him his cupbearer. Scholars have linked this myth to a Cretan initiation custom where an older individual takes a much younger man under his wing as a mentor and a lover, a cup being the traditional gift from mentor to mentee. The story of Ganymede and Zeus has been warped by Christians warring against queerness over the centuries, but Greek art depicts Ganymede as a young man (not a boy), and the pairing is most often depicted as consensual. In a more philosophical context, the abduction of Ganymede could represent the journey of the soul to a divine afterlife.[58]

The idea that Zeus's power made him unknowable was not one held by the Greeks. Certain epithets for Zeus describe a god who is downright friendly. (All the gods have numerous epithets, which emphasize a particular function or specific location of the deity.) Zeus Philios guarantees the bonds of friendship and, in the case of the Greeks, the bonds that often united quarreling city-states in times of crisis. As Zeus Xenios, the king of Olympus is the god of charity, and to honor Zeus is to help feed and clothe a stranger. Zeus also watches over those who arrive at a place in need of assistance as Zeus Hikesios.[59]

In addition to charity and friendship, Zeus was the god of justice. His justice was not just dispensed from on high; it was believed that Zeus was actively involved in the world. In the *Odyssey*, Homer writes that there are unknown gods checking in on the affairs of

---

57. Burkert, *Greek Religion*, 128.

58. Dowden, *Zeus*, 49–51.

59. Dowden, *Zeus*, 78–79.

humankind, monitoring our actions. Hesiod links these unknown deities directly to Zeus, suggesting that they act as his eyes and ears on the ground, searching for those who commit injustice.[60]

In myth, Zeus's involvement could often be far more direct. In the story of Baucis and Philemon, Zeus and Hermes dress up as peasants and ask those they encounter for a meal and a place to spend the night. After being rejected by everyone in the town they visit, father and son happen upon the cottage of Baucis and Philemon, a poor couple without much to offer. Despite their difficult circumstances, Baucis and Philemon treat their disguised guests with kindness and serve them wine.

Because Zeus and Hermes are gods, their cups refill on their own, and the couple realize who is now in their presence. Disgusted by the wickedness of everyone else in the town they are visiting, Zeus and Hermes destroy the town with a flood, sparing the lives of their hosts and making them the proprietors of a great temple. The tale ends with Baucis and Philemon becoming trees upon their deaths, where they can eternally embrace each other. The moral of the story? Zeus is active in this world and is watching.

For the ancient Greeks, Zeus was always active. Because of his ever-present lightning bolt, we tend to think of Zeus today as a storm god, but he was more than just a god of thunder and lightning. Zeus was the god of the sky and all that descended from it. Zeus was responsible for both snow and rain (and the reverse of those phenomena, drought), and in many cases was addressed explicitly as those forces. Children in ancient Athens used to sing, "Rain, rain, O dear Zeus, on the fields of the Athenians." Zeus didn't just bring the rains (or the snow), he was the rain![61]

Zeus was also the lightning that flashed in the sky and sometimes struck the ground. Sites struck by lightning were hailed as places where Zeus himself had descended. In myth, the lightning bolts thrown by the god (manufactured by Hephaestus) caused even the other Olympians to fear Zeus. Lightning is an awesome sight when it lights up the sky, but we are powerless when it strikes the earth.[62]

Apart from the sky and its storms, Zeus was the god of a realm seldom spoken of today: the ether (or aether). The ancient Greeks believed that there were two levels of air. The lower air is where people live, die, and breathe. Above our level of air, beginning where the clouds reach the tops of mountains, lies the ether. The ether was thought to be

60. Dowden, *Zeus*, 73.

61. Burkert, *Greek Religion*, 126.

62. Burkert, *Greek Religion*, 126.

a fiery realm, and it's here in the ether that Zeus and the other gods made their homes. The fiery nature of the ether is why Zeus is often equated with fire.[63]

Today we think of Mount Olympus as a single mountain in Northern Greece, but the ancient Greeks had several mountains known as Mount Olympus. The name was a way of designating the highest visible mountain, where the ether could be seen and experienced if one wanted to climb to the top and make an offering to Zeus. (No one ever built temples on the tops of the highest mountains, but they did leave offerings there.) The Olympians are Olympians because they dwell in the ether, not because they live on the top of a specific mountaintop.[64]

The fact that Zeus controlled the land where the gods dwelled should not be a surprise. The priestesses at the Oracle of Dodona sang, "Zeus was, Zeus is, Zeus will be: O great Zeus."[65] The Athenian statesman Solon (c. 630–c. 560 BCE) wrote that "Zeus oversees the *telos* [completion] of everything."[66] Zeus's place as the arbitrator of everything was the model for family life, with the husband as the supreme authority in the home.[67] Zeus established the patriarchal structure of Olympus and sanctioned that model for his children on Earth.

The Roman sky god Jupiter (sometimes known as Jove) absorbed the mythology of Zeus, and the two operated as the same deity in the age of the Roman Empire. (The word Jupiter means "father," and the god Jupiter was easily equated with the Greek *Zeus Pater*, "Zeus the father.") Not surprisingly, Jupiter was a model for many Roman emperors. The Emperor Augustus fashioned himself as a young Apollo, but in art he was often depicted as Zeus as a way to symbolize his power.[68]

Despite being the supreme god of the Greeks (and later the Romans), Zeus is mostly an afterthought among many Modern Witches. Much of this is undoubtedly due to how he's been portrayed after the fall of classical paganism. Zeus is the pagan god most easily equated with the beliefs of monotheism and the religions that embrace that ethos. Even during Zeus's reign over Olympus, pagan writers came close to describing the son of Cronus in

---

63. Dowden, *Zeus*, 56–57.

64. Dowden, *Zeus,* 57–58.

65. Burkert, *Greek Religion*, 131.

66. Dowden, *Zeus*, 88.

67. Dowden, *Zeus*, 81.

68. Dowden, *Zeus*, 113.

ways that imply an embrace of monotheism. The Latin poet Quintus Soranus (c. 140–82 CE) wrote that Zeus was the "begetter and mother of gods, one god and all gods."[69]

When a now-Christian Roman Empire outlawed the pagan practices of the Romans and the Greeks, Zeus survived as the Roman Jupiter. Stargazers and astrologers still invoke his name when looking up at the largest planet in our solar system, and in Romance languages (such as Italian, French, and Spanish) the fourth day of the week continues to be Jove's Day. As both Thor and Zeus are sky gods, the English Thursday is an indirect reference to mighty Zeus.

For much of the last 1,500 years, Zeus (most often as Jupiter) has been the Greek god most likely to be referenced in literature. The Olympian's kingly attributes and his status as the ruler of Olympus made him the Greek god most similar to the supreme God of Christianity. In English poetry, for example, Jupiter is the most frequently cited and referenced deity from 1300 (the approximate year when written records in English became common) to 1800 CE.[70] After that period of time, Zeus's supremacy in literature was eclipsed by his son/brother/grandson (depending on the myth) Pan.

If books and social media are any indication, Zeus is an infrequent visitor to modern Witch and Pagan spaces, but maybe he shouldn't be. Zeus is a far more complex god than mythology often leads us to believe, and also far more knowable. Zeus might not be cuddly, but he was a friend to worshippers in ancient Greece. The son of Cronus doesn't just sit on his throne alone lording over the earth and contemplating adulterous liaisons; he plays an active role in our world. Zeus looks down upon us from the ether, searching for injustice while sending rain, snow, and storms. Zeus was, Zeus is, and Zeus will always be.

PERSONAL INSIGHTS WITH ZEUS
by Jason Mankey

The first Pagan god I ever said a prayer to was Zeus. I remember that day quite vividly even though it happened nearly forty years ago. It was a bright, sunny, and yet still cold day in February in Illinois. I remember the wind being especially wild that morning. I was in second grade and I had a day off from school. As I left my house to go play outside, I looked up at the sun and wondered why no one prayed to the Greek gods anymore. Immediately I decided to remedy that.

---

69. Dowden, *Zeus*, 182. The writing of Soranus survives as a quotation in St. Augustine's (354–430 CE) book *City of God*.

70. Hutton, *The Triumph of the Moon: A History of Modern Pagan Witchcraft*, 43.

Raising my head up toward the sky, I asked Zeus to bless my day and keep me warm. I don't remember anything dramatic happening after my little prayer, but I must have felt something to remember that utterance all these years later. When my little invocation was complete, I pictured Zeus smiling kindly down upon me from the sky, and I hopped on my Big Wheel in search of other kids in the neighborhood to play with.

Over the years, I routinely relived that cold February morning, wondering why some people's gods are "mythology" while other gods are "religion." Didn't Zeus deserve the same honors as those figures being worshipped in all the churches nearby? Why was Zeus labeled as fiction when his stories were so much better than that other guy's? Many years passed before I came to realize that some people were still worshipping Zeus, but even during the period between being a strange second grader and embracing my inner Witch, I never believed Zeus was fictitious.

Among Witches, Zeus often gets a bad reputation. I think that's partly because he's too close to some of the deities many of us left behind when we became Witches. The vast majority of us have had enough of the nearly omnipotent male deity watching and judging us from on high.

There's also the matter of Zeus's "bad" behavior (which is putting it lightly). In mythology, Zeus takes, manipulates, rapes, kills, and continually cheats on his wife, Hera, with a multitude of (male and female) partners. This is all quite problematic (again putting it lightly), and no one I know would associate with a person like that, let alone a deity. But the stories of Zeus were written down by people—people who had their own agendas and their own flaws.

Certainly I think there is wisdom in myth, but the values present in mythology often have more to do with what the storyteller (or culture) believes than the actual deity being written about. There are dozens of instances in this book where the actual worship of a particular deity does not align very well with the best-known mythology of that deity. I don't write these words to excuse the actions of Zeus in mythology, but only to suggest that Zeus is more than just what has been written about him. It's important to also take into account how he was honored in antiquity and what it's like to work with him in the here and now.

Personal gnosis is an idea frowned upon by some in the magickal community, but I have to believe that deities progress and change over time. The worship of Zeus in 800 BCE was different from the worship of him in 8 BCE, so why would we expect the Zeus of today to be stuck in some sort of cosmic amber that has preserved an exact version of him from over two thousand years ago?

Over my decades as a Witch, Zeus has shown up when I need some guidance or a swift kick in the pants. As a god who ensures order both on Mount Olympus and in the greater world, his presence brings stability and focus into my life. Zeus helps me see the bigger picture and get back on track with whatever I'm working on. His energy is not frivolous. There's nearly always some sort of reason and purpose behind it. In my experience, Zeus is not quite friendly, but he's not frightening either. He offers guidance and insight, and that information may not always be what we want to hear. Zeus is not aloof—he'll come running when you call—but he's also a busy god. Visits are never any longer than they need to be. He seems to respect my time, so I do the same with his.

For me, Zeus is also the sky. When I look up, I can see him in the clouds observing me from a field of heavenly blue. When thunder crashes and lightning bolts streak across the sky, it's a reminder of Zeus's power and the fact that we can never completely control the natural world. While Zeus is very orderly, there's also something wild and untamed about his power when he thunders across the sky.

The first night I visited Athens, an out-of-season storm tore across the city. There were sheets of rain and booming claps of thunder. From our apartment in Athens, we could make out the Acropolis, with the Parthenon illuminated by electric lights. Brighter than those lights were the many flashes of lightning of Zeus that streaked across the sky. His show that night was a reminder that while Athena's temple is worthy of veneration, Zeus remains the king of the gods.

MAGICK WITH ZEUS
by Astrea Taylor

SWEETENING SPELL FOR PROTECTION FROM LIGHTNING

Zeus used the lightning bolt to punish the wicked, especially when he was angry. This spell uses honey, a treat Zeus was especially fond of, and the epithet Astrapaios, "lightning maker." Recite this spell at the corners of your property each year for optimal results.

Materials

• A good amount of honey or agave nectar

Go outside to one of the corners of your property and deposit a good amount of honey onto the ground. Look to the heavens and speak the following incantation. Repeat at each of the corners.

Gather your storm clouds as you will, and thunder as much as you like.
But mighty Zeus Astrapaios, spare us from harm and your lightning strikes.

SPELL JAR FOR WEALTH

Zeus had the power to grant wealth and abundance to a household. The breadwinner of the family often made offerings to Zeus in a special jar that was kept in a storeroom.[71] This spell borrows from that tradition and adds an incantation to appeal to Zeus even more. It also uses oak leaves, a plant associated with both Zeus and money. If possible, use oak leaves or acorns that fell after a storm. This is a great way to teach kids about saving money.

Materials
- A medium-size jar
- Oak leaves
- Acorns
- Coins and bills

Place a layer of oak leaves on the bottom of the jar. Add money and acorns on top. Shake the jar and say:

Thank you, Zeus, for granting abundance on this house.

Put the jar in your storeroom or in a cabinet with no lid so the leaves and acorns can dry. Add more money and leaves on paydays, on Thursdays (Zeus's day), or whenever you receive a windfall. When the jar is full, take it to the bank and deposit the money in your savings account. Alternatively, you can donate it to a charity, save it for college, or use it on something that makes you feel wealthy, such as a restorative vacation or a massage.

HOSPITALITY POTION

Whenever you travel a long distance, there's nothing like reaching your destination and being welcomed with warmth and refreshments. This was true in the ancient world—Greeks poured a libation of diluted wine to Zeus before welcoming in friends, often while singing a hymn. It's still a time-honored practice today. I always offer my guests a beverage upon arrival, even if they're staying for a brief time.

---

71. Garland, *Daily Life of the Ancient Greeks*, 134.

This potion is offered to Zeus Xenios, who maintained order through good boundaries, polite manners, and cheerfulness.[72] It can be made by hosts or by those who will soon be guests. Use juice if you prefer it over wine.

Materials

- A medium-size pot or cauldron
- 1 cup rainwater
- ¼ cup sugar
- A wand or wooden spoon
- ½ cup wine (or juice)

Pour the rainwater into the pot and heat it. Remove it from heat just as it starts to boil. Stir in the sugar until it dissolves, then add the wine. Inhale while stirring. Envision the happiest times you've had being a guest and having guests. Recall positive arrivals, fun things you did together, hugs, the food and beverages you had, and leaving on great terms. Send your happy memories and love into the potion. Take the potion outside and sit with it on the ground. Look up to the skies and say:

> *Zeus Xenios, I mix your rain from the skies above*
> *With wine, fond memories, and deepest love.*
> *May I know good hospitality and cheer,*
> *May the boundaries of hosts ever be clear,*
> *And may politeness ever be near and dear,*
> *Whether far from home or as a host right here.*
> *In your name, I pour this potion offering, Zeus Xenios.*

Pour the mixture onto the ground.

SEVEN-DAY CANDLE RITUAL FOR JUSTICE

Justice is an important part of a functioning society. Without it, there is no respect for the law or those who uphold it. This seven-day candle ritual calls upon Dike, the goddess of justice for humankind. She is often portrayed blindfolded and holding a set of scales in one hand and a sword in the other. Her image can be found in courtrooms across the world. Whenever Dike learns of injustice, she relays her concerns to her father, Zeus, until he acts.

---

72. Smith, *Dictionary of Greek and Roman Biography and Mythology*, 1288.

Materials

- A seven-day candle encased in glass
- A candleholder to prevent scorching
- A black marker
- Rubbing alcohol
- A cotton ball
- A lighter

Make a special place for this candle (and candleholder) so it can burn for long periods of time. On the candle, use the marker to draw the scales of justice unevenly, with one side higher than the other. Say:

Dike, goddess of justice, I implore you to correct an injustice that harms my community.

Speak your concerns, including what happened, who is in the right, and who is in the wrong:

I beseech you to enact justice upon _____ (person in the wrong). Please tell your father, the almighty Zeus, about the unfair conditions, the pain, and the strife until Zeus changes the situation. I offer you the light of this candle, that it may inspire the light of more justice in the world.

Light the candle. Let it burn as long as you can. If you have to leave the room, blow it out. The next day, soak the cotton ball with alcohol and remove the uneven scales from the glass of the candleholder. When the alcohol is dry, redraw the scales a little more evenly but still uneven. Repeat the entreaty to Dike for six more days, each day making the scales more even but not quite. On the seventh day, draw the scales evenly. Repeat the entreaty to Dike and then speak these words to Zeus:

Zeus! I call upon you, heavenly sky father. Your daughter Dike has spoken of _____ (person in the wrong) and the injustice they caused. I ask you to bring swift justice to this matter and use your almighty powers to correct this wrong in the world. Bestow order and instill truth and justice in the world. As I speak these words, I give thanks to you, knowing you can see all and you will work to find justice.

Let the candle burn out completely if possible. Light it again for the same matter whenever you need to send more energy to justice.

TRUTH-BINDING SPELL

Zeus loathes liars and oath-breakers. One of his responsibilities was to ensure that humans told the truth, and he punished those who lied. This spell calls upon Zeus to bind someone to tell the truth. It may remove some of the person's free will, so only do it if you're comfortable with those ethics.

Materials
- A small candle
- A lighter
- A large bowl made of ceramic/metal
- A rectangle of paper (about one-quarter the size of a sheet of paper)
- A pen
- Peppermint oil
- Clove oil
- A piece of thin metal wire or a twist-tie stripped of its plastic
- Incense
- An incense holder

Light the candle and place it near the bowl. Stare at the flame for a moment and get in touch with your anger. On the piece of paper, write the name of the person who will be bound to tell the truth, their relation to you, and the words "from now on, will only speak the truth to me." If you're angry, scratch the paper with the pen until you start to feel better. Open the oils and let two drops of each oil fall onto your words. It's okay if the words smear. When you are finished, say:

By clove and mint, I empower these words.

Roll the paper into a tight scroll. Tie the metal wire around the scroll in the middle, then twist the ends of the wire together. As you do so, imagine your will strengthening. Hold one end of the scroll over the flame and light it on fire for a second, then quickly stub it out in the bowl. When the fire is out, repeat this action on the other side of the scroll. Then say:

Mighty father who punishes the liar,
I request your help with my desire.
I ask that _____ (name of person) only speak truth to me,
I ask this to also be your decree.

For as long as this scroll is bound with wire,
They'll tell the truth or feel the fire.

Give sincere and humble thanks. Light the incense and let the purifying smoke waft into the air. Let the incense burn out completely if possible. Store the bound scroll in a safe place. If you ever wish to release the binding, untwist the wire and burn the remainder of the paper.

HERA
by Jason Mankey

There is sometimes a very large disconnect between how a deity is written about in Greek mythology and how that deity was actually perceived within ancient Greek religion. Perhaps the greatest example of this is Hera, the wife (and eldest sibling) of Zeus. Among the Greeks, Hera played a major role in religion. Not only was she revered, but she was also an extremely powerful goddess. But if what you know about Hera comes only from mythology and the works of Homer, you might have an entirely different perception of the queen of the gods.

In myth, Hera is a jealous and most often unsympathetic figure. She is probably most famous for punishing Zeus's love interests and their resulting children. After Zeus begins an affair with the mortal woman Semele (the mother of Dionysus), Hera reacts by persuading Semele to ask Zeus to reveal his true form to her, knowing that such a revelation will instantly kill Semele and the child she carries. When the Titan Leto was pregnant with Artemis and Apollo, Hera lengthened Leto's pregnancy simply to bring her extended suffering. After the nymph Callisto was unwillingly impregnated by Zeus, Hera turned her into a bear as a form of punishment. None of this casts Hera in a flattering light.

Perhaps the greatest example of Hera's cruelty in myth can be found in the legends of the god and hero Heracles. After Hera gave him a bout of madness, Heracles killed his wife and children. His legendary twelve labors were punishments for these actions. Hera was clearly the villain in this story, and yet the warrior god is named after her (his stepmother). Heracles means "the one who won fame through Hera," and it's likely that Heracles was originally a servant of the goddess.[73] In Olympia, it's possible Hera was wor-

---

73. Kerényi, *Zeus and Hera*, 137.

shipped as a moon goddess while being partnered with the stepson whom mythology suggests she despised.[74] Hera and Heracles do make up eventually, but not until the latter's death and eventual ascent to deity. So what's the real story behind Hera?

While the popularity of many Greek deities waxed and waned from city to city and region to region, Hera was worshipped nearly everywhere in the Greek world. Her temples are among the oldest in Greece, and her relationship with Zeus dates back to the Bronze Age.[75] An ancient temple at Olympia suggests that Hera, perhaps for a time, was the most important deity among some of the Greeks, even after the arrival of Zeus. The Greek geographer Pausanias (c. 110–c. 180 BCE) described an image at Olympia showing Hera seated on a throne, with Zeus standing beside her in a subservient position.[76] That's power!

Despite such suggestions of Hera's true power and her early presence in Greek religion, we know very little about her origins. Her name might be connected to the Greek word *hora*, which translates as "season."[77] If so, her specific season would likely be the time when a young woman is eligible for marriage. Most scholars also believe that Hera was originally an earth mother type of goddess, and the season reference could be related to honoring all seasons, what most modern Witches call the Wheel of the Year.

In many ways, Hera is a goddess of order. She rules over many of the institutions that defined life in ancient Greece, including marriage. Hera rules over both marriages and their preparation. During weddings she was invoked as the "uniter," and then ultimately the "fulfilled," since marriage was seen as a means of personal fulfillment.[78] The marriage and partnership of Hera and Zeus was described by Hungarian historian Carl Kerényi as "the archetypal image of father, husband, and wife."[79]

The marriage of Zeus and Hera might have been something to celebrate, but their romantic relationship began with deception. Fed up with Hera ignoring his romantic overtures, Zeus turned himself into a cuckoo bird and appeared to his love interest in that form, wet and ragged. Taking pity on the bird, Hera took it in her arms and cradled it in her bosom. Zeus then resumed his true form and ravished Hera. The two were wed shortly thereafter.

---

74. Kerényi, *Zeus and Hera*, 138.

75. Giesecke, *Classical Mythology A to Z*, 61.

76. Kerényi, *Zeus and Hera*, 135.

77. Burkert, *Greek Religion*, 131.

78. Burkert, *Greek Religion*, 133.

79. That's the subtitle of Kerényi's 1972 book on the couple, *Zeus and Hera: Archetypal Image of Father, Husband, and Wife*.

This is a disturbing tale. There's no reason Zeus should be rewarded for his awful behavior, but the story might be a metaphor for how Zeus usurped Hera's power in areas where her worship was more dominant than that of her husband. Cuckoo birds are tricksters. They visit the nests of other birds and push out the eggs in those nests. They then lay their own eggs in those nests and let other birds raise their young. Zeus is a lot like a cuckoo. He sneaks onto Hera's throne and then pushes out much of her influence and takes it for his own.

Hera's power extended to other aspects of civilization beyond marriage. She was the protectress of cities and settlements and those who built their homes in such places.[80] Hera also had a special connection to cattle, which might date back to the Indo-Europeans. Throughout the *Iliad*, Hera is described as "cow eyed," "sow eyed," "ox eyed," or "cow faced," depending on the translator. It's hard to imagine anyone today desiring such a description, but to the Indo-Europeans, cattle were a source of money and power.[81] During the Mycenaean period, cattle sacrifices to Hera outnumbered those to Zeus.[82] That's power.

Despite Hera being a goddess of marriage and social order, motherhood is largely absent from her story. With Zeus, she is the mother of Ares and Hebe, but even Ares, despite being an Olympian, is mostly a minor god in most of ancient Greece. Zeus's children from his mistresses are given much more prominent roles. Both Hera's lack of connection to motherhood and her tremendous power can be seen in the birth of her son Hephaestus. Jealous that Athena was born from Zeus's head, Hera creates and gives birth to Hephaestus without the help of her husband. But because of Hephaestus's physical challenges, she hurls the child to Earth shortly after he's born. Hera is capable of tremendous wonders but also of cruelty if things don't go exactly as she wants them to.

Hera is never depicted as a mother in ancient Greek art, and when she is portrayed sitting next to her children, they are always fully grown.[83] Perhaps this is because Hera refuses to be defined by anything or anyone else. While the goddess often comes across poorly in the works of Homer, at the same time she is doing what she wants and she refuses to submit to the will of anyone else, even Zeus. With Zeus, Hera is an equal partner, not a secondary one. Homer pays her the ultimate compliment when he describes Zeus as "the loud-thundering husband of Hera."[84] Hera, despite all her difficulties with Zeus, sits on one of the two thrones of Olympus.

---

80. Giesecke, *Classical Mythology A to Z*, 61.

81. West, *Indo-European Poetry and Myth*, 184–85.

82. Graziosi, *The Gods of Olympus*, 20.

83. Burkert, *Greek Religion*, 133.

84. Burkert, *Greek Religion*, 132.

Because of how she's portrayed in myth, Hera often feels remote to some people, but that was not how her worshippers interpreted her. The poet Sappho (c. 630–c. 570 BCE) most often wrote about Aphrodite in what survives of her poetry, but she also wrote about Hera, and in a familiar sort of way. In one poem, Sappho calls the goddess "Lady Hera, gracious in all your majesty," and she asks Hera to "help me as in the days of old." [85] In a recently discovered poem, Sappho offers the goddess "many prayers." [86]

To the individuals who wrote the surviving Orphic hymns some five hundred years after Sappho's death, [87] Hera was also a welcome presence. To the Orphics, Hera was more than a goddess of marriage and civilization; she was a goddess of air and "the sweet breezes to nourish the souls of mortals." [88] Her power is clearly stated by the Orphics. Hera is the ruler of all things, and from Hera "all things have their births." [89] Instead of the scowl that Hera seems to wear in most myths, the Orphics mention her "beautifully smiling face." [90] This is the goddess you want with you on your journey through life.

The Romans equated Hera with the goddess Juno, and the two oversaw similar functions in society. Juno was also a goddess of marriage and of cities, and she was also a protector of wives and mothers. Unlike Hera, Juno also looked out for young soldiers. She was both "the one who warns" and the "safe keeper" of the Roman legions. Juno was also a bit more violent than Hera. The Romans also called her Juno Curitis, the goddess of the lance. Eventually, when the Christian church rose to power, the prayers spoken by women in childbirth to Juno Lucina, goddess of light, became the prayers spoken to Saint Anna, a saint of women and childbirth who was also associated with candles. [91]

In the ancient world, Hera was a goddess of women, and Cronos's eldest daughter still fulfills that role for many Witches today. But perhaps Hera's most important role in Witchcraft involves the *hieros gamos*, the sacred marriage, and that idea's influence on the practice known as the Great Rite. The sacred marriage most often involves two fertility or nature deities coupling, the result of their actions then being the continued fertility of the earth.

---

85. Sappho, *The Poetry of Sappho*, 17.

86. Whitmarsh, "Read Sappho's 'New' Poem."

87. The Orphic hymns were written during the first few centuries of the Common Era, though which exact century is an open question.

88. Dunn, *The Orphic Hymns*, 75.

89. Dunn, *The Orphic Hymns*, 75.

90. Dunn, *The Orphic Hymns*, 75.

91. Laing, *Survivals of Roman Religion*, 13.

In the *Iliad*, Hera seduced Zeus in order to distract him from the ongoing Trojan War. As the couple made love, flowers bloomed and grasses sprung up from the soil, creating a cushion for their romantic encounter. As their lovemaking continued, a golden cloud emerged around them, sending rain or dew down upon the earth. Glorious things were created simply by these two powerful deities being together.

What's most striking about this passage is that it illustrates what comes from the union of a sky god (Zeus) and an earth goddess (Hera). Zeus is the rain and the sun, while Hera is the soil and the land. United together, earth and sky (Hera and Zeus) create new life. In Witchcraft, the Great Rite is a celebration of two forces coming together to create something new. Often this is simplified into an idea focused exclusively on penises and vaginas, but plants and flowers aren't emerging from the womb of Hera here. They are simply created by the combined powers of earth and sky.

Perhaps the power of Zeus is not even needed, so great is Hera's power. She did create an Olympian all on her own, while Zeus had to eat the Titan Metis to accomplish something similar. An ancient worshipper once called Hera the "origin of all things."[92] For a goddess of marriage, civilization, and creation, it's certainly an apt description.

PERSONAL INSIGHTS WITH HERA
by Maria Shell

Hera came to me when I was in elementary school, shining out of the pages of a book. She came into my awareness again on the television screen as a pair of vengeful eyes with peacock centers that appeared in the aether when she cursed her nemesis, Hercules, in the TV series of the same name. There was something sexy and powerful in those eyes, and they called to me in a very primal way.

In the form of the mother, Hera came to me again. I was a young wife with three kids, the youngest of which was fourteen months old when I attended my first Pagan gathering. As I began to educate myself on polytheistic religion and Wicca in particular, I was called to choose a mother, someone to whom I could pay homage on my new altar honoring the God and Goddess. I immediately knew it would be Hera. As the queen of heaven, she is the goddess of wives and mothers and a protectress of children. Hera was the power I never learned from a mother, who left our home when I was eleven, leaving me to raise

---

92. Kerényi, *Zeus and Hera*, 114.

my brother and sister and defend myself against predators disguised as family, friends, and neighbors. She was the magick I possessed but was unsure how to access.

Then one day, while I was doing a guided meditation, Hera came to me in a vision. I was guided to a cave in which a shaman sat before a fire. I sat across from him and looked into the fire, seeking signs and sigils in the leaping flames and throbbing coals. As I sat, my spirit animal, a sleek black panther, came to me and rested its head on my lap, allowing me to pet her. Then the shaman gestured for me to rise and look behind me. I turned to see the tip of a peacock feather brush my arm. And there Hera was, transforming from her form as peacock into the goddess herself. We looked into each other's eyes, and then she beckoned me to her. As she took me into her embrace, she whispered, "My child." I knew in that moment that I was her priestess, then and forever.

As such, Hera demanded certain things from me: adoration in the form of representation on the physical plane, both in my person and in my behavior. She was by my side as I learned the arts of magick, ritual, tarot, and oracle, giving me the knowledge, insight, and foresight for which I prayed. She empowered me to become a more present parent and to think about things in a different way, making my roles as mother and wife my focus. She was my judge and jury when I had moments of infidelity in my marriage. She called me to task with lessons and karma that both punished and aided me. When I finally heeded her call, I ended my marriage and became true to her in practice as well as form. Fidelity, service to self and others, and love would be my way of being in all things.

Hera comes to me still, in moments of joy and sorrow, moments of magick and meditation, moments of work and play. She was the protectress of the old gods, of the ways of the ancients, and I am called to bring those concepts forward into the modern-day world. But she holds the covenant to which she was sworn—to bring the knowledge and wisdom of the gods to people throughout all times. In this way, she works through me and with me, lifting me up and guiding me to praise her name.

I have worked with many gods and goddesses over the past thirty years, but Hera remains my mother. At times I wear her like a robe, adorned in finery and jewels that represent her in her many forms. Other times I become her, drawing down her power to perform transformative rituals for myself and others. And at other times still, she is there with me in stillness, speaking words of love and wisdom that guide my steps on her path. For all this and so much more, I will remain true in devotion to her even as I work with other goddesses and gods, as the mother of this priestess, and as Queen of Heaven.

Maria Shell is a Wiccan High Priestess, author, and owner of Baba Yaga's Hut, a spiritual and wellness business in Dayton, Ohio, that builds Pagan community through public rituals

and events. With over thirty years of experience, she has walked the crooked (left-hand)
path with many gods and goddesses, but Hera is her primary mother figure.

MAGICK WITH HERA
by Astrea Taylor

QUEEN OF ATMOSPHERE GLAMOR SPELL

The Homeric hymn to Hera says she is the equal of Zeus, the most powerful god in the world. Hera was known to use her glamor and exquisite beauty to get what she wanted. Some people thought of her as the personification of the atmosphere,[93] which was interpreted as the upper part of the sky, the starry heavens, aether, and/or Olympus. This glamor spell uses the concept of Hera's diadem (crown) and lilies (her flower) to invoke her power.

Materials
- About 5–6 lilies
- A small jar (about 4 ounces)
- Water
- A vase
- A marker
- A strainer
- 1 ounce pure alcohol

Place the petals from all but one of the lilies in the jar and cover them with water. Place the other lily in a vase and offer it to Hera. Say:

Queen of Heaven, Hera divine, grant me a glamor that is perfectly sublime.

Draw stars all over the outside of the jar with the marker. If possible, place the jar in starlight, but not sunlight. The next day, strain out the petals. Squeeze any remaining moisture from the petals into the jar, then discard them. Add the alcohol to the mixture. Say:

With starry heavens, lilies sweet, and Hera's blessing, my glamor is complete.

---

93. Theoi Project, "Hera."

Put a finger in the liquid and draw a star on the center of your forehead. Continue this action across your entire head until you have a crown of stars blessed with her aroma. The glamor will last as long as the diadem is not washed off. Store the jar in the refrigerator and use it until it goes bad.

Pomegranate Anniversary Blessing

While writing this book, I decided to make a special anniversary dish that incorporates pomegranates, one of Hera's correspondences that symbolizes marriage. This simple dessert can be enjoyed any time around the date of your anniversary. The richness of the chocolate mousse complements the sharpness of the fruit exquisitely.

Materials
- 2 servings chocolate mousse (or pudding)
- A fancy serving dish
- Fresh pomegranate seeds
- Metal spoons

Place the mousse in the fancy dish and sprinkle the pomegranate seeds on top. Say:

Hera, goddess of marriage, I ask you to enchant this dessert with sweet happiness. As my partner and I celebrate one more year together, we thank you for blessing us with happiness.

Clink your spoons together as many years as you've been married or together. Dig in and savor the sweetness of Hera's gift.

POSEIDON
by Astrea Taylor

Poseidon is the personification of moisture and the god of freshwater springs, the seas, and coastal areas.[94] He was an important figure for the Greeks, as most of their cities were near the sea, which provided food and routes for trade and travel. He is also known as the Earth Shaker and the god who made earthquakes. He is depicted as a nude, mature, and muscular man with long hair and a beard. His symbol is the trident, and he is known to ride through the sea in a golden chariot drawn by horses that ride the waves. His animals are the bull and the wild horse. He is also known as the lord of water monsters, sea creatures, and water nymphs and the tamer of wild beasts.

Poseidon is thought to have originated from an Indo-European deity named Potei-Dan, which translates as "lord or husband god."[95] He was a sky father deity who wielded a forked lightning bolt. His thunderous horses rode the wind and galloped through the grain, causing thunder.[96] He arrived in the region at the same time as Demeter, sometime before 1400 BCE. Together, they were the sky father and the earth mother who had a daughter (Kore). The Mycenaeans built him temples and offered him great sacrifices.[97]

If you think these stories of Poseidon seem more like the myths of Zeus, you're correct. Some historians believe they were originally the same deity, and the name got

---

94. Graziosi, *The Gods of Olympus*, 56.

95. Seltman, *The Twelve Olympians*, 139–40.

96. Seltman, *The Twelve Olympians*, 141, 148.

97. Graziosi, *The Gods of Olympus*, 20.

scrambled with the evolution of language.[98] Centuries after Poseidon's adherents arrived in Greece, Indo-European worshippers of Zeus arrived and became the dominant force.[99] Despite the numerous similarities between the two gods, the newcomers rewrote the myth into what is commonly known today. In it, Zeus retained the lightning bolt, the rulership over the sky, the partnership with Demeter, and the parentage of Kore. Poseidon became a brother of Zeus and was given dominion over the sea. His forked lightning bolt became a trident, which is a tool commonly used by fishers.

Poseidon also became responsible for earthquakes and their damage, and this is evident in two of his epithets: the Holder of the Earth and the Earth Shaker. Every time there was an earthquake in Greece, people sang a special song to him to calm his shaking. Considering the many active fault lines and tectonic plates in Greece, he was likely thought of as a powerful and temperamental deity.

Poseidon was also associated with storms, hurricanes, sea swells, and giant waves, as well as the destruction that came with these kinds of events, which made people afraid of his temper.

In the *Odyssey*, Odysseus blinded the cyclops Polyphemus, Poseidon's son.[100] Seeking revenge, Poseidon delayed Odysseus on his journey home by sending massive storms and waves that destroyed all his rafts. When Odysseus became a priest of Poseidon and founded a new oracle in Poseidon's name, all was considered mended between them.[101]

Poseidon's lesser-known attribute is being the god of oracles. As Lord of the Deep, he ruled over Delphi after Gaia,[102] and he also ruled over the Oracle of the Dead at Cape Tainaron. Oracles of the dead were associated with shores, beaches, or any place where there was a body of water.[103] This underworld aspect, along with Poseidon's earthly titles and the fact that horses were considered chthonic (underworld) animals, suggests he is a chthonic deity.[104]

Poseidon competed with Athena to be the ruling deity of Athens. He caused a salt spring to appear on the elevated Acropolis, and the first horse leapt out of it, while she

---

98. Seltman, *The Twelve Olympians*, 140.

99. Seltman, *The Twelve Olympians*, 38.

100. Seltman, *The Twelve Olympians*, 147.

101. Burkert, *Greek Religion*, 139.

102. Burkert, *Greek Religion*, 139.

103. Stratton-Kent, *Geosophia*, 149.

104. Burkert, *Greek Religion*, 138.

grew an olive tree. Athena won the contest, but the people of Athens still venerated Poseidon greatly.

Poseidon coupled with many goddesses, nymphs, and even a king of Pisa. One of his early myths tells of his love for Medusa, with whom he lay in a flowery meadow. At the time, she was a half-horse woman. They had two children, Chrysaor and Pegasus. (For more on Medusa, see the chapter dedicated to her toward the end of the book.) Poseidon also married Amphitrite, the queen of the sea. She grew jealous of his affair with the sea nymph Scylla, so she poisoned her water with herbs and turned her into a monster.[105]

The Greeks made offerings to Poseidon on the seashore and in the sea. They used seawater to cleanse themselves because they believed in its power to cleanse and purify.[106] A common offering at Poseidon's sanctuaries was the first fishes caught, which were used in a celebratory meal. He also received sacrifices of bulls, and horses were drowned for him in the Whirlpool of Argos.[107] Another offering to Poseidon was wine, poured directly into the sea. He had several temples all over Greece, mostly in coastal cities, but his home was Corinth.

The oceans were an important source of food, especially due to the poor soil in the majority of Greece. Fishers petitioned Poseidon to help them catch fish, especially tuna, for which the trident was used. In the Homeric hymn to Poseidon, he was petitioned as a savior of ships and helper to sailors.[108] His vast temple at the peak of Cape Sounion shone brightly and reminded sailors of his power. With Athena's gift of ship building came many activities that involved Poseidon, including navigation, map making, trade, and travel. He also ruled over naval fleets and sailing leagues. Prayers and offerings to Poseidon could decrease turbulence and help ships arrive safely to their destination. He was honored at Corinth in the Isthmian games of sports and music every four years.[109] As the god of springs and wells, he must have been important to everyday life, too.

The Greeks entreated Poseidon for magick. In the *Iliad*, Poseidon cast a spell on the warrior Alcathous, blinding him and making him immobile in war. Poseidon was also petitioned in a curse to block an opponent's spear and give the petitioner more power in athletic contests.[110]

---

105. Seltman, *The Twelve Olympians*, 145–46.

106. Mylonas, *Eleusis and the Eleusinian Mysteries*, 249.

107. Burkert, *Greek Religion*, 136–38.

108. Seltman, *The Twelve Olympians*, 144.

109. Seltman, *The Twelve Olympians*, 147.

110. Faraone and Obbink, *Magika Hiera*, 11.

Many cities in Italy were named after Poseidon. In Rome, his myth was merged with that of Neptunus, a preexisting deity who originally wasn't associated with the sea and was also associated with Mercury/Hermes and overseas trade.[111] The Roman writer Ovid rewrote the story of Poseidon and Medusa to make him violate her, which is far from the original story.

Eventually, when Rome expanded its territory into Britain, Poseidon's trident was included in the imagery of Britannia, the goddess of the land. Many centuries later, this imagery was adopted by Great Britain, and at the time of this writing, the trident is on the back of the British penny.

At Neptune's festival, fishers and priests took his statue into the sea with hundreds of boats. This celebration is now performed for St. Nicholas, who is also said to command the sea. He's a popular saint at the original places of Neptune's worship.[112]

These days, many Witches work with Poseidon for water magick. He is called upon to quell hurricanes and still the earth's shaking. Horse trainers and animal tamers invoke him for his influence. Some Witches work magick with the Lord of the Deep when they are swimming in a body of water, on a shore, or in a boat so they can truly commune with his watery essence.

PERSONAL INSIGHTS WITH POSEIDON
by Autumn Pulstar

When I was two years old, my parents took me to the beach for this first time. As soon as I saw the ocean, I made a beeline for the water, screaming at the top of my lungs, "Daddy! Daddy," and I threw myself in the water. My father told me I was definitely talking to the ocean and not him. Every year, we went to the beach, and my parents had to drag me out of the water when it was time to return to our cottage. I played games with the waves. I sat on the sand for hours, conversing with the entity I knew was there. One year I was so deep in meditation while in the water that I didn't realize I had gone under. Suddenly I could hear his voice, much louder, saying, "My dear, you have to *breathe!*" I popped up to the surface.

When I got older, I would go to the beach at dusk, journal in hand, and write. I recognized quickly that the words were messages to me. Advice. Requests. Sometimes I just sat

---

111. Laing, *Survivals of Roman Religion*, 114.

112. Laing, *Survivals of Roman Religion*, 114–15.

there, deep in meditation. Other times I would walk the beach at the water's edge in silence, listening to the message of the waves. I brought home a jar of sand and a jar of water to place on my dresser. I created a ritual for gathering both jars, as well as returning them to the ocean the following year.

At a very young age, I understood that the presence I felt was Poseidon. I still experience him as a father figure, and when I can get to the coast, the very first thing I do is head to the water and say hello. I continue to bring a journal to the beach, only now at sunrise. I love rereading what I have written in the very early morning hours, even years later. A statue of Poseidon sits on my altar in front of a framed picture of the ocean. Shells and sea glass also decorate the space, kept in handmade pottery bowls. I still collect a container of ocean water during every trip and use the water for libations or for blessing myself during ritual. I burn incense, particularly myrrh and frankincense. I write my own prayers for more formal rituals, but I usually just speak to Poseidon as I would a beloved parent.

Though some view Poseidon as a god with a temper, I have not found that to be the case. In fact, he can have a sense of humor. For years I asked to have a place by the beach, no matter how small my new home would be. Without making the connection, we set up a recreational vehicle (RV) at a lake, only steps from a beach. When it occurred to me that I had gotten exactly what I had asked for, I questioned Poseidon about it. His response was an amused "Blame Neptune." We named the RV "Neptune's Revenge."

Autumn Pulstar celebrated fifty years in the Craft in 2020. She is currently High Priestess of a local coven in North Carolina, and she continues to enjoy Neptune's Revenge throughout the year.

MAGICK WITH POSEIDON
by Jason Mankey

A RITUAL FOR SAFE TRAVELS

Though Mercury is most often hailed as the god of travelers, for many in the ancient world Poseidon played a similar role. As a god of oceans and rivers, Poseidon was frequently petitioned by sailors for safe passage when going on a long sea voyage. His dominion was not limited to the waters, and anyone traveling by horseback would have sought the blessings of Poseidon, as the god of horses.

In mythology, Poseidon was frequently depicted as a moody and vengeful god. Displeased with the Greeks after their sacking of Troy, Poseidon made sea travel difficult for the victors of the Trojan War. Poseidon reserved his most intense loathing for the hero Odysseus, who blinded the sea god's son Polyphemus, the cyclops. Poseidon's wrath was so great that he extended Odysseus's journey by ten years! Staying in the good graces of Poseidon while traveling is of the utmost importance.

Most of us today don't travel long distances by ship or on horseback, but I think Poseidon is still watching over us when we're away from home. Before going on any lengthy trip (especially overseas, which requires flying over very large bodies of water), I like to make an offering to Poseidon to ensure safe travel and a timely return. This magick requires a connection to water. I like to do this activity when visiting an ocean, a river, or a lake, but a large bowl of water will work just fine too.

Materials
• A connection to water (a body of water or a bowl of water)
• Local flowers, one for each day of your trip (or one flower petal for each day of your trip)

Start by taking a moment to connect with the water around you. Hear, smell, see, and feel the water. Notice the crashing of the waves or the gentle flow of the river. Get close to the water and touch it if possible. Dip your toe in and notice the water's heat or cold. Know that in the ripples and waves, you are exploring the place where Poseidon dwells.

If you are indoors and using a bowl of water, there's still much to explore. Put a finger in the water of your bowl and swirl it around. As the water spins around, feel yourself connecting with bigger bodies of water. Use your bowl and its contents as a portal to the world's lakes, rivers, and oceans.

Once you feel connected to the waters and Poseidon, petition the sea god for safe travels. When I do this exercise, I usually say something like this:

Great Poseidon, ruler of the oceans, shaker of cities, and master of the horse, I seek your blessings. Watch over me (and my loved ones, if applicable) as I journey far from home. May my travels run on time, with nothing keeping me from my end goals. Watch over me as I journey, helping to keep me safe from all harm. O powerful Poseidon, as I ask for this boon, I also give to you. Take these flowers (or petals) as a gift, one for each day I will be away from home.

Begin tossing your flowers (or petals) one by one into the body (or bowl) of water. As you throw each flower into the water, ask for one of the following blessings or whatever else you wish for Poseidon to provide:

- *That I will safely return home.*

- *May my journey proceed as scheduled.*

- *That nothing will be lost on this trip, only gained.*

- *That your waters will be gentle.*

- *May the wind always be at my back.*

- *That I will be welcome in foreign lands.*

- *May all who journey with me be safe.*

- *For our connection in all places and all times.*

- *For success in this endeavor.*

- *May fresh water be plentiful in my travels.*

- *For experiences that will make me a better person.*

As you cast each flower into the sea, envision in your mind's eye the things you want to see happening. Within every mental picture, see Poseidon watching over your journey and guiding you toward that which you seek or desire.

After all your gifts have been given to Poseidon, ask him to accept your offering:

Mighty Poseidon, sovereign of the seas, accept this offering of beauty from me. May these flowers brighten your world and provide sustenance for the creatures you watch over. Protect me on my journey, O powerful god!

If you've done this exercise using a bowl of water, pour the water (along with your gifts) someplace outside near a tree or other green growing thing. No matter where you've performed this ritual, pick up some trash or litter in the area where you made your offerings to Poseidon in honor of him.

DEMETER
by Astrea Taylor

Demeter is the goddess of plants and agriculture, especially grain. Her name, which is sometimes synonymous with a loaf of bread, is a combination of the Greek words *da* (earth) and *meter* (mother).[113] As the earth mother, Demeter has the power to bring seeds to life and make them flourish as well as the ability to cause the fields to be barren or make the crops die. Greece had poor soil, and grain was considered the most basic necessity for survival. The Greeks made offerings to Demeter to survive blights, droughts, and pests. Demeter is associated with several agricultural festivals and rituals throughout the year, the most important of which is the Eleusinian mysteries. She is often portrayed as a seated woman with rich, golden hair, the color of ripe grain. She wears a dark robe and holds a scepter, a poppy flower, or a sheaf of grain. Her animal is the pig, though she can also turn into a horse. Over the years, her sacred mysteries spread across the Mediterranean to several locations.

The grain mother is found in several different cultures due to the shared agricultural practices of ancient people. Demeter is thought to have originated in the Bronze Age, where she was worshipped as a mother goddess or as nature itself.[114] There are parallels between the seasonal myth of Demeter and that of the Mesopotamian goddess Duttur, who searched

113. Seltman, *The Twelve Olympians*, 38.
114. Burkert, *Greek Religion*, 6.

for her son after he was taken to the underworld.[115] There are also associations with the pre-Hellenic version of the goddess Hera as well as the great mother goddess.[116]

It's unknown exactly when Demeter arrived in Greece, as there is evidence in Hermione, Thessaly, and Trace, where rituals to her were held in stone circles. Ancient records place Demeter at Eleusis, her most powerful sanctuary site, at about 1400 BCE, when the first field of wheat was planted.

Demeter and the hero Iasion made passionate love in the thrice-plowed fields to make the crops grow. Their union produced Ploutos, the generous god of wealth, also known as the god of grain underground. According to Hesiod, it may have been common for people to practice ritual fertility magick as well. In *Works and Days*, Hesiod advised farmers to "strip down when you sow, and strip down again when you plow or reap, if you want … Demeter's gifts."[117]

Zeus pursued Demeter while they were horses. Afterward, she gave birth to Kore, the goddess of flowers, who was also known as the maiden. Their union may have been a reference to how fertile rains and lightning (blessings from Zeus) fertilize the fields and help the crops grow.

The most popular myth of Demeter was the Homeric hymn to her, which reveals her life-sustaining powers and her great love for Kore. It was an important myth that showed how the seasons were created. It was also part of the Eleusinian mystery rituals. To summarize the myth, Kore was gathering flowers in a meadow when the earth opened up and Hades abducted her. Demeter searched for her, mourning. Eventually, Helios told her that Hades had absconded with Kore because Zeus, Kore's father, allowed them to marry. Demeter grieved so much because she feared she'd never see her daughter again. She allowed all plant life to die, and she wandered the earth, disguised as a mortal. Eventually, she found maidens at a well who told her about a royal baby who needed care.

After speaking with the baby's mother and accepting a drink of kykeon (barley water), Demeter agreed to care for the child. However, every night, Demeter bathed him in ambrosia and put him in the fire to make him a god. When the boy's mother discovered this, Demeter revealed her goddess nature to the family. Curiously, this myth, from the maiden well to this point, is nearly the same as that of the Egyptian goddess Au Set, whom

---

115. Penglase, *Greek Myths and Mesopotamia*, 134–35.

116. Seltman, *The Twelve Olympians*, 148.

117. Hesiod, *Theogony; Works and Days; Shield*, translated by Athanassakis, 390–94.

the Greeks called Isis—another earth mother who created the seasons. Historians have determined that the Greek myth influenced the Egyptian one.[118]

Demeter asked for a sanctuary to be built and left to wander the desolate world alone in her sadness. Shortly thereafter, the Greek messenger goddess Iris recognized her. Iris pleaded with Zeus for the return of Kore. He agreed to it, but only if Demeter would allow the plants to grow again. Of course, she agreed.

Kore was overjoyed at the news, but before she left the underworld, Hades gave her pomegranate seeds to eat. The liminal goddess Hekate assisted Kore as she traveled from the underworld to the world. They met Demeter in a happy reunion. Demeter restored the fertility of the land, and the crops and plants all flourished. However, because Kore had eaten the pomegranate seeds, Zeus decreed that she must return to the underworld for one third of every year to be the queen of the underworld. This cycle explains the seasons: when Persephone is away, the crops die, but when she returns, plant life returns and blooms. Demeter taught her mysteries to Triptolemos, specifically how to plant fields of grain, which had previously been sown amid other plants.[119] He shared this wisdom with all of Greece.

This myth is likely an allegory for agricultural cycles that happen with the seasons. Mature crops, which are represented by Demeter, produce seeds, which are represented by Kore. The descent of Kore into the underworld represents either the planting of the seeds underground or their storage in vessels underground. When the seed is sown, it partakes in a kind of marriage with the nutrients below the surface of the earth. This union happens in accordance with gentle rains, or blessings from Zeus. The seed grows, sets down roots, and becomes much greater than it once was. Finally, the seedling grows green tendrils, thus returning to the world with the help of Hekate, who aids in transformations and changes. The young plant reencounters Demeter and comes under her purview.

The Eleusinian mysteries, also known as the Greater Rites, were held at Eleusis, a ritual sanctuary site thirteen miles northwest of Athens, near the sea. Its high stone walls contained all of the places mentioned in Demeter's myth as well as other temples.[120] These rites have been called the most important ritual of Greek society. Thousands of people were initiated every year; however, the initiates were carefully chosen. Potential initiates were required to undergo a preparation ritual, and only those who had not killed anyone,

---

118. Penglase, *Greek Myths and Mesopotamia*, 150–52.

119. Mylonas, *Eleusis and the Eleusinian Mysteries*, 20–21.

120. Bowden, *Mystery Cults of the Ancient World*, 29.

who were properly cleansed, pious, and inherently good, were accepted.[121] In order to be fully initiated, participants needed to experience the mysteries twice, usually in consecutive years.[122]

The Eleusinian rituals were lauded by many people as life-changing, which is why they persisted for so long. Demeter's lessons of agriculture gave the Greeks better nourishment, which fostered civilization and elevated them above many other cultures. But her blessings didn't stop there—her rituals also ensured a better afterlife. The details of the rites were kept secret by the oath-bound participants. If they were revealed, it was punishable by law. There are no exact records of what took place, but much can be surmised from the layout of Eleusis, archaeological evidence, carefully worded documents, etymology, reports from oath-breakers, and records of punishments for revealing the secrets and reenacting the mysteries.

The Eleusinian rites started with several events in Athens on the 15th of the month of Boedromion.[123] The first five days consisted of festivities, lessons to prepare the initiates, and purification rituals such as cleansing in the sea and the sacrifice of piglets. On the fifth day, participants donned myrtle garlands and walked in a grand procession on a fourteen-mile journey. For eight days, they walked through sacred locations.[124] Eventually, the initiates reached the maiden well on the outskirts of Eleusis, where the priestesses sang and danced and the initiates were purified with water.[125] The first-year initiates may have been blindfolded here as well.

When the skies were completely dark, the sanctuary doors to Eleusis opened. The participants walked by torchlight, silent and perhaps with a chorus of singers. Priests and priestesses dramatically acted out the parts of the gods as the initiates journeyed through the places mentioned in the Homeric hymn to Demeter. They even walked past the entrance to Hades. It's likely that the initiates helped Demeter search for Kore with torches.[126] Before the climax of the ritual and entrance into the largest temple, the priests gave the initiates kykeon, a mixed potion of water, barley, and pennyroyal, a kind of mint.[127]

121. Mylonas, *Eleusis and the Eleusinian Mysteries*, 7, 247–48.

122. Bowden, *Mystery Cults of the Ancient World*, 44.

123. Mylonas, *Eleusis and the Eleusinian Mysteries*, 247–52.

124. Mylonas, *Eleusis and the Eleusinian Mysteries*, 247–52.

125. Mylonas, *Eleusis and the Eleusinian Mysteries*, 73, 232, 236.

126. Mylonas, *Eleusis and the Eleusinian Mysteries*, 231.

127. Faraone and Obbink, *Magika Hiera*, 144–45; Mylonas, *Eleusis and the Eleusinian Mysteries*, 260.

WAS KYKEON HALLUCINOGENIC?

Some scholars believe the kykeon offered to initiates was made with ergot, an entheogenic fungus commonly found on barley and other grains, while other scholars believe it's not likely whatsoever. The theory remains highly contested, with respected scholars on both sides.

Critics of the concept iterate how poisonous ergot is. The side effects of ingesting it in high concentration include hallucinations, painful convulsions, and possibly even death.[128] It's likely that the painful effects would have been commented on by people who attended the mysteries, and there are no such accounts.

Those against the hallucinogenic theory also believe the vast amount of ergot collected would not have been enough for everyone who participated in the rites every year.[129] The amount of ergot needed to intoxicate all of the initiates would have left a huge agricultural footprint, and there is little evidence to back it up.

The proponents of the "spirited grain" concept believe that it is the reason behind Demeter's epithet *Erysibe*, the Greek word for *ergot*,[130] as well as her association with purple (the color of ergot) and the fact that a sheaf of grain was the symbol of the mysteries. In archaeological investigations, ergot was detected at a Spanish mystery temple dedicated to Demeter.[131] However, this evidence is limited and circumstantial.

Regarding the effects of ergot, the scholars in support of the mystery use of it believe that it must have been in very low concentrations, so as not to cause extreme side effects. Modern science appears to support this, as ergot is used in low dosages to treat migraines, and the side effects may include tingling, nausea, and dizziness or a spinning sensation.[132] This is somewhat similar to the reports of the mystery participants who experienced disorientation, vertigo, and trembling. Furthermore, when one modern chemist prepared a weak dose

---

128. Bowden, *Mystery Cults of the Ancient World*, 43.

129. Burkert, *Ancient Mystery Cults*, 108.

130. Rinella, *Pharmakon*, 85–101.

131. Samorini, "The Oldest Archeological Data Evidencing the Relationship of *Homo sapiens* with Psychoactive Plants: A Worldwide Overview," 70.

132. Drugs.com, "Ergotamine."

from the medicine, he reported it was a fast-acting, hypnotic drug that produced soft visions in low light as well as gastric problems.[133]

It's also possible that some other herb was used. An opium pipe was discovered at one of Demeter's sanctuaries in Cyprus, and she was also associated with poppies.[134] If a hallucinogen was used, it may have promoted a more primitive mindset. Plutarch said that Kore "gently and by slow degrees detaches the mind from the soul,"[135] which could have been an allusion to the hallucinogenic feeling. Hades was also associated with ritualistic hallucinogens in his temple, and he was part of the rite.

Whether a hallucinogen was used during the rites or not isn't as important as the meaning behind it. The expectation alone of imbibing a "magickal drink" after a prolonged time of unfolding mysteries could promote an altered mind state, much like a placebo.

ꙮꙮꙮꙮꙮꙮ

The final stop of the Eleusinian rites was the massive Telesterion, an enclosed palace and one of the largest temples ever constructed in the ancient world.[136] One at a time, the people attested to their worthiness to be initiated by the hierophant, Demeter's high priest.[137] He spoke sacred words and revealed the secret items to the initiates. One oath-breaker reported that the big reveal was a sheaf of grain.[138]

Next, the initiate came face-to-face with a priestess acting as Demeter. She crowned them with a myrtle garland, which represents a peaceful victory.[139] It's likely that a play occurred with all of the initiates inside the Telesterion, which, at its largest, could hold up to three thousand people in tiers. This likely introduced the concept of a special afterlife and eventual reincarnation, both of which were gifts from Persephone.

Afterward, the initiates were probably released into the fields and meadows surroundings the sanctuary, where a celebration was held.[140] Plutarch mentioned beautiful mead-

---

133. Ruck, *Sacred Mushrooms of the Goddess and the Secrets of Eleusis*, 182–85.

134. Burkert, *Ancient Mystery Cults*, 108–9.

135. Plutarch, *Plutarch, Moralia, Volume XII*, 199.

136. Bowden, *Mystery Cults of the Ancient World*, 37.

137. Mylonas, *Eleusis and the Eleusinian Mysteries*, 238.

138. Bowden, *Mystery Cults of the Ancient World*, 32.

139. Mylonas, *Eleusis and the Eleusinian Mysteries*, 239–95; Julia Blakely, "Myrtle."

140. Seltman, *The Twelve Olympians*, 158–59.

ows, views, sounds, and dances.[141] Only the best people went to the Eleusinian fields in the afterlife, so a party there after the ritual would be symbolic of what could be expected in the afterlife. This would also return the initiates to a place similar to the beginning of the myth, the place where Persephone was taken by Hades. The ancient Greek poet Pindar hints at this, saying the initiates know "the end of life [and] … the beginning given by Zeus."[142]

The Eleusinian mysteries bound the people of Greece together and gave them a transcendent, firsthand experience of the gods. Demeter and Kore's relationship is one of profound love and closeness. Although many Greek goddesses had children, this appears to be one of the only loving mother-daughter relationships in all of Greek mythology.

Demeter took part in other seasonal rituals. One of the important festivals that occurred all over Greece was the Thesmophoria, a three-day retreat for married women and concubines. They camped out on Demeter's hilltop sanctuary, dug pits, and made offerings of piglets into the pits. But it wasn't all serious. They also told each other indecent jokes and baked bread shaped into snakes and male genitalia, which were also sacrificed.[143] The women also acted out the loss of Kore and held a feast to honor childbirth. It's thought that the festival helped transition girls into wives and promoted the fertility of women and the land. The name Thesmophoria relates to Demeter's epithet *Thesmophoros,* "law-giver."[144]

In 760 BCE, a severe famine ravaged the crops near Athens. The people consulted the Oracle of Delphi, who told them to make a sacrifice to Demeter before the harvest. They made the offering to her at Eleusis, and the famine disappeared. Every year thereafter, the Greeks made offerings to Demeter in the form of first fruits to ensure the fertility of the land.

Demeter assisted in nonagricultural Greek magick as well. Her name was found on several curse tablets: they were often from a woman who wanted to curse another woman who had done her wrong. Other magickal requests to Demeter included justice, punishments, and curses for others to feel illness and pain.[145] Demeter was also invoked for protection against Witchcraft.[146]

---

141. Bowden, *Mystery Cults of the Ancient World,* 40.

142. Bowden, *Mystery Cults of the Ancient World,* 47.

143. Bowden, *Mystery Cults of the Ancient World,* 124.

144. Bowden, *Mystery Cults of the Ancient World,* 79.

145. Faraone and Obbink, *Magika Hiera,* 99, 70–78.

146. Stratton, with Kalleres, *Daughters of Hecate,* 401.

The Eleusinian mysteries were popular in many parts of the world, and people traveled long distances to partake of them. They were one of the longest-lasting Greek traditions. Sanctuaries to Demeter abounded all over Greece, some of which had their own festivals and mysteries. The Romans syncretized Demeter with Ceres, the Latin goddess of growth, but they retained the mysteries. In 395 CE, Eleusis was sacked by the Goths, who destroyed the temples.[147] It lies in ruins to this day.

Demeter's rites are thought to have greatly influenced Christianity. The most notable similarities include an earthy mother who conceived a child with a sky god, a child who was taken, sorrow for the loss, and a reunion. Another parallel among the two spiritual tales is the sacrifice of the child to create life after death and later assisting those who were initiated to a better afterlife. Demeter's priestesses, who lived together in chastity and gardened, may have been the precursor for Catholic nuns.

The title of Demeter's high priest lived on. The Hierophant became a title in a Catholic order called the Illustrious Brotherhood of Our Blessed Lady, the mother of God.[148] One of their disciples was the painter Hieronymus Bosch (c. 1450–1516), who chose a derivative of Hierophant for his magickal name.[149] The Hierophant also survives today in the form of a tarot card of the major arcana.

Until the removal of Demeter's statue from Eleusis in the early 1800s, local villagers continued to give her garlands of flowers in return for a good harvest.[150] One of Demeter's oldest myths lives on to this very day—ritualized sex still happens in the thrice-plowed fields in many areas of Greece to secure Demeter's blessings on the crops.[151]

These days Demeter is used in motherly/parental magick as well as to protect children from harm. She is also called upon in green Witchcraft for growing plants and fungi. Demeter can assist with accepting natural cycles because, like the seasons and the crops, parts of us bloom, mature, bear fruit, grow older, and die. She can also help cause change in accordance with one's will, especially for justice or retribution. Some Witches call upon Demeter at the harvest sabbats Lammas and Mabon.

---

147. Bowden, *Mystery Cults of the Ancient World*, 198.

148. Mylonas, *Eleusis and the Eleusinian Mysteries*, 230.

149. Time Magazine, "Art: Blood and Roses."

150. Seltman, *The Twelve Olympians*, 159.

151. Hesiod, *Theogony; Works and Days; Shield*, translated by Athanassakis, 55.

PERSONAL INSIGHTS WITH DEMETER
by Lady Belladonna LaVeau

The Great Mother, Demeter, goddess of grain, provides for all our needs. She has given us this earth and everything on it to sustain our lives, to bring us joy, and to encourage our growth. She takes delight in watching us succeed. She also experiences sadness with our failure. She is responsible for our safety and for keeping the entire world in balance. Her daily rituals involve prayer upon waking, eating, and sleeping. She gives us the Wheel of the Year, the sabbats which revolve around the agricultural rituals of manifesting food for civilization to flourish. She desires prayers of gratitude and awareness that she provides literally everything you have.

Working with Demeter is very tangible. She appreciates that we look for symbolism in a seed, but she tells us a seed is food, and without food, we can't grow spiritually. We must first take care of our basic physical needs to be able to focus on anything else. She loves her children. She delights in giving gifts and nurturing us. It is my honor to be one of her voices, as her Hierophant. The Aquarian Tabernacle Church (ATC) produces Demeter's mysteries at the Spring Mysteries Festival every Easter weekend, the same mysteries that were shared in ancient Greece at Eleusis. I am the Archpriestess of the ATC, and I am sworn to reproduce her mysteries. She called us to do this festival when the church was very young. We have successfully fulfilled this duty for thirty-six years.

The goddess has a strong and powerful voice that is also filled with delight and anticipation. She speaks to us clearly, and she often wakes me up with her instruction. There is no question when the Great Mother is sharing information. It's clear, concise, and memorable. Although I do not physically see the goddess when she speaks to me, she feels very large and she speaks to me as a student and as her child.

Each year at the Spring Mysteries Festival, a different vessel is chosen by the gods to carry the deities. I was chosen to carry Demeter in 2018, the year before the first indications of the upcoming COVID-19 pandemic. She was in a state of unrest, concern, frustration, and dread. She instructed to me go around the United States and warn people of an impending disaster where food might be scarce. She warned of losing our food supply and of the perils of eating genetically modified foods. She insisted that our illnesses were because of our food and diet, and that we had lost the basic rituals that she had taught to humankind—the rituals that created civilization.

Demeter is alive and real. One of her biggest desires is that we know her. She told me that we have been separated from her. She desires that we be free and gain our abundance from the earth. She says we are unhappy because we are bound to money, and our current lifestyle is not good for the planet or anyone on it. She tells me that even those who hold wealth and control this world are not happy. She is working to right the balance and restore our freedom. I am still not sure what that will ultimately look like.

She wants every person to learn to grow their own food. Demeter says that you are not free until you have secured a food source. She wants family farms and prayers of gratitude expressed before eating. She wants us to return to a spiritual society where we know that she is alive and operating daily to take care of each of us. She prefers we live in smaller tribes where we provide for each other's needs through cooperative endeavors.

Demeter asked me once what it would be like if you called your child or your mother and they were so surprised that you existed and wanted to talk to you that you couldn't have a conversation past their incredulousness about the fact that you were alive and speaking to them. How would that make you feel? Her greatest desire is for you to know her, beyond faith and question. She needs humanity to remember her, know her, care about her, and be grateful for her. She works to sustain our lives, and she cares for us infinitely.

Lady Belladonna LaVeau is the Archpriestess of the Aquarian Tabernacle Church, and she has been fighting for Pagan civil rights for over forty years. A published author and responsible for bringing WiccanSeminary.edu online, Bella is the Hierophant of Demeter and produces the restored rites of Eleusis.

MAGICK WITH DEMETER
by Jason Mankey

AN ABUNDANCE RITUAL

Over the course of the year, I reset the public altars in my house several times. Often this is done to celebrate specific holidays—Samhain and Yule come to mind immediately—but most often it's done to celebrate the seasons and the deities I most associate with them. At the end of August, our summer altars are replaced with ones celebrating the beginning of autumn, and every year, Demeter is given a place of honor on our most visible altar. With a sheaf of grain in one hand and a cornucopia nestled in her other arm, the daughter of Cronus and Rhea rules the harvest season in our home, ensuring abundance and ridding the house of any unwanted energies.

But before placing Demeter in her space of honor, I cleanse the space that her statue will be occupying with grain. The ancient Greeks threw barley on their altars both indoors and out in order to purify them at the start of ritual. While that's not a custom I've adopted, I do cleanse with cereal grains and use those grains to bring abundance into my home during the autumn and winter months. Since Demeter is the grain goddess, it feels appropriate to ask for her blessing while utilizing her most famous association: grain. I recommend using something that is commonly grown in your geographic area. Wheat, corn (maize), rye, rice, millet, and of course barley all work equally well. Whatever you use, it will be more powerful if you've grown it yourself or purchased it locally.

While I use this rite to cleanse my altars, you can also use it to cleanse a room or your backyard. If what you want to cleanse has a surface on which you can scatter grain, you can use this rite to cleanse that space.

Materials
• Several handfuls of grain kernels
• A libation such as honey
• Olive oil or wine

Start by invoking the goddess Demeter and asking for her blessings:

Universal mother, blessed and divine, I call to thee. Great Demeter, be with me as I bless, cleanse, and renew the sacred space in my home. Know that you are ever welcome here in this space. Blessed be!

Now physically clean your space. In the case of my altars, that means moving everything off the altar and wiping down the space with surface cleaner to remove any dirt or dust. In addition to cleansing the space, make sure everything you plan to put on the altar is clean. This might mean cleaning a statue, an incense holder, or other items. Once you've cleaned the surface and everything going on top of it, call to Demeter once more:

Goddess of seed and fruits abundant, I cleanse this space with the grain you have graciously given to us. May these kernels remove all negative energy and anything that's unwanted from this space. In the name of Demeter, I remove all that's undesirable and unwelcome here. May all negativity be banished from this place. So mote it be!

Pick up a handful of grain and scatter it over the altar and the items you've put there. As the kernels fall from your hand, visualize them soaking up any negative energy that has accumulated in your space. Once the grains have been scattered upon the altar, let them sit in your space to allow them to do their work. After a suitable amount of time (a minimum of fifteen minutes to a maximum of one day), carefully pick up the grains and dispose of them outdoors and away from your home, in the compost pile, or in the trash.

Pick up a second handful of grain and hold the kernels in your dominant hand. Feel all the potential the kernels possess. The grain you hold in your hand has unlimited potential. It can be used as seed to ensure the next harvest, or it can be a foodstuff capable of surviving the hottest summer or the coldest winter. Contemplate the power and possibilities you hold in your hand. Imagine your kernels sprouting in the ground or being turned into bread or beer, and reflect on the generosity of great Demeter. Sprinkle the seed on your altar a second time and ask for the blessings of Demeter once more:

Goddess of the harvest, goddess of threshing, goddess of transformation and growth, bless this space with your gifts. Like the seeds that fall, may this space flower and be one of increase and advancement. Great Demeter, Earth Mother, let this altar (or other spot) be touched by your power and blessings. So mote it be!

Let the kernels you've scattered remain on your altar, again for at least fifteen minutes or up to a day. When you feel as if Demeter's power has been absorbed into your space, carefully pick up the grain while saying:

This space has received the gifts of Demeter. Universal Mother, ever be welcome here, and may my Witchcraft grow like your fruits. So mote it be!

Dispose of the grain however you choose, or save the kernels to use in magickal sachets and bundles.

When the grain has been gathered, be sure to thank Demeter by leaving her an offering. Honey, olive oil, and wine are all appropriate here and can be poured directly onto the ground in honor of Demeter or placed in a libation bowl to honor her.

APOLLO
by Jason Mankey

One of the most important stops for my wife and me on a recent visit to Greece was Delphi, home to the god Apollo's most famous oracle. Delphi is more than just the remains of one temple; it's an entire compound literally carved into the side of Mount Parnassus. Most of Delphi is in pretty bad shape—there are more broken pillars than whole ones— but the space is still inspiring. Our visit began at 8:00 a.m. with the rising sun (and before most of the other tourists had arrived).

Unlike most other sites related to the gods of Olympus, Delphi was a place for all Greeks, regardless of origin. Every major Greek city-state helped finance the goings-on at Apollo's sanctuary during its heyday. Sparta and Athens were often at odds with each other, but they always agreed on the importance of Delphi in antiquity. More than just a temple dedicated to the prophecy of Apollo, Delphi was also home to an amphitheater and the *omphalos*, a stone once wrapped in swaddling clothes swallowed by the Titan Cronus, who believed he was swallowing his infant son, and future rival, Zeus. The omphalos ensured that the gods of Olympus as we know them today would rise up and overthrow the Titans who gave birth to (most of) them.

The holiest spot at Delphi is the temple where Apollo shared his prophecies with his high priestess, the Pythia. *Pythia* was the title of the oracle at Delphi, and seekers came from across the Mediterranean and beyond to hear the messages of Apollo given through his priestess. The word Pythia comes from the Greek word *pytho*, another name for Delphi.[152] There's not much left of Apollo's temple, but its position and remaining footprint on Mount Parnassus give the impression that it was once impressive indeed.

---

152. Graf, *Apollo*, 65.

Curiously, all the pictures I snapped of Apollo's temple that morning featured a clear beam or two of light shining directly down onto the temple. Apollo's rays were not visible to my naked eye, but they showed up in every picture my wife and I took at the temple. We initially assumed there must have been a bit of glare plaguing my cell phone's camera, but the rays appeared on her photos, too, and with all three devices we used. Eventually we came to the conclusion that the rays of the sun were Apollo's way of sharing his continued presence at Delphi.

Apollo is a god of many talents, but because of Delphi, Apollo might be most famous for sharing the gifts of prophecy and divination. Delphi was oracular prophecy on a large scale. The pronouncements from the Pythia were the very words of Apollo and were heeded by kings, despots, and, later, the Roman Senate, but Apollo's prophetic gifts could be used more intimately as well. Professional seers who inspected the entrails of sacrificed animals were followers of Apollo. Less bloody means of gauging the future could be determined by throwing dice or casting lots, with the wisdom revealed coming from Apollo.[153]

As with most of the Greek gods, there were hundreds of temples and sanctuaries dedicated to Apollo scattered throughout the ancient world. In many of these it was possible to consult Apollo directly through a process known as incubation. Incubation involved a small ritual and then a good night's sleep in a specific sanctuary room dedicated to Apollo. It was believed that the querent (questioner) would meet Apollo in the dreamworld at such locations. The next morning temple priests would help interpret the dream.[154]

With the exception of throwing dice or casting lots, all of these prophetic services required a payment of some kind. Delphi, for instance, required a monetary fee (which could vary) and the sacrifice of a goat.[155] The prophecies of entrails readers and seers such as the Pythia came to Earth from Apollo but originally manifested in the mind of Zeus. Apollo essentially functioned as his father's spokesperson, sharing the sky god's wisdom in an approachable fashion.[156]

While Greek religion could be frustratingly patriarchal, the most important people at Delphi, the Pythia, were always women. Originally the Pythia were required to be young, but after one of the young Pythia was raped by a Thessalian, all Pythia were required to be at least fifty years old. (It was believed that an older woman was less likely to be a victim

---

153. Graf, *Apollo*, 53.

154. Graf, *Apollo*, 52.

155. Graf, *Apollo*, 65.

156. Graf, *Apollo*, 53.

of rape.) In a nod to the original custom, these now-older Pythia had to dress as younger women, and they had to remain celibate while working for Apollo. The celibacy might have been a requirement because becoming one of Apollo's seers was seen as an extremely intimate connection, very close to sex, and Apollo was often a jealous lover in myth.[157]

It's often assumed that the advice of the Pythia came from more than just divine intervention and that some hallucinogenic substance must have played a role. Ancient chroniclers frequently wrote that the Pythia inhaled "vapors," leading to speculation about various drugs and most often some sort of intoxicating gas from deep within the earth. Delphi does sit on two fault lines, and the result is that gases such as ethane, methane, and ethylene often drift toward the surface and find their way into the nearby springs.[158] The Homeric hymn to Apollo suggests goats played a large role in determining the site of Apollo's most famous sanctuary. According to the hymn, the shepherds watching the goats noticed the animals getting high from gases emanating from the ground. The shepherds then attributed the wonder to Apollo.[159]

Accounts of the Pythia often mention that she answered questions while in a state of mania, *kátochos*, which was controlled by Apollo.[160] Those who believe that the Pythia's power came from a chemically induced mental state often point to references of mania as a way to support their ideas. But the Pythia did not breathe their vapors in isolation. Male priests of Apollo were always nearby supporting the Pythia. In addition, the Pythia were recorded as being lucid and speaking in complete and coherent sentences while sharing their prophecies.[161]

That the Pythia's pronouncements were coherent shouldn't come as much of a surprise, as Apollo has long been seen as the god of both music and poetry. But long before Apollo was the god of poets, he was the god of *mousikē*. (Yes, that's where the word *music* comes from.) Greek mousikē was more than just instruments or singing; it was a combination of dance, instrumental music, and sung text, and was designed for public consumption.[162] Apollo's dance was not the ecstatic free-form leaping of the god Pan, but rather was precise and designed to bring the populace of a city or town together as a show of

---

157. Graf, *Apollo*, 65.

158. Broad, *The Oracle*, 189, 194.

159. Graf, *Apollo*, 69.

160. Graf, *Apollo*, 68.

161. Graf, *Apollo*, 67.

162. Graf, *Apollo*, 34.

civic virtue. The combination of instrumental sounds, sung verse, and dance was a show of beauty, a trait highly valued by the ancient Greeks.

Over time, mousikē faded into its individual components. Apollo became the god of our music, most specifically the god of the lyre, the instrument of civilization. The power of the lyre was so revered that it was said to bring about sleep, extinguish Zeus's thunderbolts, and make Ares forget about war.[163] Today, many of us think of Orpheus when we picture the lyre, but it was Apollo who taught Orpheus the secrets of the instrument.

Music was so mysterious and powerful to the Greeks that the word ōdē (which we know obviously as *ode*) is related to the Greek word for spell, *epōdē*.[164] (Never let anyone tell you that going to see a concert or your favorite DJ isn't magickal.) Apollo's power was so great that he became the template for most individuals capable of doing beautiful and extraordinary things. Healers, poets, musicians, singers—anyone capable of creating magick on Earth through their own abilities was thought to be inspired by Apollo.

The word *paean* (which is a song of praise) is also related to Apollo. Originally, Paean was a Mycenaean deity who functioned primarily as a healer and an averter of evil.[165] Over time, Paean faded into the background, and the name Paean became an epithet for Apollo in his role as a healer. Apollo's role as a healer would eventually be eclipsed by that of his son Asclepius, which is probably for the best considering that Apollo was also the god of sudden death and the plague and a master of the bow.

It was not uncommon for a dominant god like Apollo to absorb the attributes of other lesser deities. The deity whose influence waned the most as the result of Apollo is probably Helios, who was once the unquestionable god of the sun in Greek myth. Over time the two deities became conflated, with Apollo becoming a sun god in his own right. In certain places the names Helios and Apollo were even used interchangeably.

Apollo is sometimes called "the most Greek of all the Greek gods" because he represented so much of what the Greeks valued in society: moderation, eternal youth, beauty, art, poetry, and music.[166] The problem with Apollo being the most Greek of the Greek gods is that he is not mentioned in the first lists of Greek gods found in the Linear B tablets. Later he is a part of Homer's *Iliad*, but he takes the side of the Trojans and actively battles his half-sister Athena during the war.[167]

---

163. Graf, *Apollo*, 40.

164. Graf, *Apollo*, 46.

165. Graf, *Apollo*, 44.

166. Seltman, *The Twelve Olympians*, 109.

167. Graf, *Apollo*, 10–11.

Over the last two hundred years, numerous theories for the development of Apollo in antiquity have been proposed by scholars, with many arguing for a foreign birth. The truth probably lies somewhere in the middle, with Apollo the result of two very different cultures uniting. The Dorians, the last wave of Greek-speaking people to descend southward into the land we today call Greece, held tribal gatherings they called *apellai*, which were similar to what today we might call a tribal moot.[168] Dorian Greeks often referred to Apollo by the name Apellon. The Dorian influence on Apollo, a god concerned with civic pride and community, seems logical.

To the east in Asia Minor, Apollo was called Lykios, a name that derived from the city of Lycia, one of the strongest centers of his cult. Lykios became such a popular epithet for Apollo that the god was recognized by this name in much of the Greek (and later Roman) world. On the island of Cyprus, Apollo was honored as Apeilon.[169] Cyprus is located near both the Middle East and Greece, so if Apollo was worshipped there early in his existence, he likely would have come in contact with a large variety of influences.

Though the precise origins of Apollo will never be known, what is known is how influential the god became in Greek society. As the favorite son of Zeus, Apollo was the heir to the throne of Olympus (not that his dad would ever relinquish it).

Apollo is also the only Greek god to be fully integrated into the Roman pantheon by name. Whether in Greek or Roman myth and religion, Apollo is simply Apollo. The first Roman Emperor, Octavian (63 BCE–14 CE), later known as Augustus, built his empire around identifying with the youthful Apollo.[170] Other emperors would do the same, but the results would be less dramatic. The notorious Emperor Nero styled himself as Apollo incarnate, and the Emperor Constantine would adopt Apollo as his own before turning to the Christian God.

As Christianity began to grow in popularity beginning in the 30s CE, Christians appropriated the appearance of Apollo for their god, Jesus the Christ. Early images of Jesus are very different from the ones we know today, and often depicted a young, beardless man who greatly resembled Apollo.[171] Christian writers also liked to claim that Jesus was the "true Apollo,"[172] and they reinterpreted myths featuring Apollo into allegories for Jesus.

---

168. Burkert, *Greek Religion*, 144.

169. Graf, *Apollo*, 138.

170. Graf, *Apollo*, 127.

171. Yeomans, "Borrowing from the Neighbors: Pagan Imagery in Christian Art."

172. Graf, *Apollo*, 148.

The tale of Apollo slaying the Python dragon at Delphi was turned into a story of Jesus killing a snake from hell.[173]

In addition to twisting Apollo's image and stories for its own purposes, Christianity provided a second life for the god as a representative of the sun. Italian frescoes in Christian churches often depicted the seven (known) planets as Roman deities, with Artemis and her brother Apollo playing the role of the moon and sun (which were thought to be planets during medieval times). This helped to keep Apollo alive in the public imagination long after other figures such as Helios had been mostly forgotten.

In antiquity, Apollo had a decent relationship with his half-brother Dionysus, but the nineteenth-century philosopher Friedrich Nietzsche (1844–1900) painted the two Olympians as being in conflict. Coning the terms Apollonian and Dionysian, Nietzsche saw two distinct sides to life: order (Apollo) and madness/lack of order (Dionysus). Dionysus was the ecstatic, while Apollo was the rational. Apollonian traits preserved the individual's sense of self, while Dionysian traits subsumed the self in service to a greater whole.

Apollo would also play an indirect role in the reemergence of Witchcraft near the start of the twentieth century. Charles Leland's (1824–1903) *Aradia, or the Gospel of the Witches* (1899) is most famous for introducing the goddess Aradia, daughter of Diana (Artemis), to the world, but Apollo makes what must be a cameo in the book's opening pages. Leland writes of Diana loving her brother, "the god of the Sun and of the Moon, the god of Light."[174] Leland gives this figure the name Lucifer, the infamous angel who falls from heaven due to his pride. But the figure feels much more like Apollo than Lucifer, and the connection of Diana with the moon and Apollo with the sun was a long-standing one by 1899. Later in *Aradia*, Leland includes a tale unrelated to the main text but places it in his book because "the whole conception is that of Diana and Apollo in another form."[175] Leland must have seen the similarities between *Aradia*'s "Lucifer" and Apollo, too.

For Modern Witches, Apollo remains an important deity. His name is invoked in healing spells, and his presence can be felt every time we work with the tarot. Apollo continues to shine down upon us as the sun, and his magick can be felt any time we write poetry or create music. Apollo remains just as beloved today as he was two thousand years ago.

---

173. Graf, *Apollo*, 148.
174. Leland, *Aradia*, 1.
175. Leland, *Aradia*, 86.

PERSONAL INSIGHTS WITH APOLLO
by Derrick Land

It wasn't until I was in college working toward my degree in criminal justice that I really connected with Apollo. I know what you're thinking. When you think of Greek deities of justice, Themis or Athena typically come to mind, and I'm inclined to agree. However, something pushed me to look past that. To my surprise, I found that Apollo also has associations with justice, law, and order—specifically at Delphi. Intrigued, I was led down a rabbit hole of his mythology and associations. The more I researched and read about Apollo, the more commonalities and synchronicities I found between him and me to the point where I started to feel almost as if he knew me as much as I was getting to know him. One time during meditation, I had an epiphany that the "something" pushing me was him all along. I set up an altar devoted to him and started to work with him directly in my practice, which has been over a decade now.

When working with Apollo, I typically do a devotion that consists of a meditation while burning orange or gold candles (or sometimes purple for prophecy/psychism) anointed with laurel leaf oil. Once the devotion is over, I snuff the candle and will relight it the next time. Burnt offerings include laurel leaves and/or frankincense. I leave a bowl of sunflower seeds on the altar, replacing them ever so often with fresh ones and tossing the old in the backyard, which the birds just love! Sometimes I play music to honor Apollo, and while any music will suffice, I tend to stick to instrumentals as opposed to those with lyrics. I've always gotten the sense that he prefers that.

I really can't count the number of times that Apollo has helped me out. He is always willing to help whenever I need healing, for myself or another, or inspiration to create something—from writing a ritual for my coven to making a PowerPoint presentation for work. He helps when I'm contemplating a course of action, encouraging me to take a path and/or showing me a path that is fair and just. At the entrance to his temple at Delphi, there are three maxims inscribed: "Know thyself," "Nothing in excess," and "Surety brings ruin." It has been an ongoing process to incorporate these maxims into my life. Apollo helps guide me in these, but still leaves the final decisions up to me. Through the wisdom of these maxims, and the lessons learned when I've strayed, I have benefited by finding general success and optimism, qualities of the sun that he embodies.

Perhaps the most meaningful way that Apollo has helped me is by being a protector. I sometimes am a little too trusting and wear my heart on my sleeve. If I'm about to get into an unfavorable situation, he will often send me a warning, usually manifesting in an intuitive, prophetic dream or through another divinatory medium, such as tarot. Sometimes it's a gentle nudge, while other times it's a full-blown push, as I can be stubborn. He is also more than willing to assist should more baneful measures need to be taken. Thankfully, those times have been few and far between, but Apollo will unleash those poison arrows if need dictates.

Derrick Land is a third-degree High Priest in the Phoenix Tradition. Operating out of Austin, Texas, he helps run a coven and puts on an annual festival called Austin Witchfest.

MAGICK WITH APOLLO
by Astrea Taylor

SPELL TO AVERT EVIL OR BREAK A CURSE

This spell calls upon Apollo in his Alexikakos epithet, which means "to ward off evil or break curses." Ancient petitioners gave him votive offerings, or figurines, usually with a request written upon them. You can make your own votive offering from wood or clay, as many of the Greeks did, or you could buy something from a Witch store, craft store, or thrift store. Choose a figurine that represents you.

This spell requires a shrine to Apollo. Ideally it will occur during the day to use Apollo's association with light.

Materials
• Lyre music
• Incense (preferably frankincense)
• A lighter
• A votive offering
• A pencil or a fine-tipped marker to write on the votive

Turn on the music and light the incense. Cleanse the votive with the incense and sunshine. Write your request on the votive, such as "Thank you, Apollo, for protecting me from all harm," or "Break any curses laid upon me: past, present, or future."

When you're done writing, say:

Apollo Alexikakos, breaker of curses and averter of evil, I ask for you to _____ (your request, such as "protect me from all harm"). I offer you this votive as a token of my appreciation.

Place the votive on your altar. Allow the incense to burn as long as possible. When it is no longer burning, turn off the lyre music. Recharge the offering whenever you need a boost in protection.

Pythia Divination Ritual

This divination ritual mimics that of the ecstatic possession of Pythia, the High Priestess and Oracle at Delphi, by Apollo. She predicted the future, used telepathy, and viewed events from far away. The incense smoke mimics the vapors used to divine the future. A hallucinatory incense such as nutmeg or mugwort is recommended to achieve an ecstatic state; however, any incense can be burned, as it will likely produce ethylene, a mildly hallucinogenic gas, as a by-product.[176] This is the same gas predominantly found at Delphi.[177] We recommend using an audio recording device to keep with the verbal tradition of the ritual, and many smartphones have this capability. If this is not available, a pen and a book of shadows is recommended to record the transmission. If possible, do this work on the seventh day after the new moon, as that was the day that was associated with Apollo and the day the Oracle was opened to receive petitions.

Materials
- Incense
- A lighter or matches
- Spring water
- A small, light-colored, shallow bowl (or plate)
- Bay leaves (fresh if possible)
- A recording device

Cleanse yourself and the ritual space, then cast a circle for protection. Light the incense. Meditate upon the Oracle's saying: *know thyself.* Pour the water into the bowl and take a drink. Chew the bay laurel leaves and enter an ecstatic trance state. Say:

Apollo, god of light, poetry, and music, god of prophecy, I ask you to come to me now. Come to me and fill me with your being. Inhabit this body with your divine spirit so that I may prophesy the future.

Feel Apollo's divinity settle into your body and saturate every molecule. It may feel like a light energy. With each breath, let your trance state get deeper and deeper. Merge

---

176. Erston Miller, "The Story of Ethylene."

177. Broad, *The Oracle*, 199.

with Apollo and open your mind to feel transcendent bliss. Move your body to release any physical blocks. Exhale and inhale loudly for three breaths. With your next inhalation, allow Apollo to possess your body with his spirit. When you feel the shift, gaze at the surface of the water. Allow your eyes to unfocus. You might see something on the surface of the water or in the depths of the water. If any shapes appear, watch them for your answer. If the divination is unclear, write down the vision and plan to look at it another time.

When you're done with the divination, say:

I thank you, Apollo and Pythia, for your wisdom. I release you.

Exhale completely and feel Apollo's presence leave. Open the circle. Extinguish the incense (if it's still burning). Ground into your body by resting, eating food, and drinking. Go over the messages later when you have a more revived headspace.

ARTEMIS
by Jason Mankey

Unlike most of the other goddesses who resided upon Mount Olympus, Artemis existed in a state of perpetual youth and virginity. Hera, Demeter, and Aphrodite were always depicted as fully grown adult women. Artemis, on the other hand, was most often depicted as a young adult, just on the cusp of womanhood. And, just like many young people, Artemis was quick to anger in myth, often lacking the patience of her older peers.

The youth of Artemis is on full display in the *Iliad* during a confrontation with her stepmother Hera:

> "But since you'd like a lesson in warfare, Artemis.
> just to learn, to savor how much stronger I am
> when you engage my power—"
>
> She broke off,
> her left hand seizing both wrists of the goddess,
> right hand stripping the bow and quiver off her shoulders—
> Hera boxed the Huntress' ears with her own weapons,
> smiling broadly now as her victim writhed away
> a showering arrows scattered. Bursting into tears
> the goddess slipped from under her clutch like a wild dove…
> so she fled in tears, her archery left on the spot.[178]

---

178. Homer, *The Iliad of Homer*, translated by Robert Fagles, 535–36. Spacing in the original.

While Homer does not paint the most flattering picture of Artemis, the youngest daughter of Zeus and Leto was worshipped in a large swath of the ancient world, from modern-day Afghanistan to modern-day Spain.[179] The Temple of Artemis at Ephesus was one of the Seven Wonders of the Ancient World, and depictions of the statue at that temple (often thought to show Artemis with dozens of breasts) are among the most striking pieces of art from the Classical period. Today, Artemis continues to cast a large shadow and, due to her association with the Roman Diana, has become one of the most popular goddesses in Modern Witchcraft.

Artemis is one of the oldest deities of the Greeks appearing on the Linear B tablets, but there are even older pieces of evidence suggesting a goddess similar to her. Perhaps the most striking is a mural from the doomed city of Akrotiri on the island of Thera (Santorini),[180] which depicts a young female deity being presented offerings by a monkey, along with several young female followers in the background. The age of this goddess figure and its clear associations with nature suggest some sort of proto-Artemis, since the connections to youth and nature are two of the more consistent ideas in Artemis's iconography.[181]

Despite Artemis's appearance in the Linear B tablets, her origins were debated in the ancient world, a controversy that has persisted into present-day scholarly circles. Roman historians believed her worship originated in either Crete or Ephesus, the latter of which is located across the Aegean Sea from Greece in present-day Turkey. Many modern scholars believe that she was an import to the Greek mainland, coming from Anatolia (or Asia Minor, most of present-day Turkey).[182] As one of the most syncretic goddesses among the Greeks, Artemis might possibly be a combination of several different goddesses from across the Mediterranean and a merging of an Eastern deity with a young Greek nature goddess.

No matter her origins, Artemis's attributes are well established. Artemis is a goddess of hunting and the natural spaces where that activity takes place. While Demeter is the goddess of agriculture, Artemis is the goddess of the natural world, the sovereign of the forests and the world's wild spaces. Artemis is not a hunter because she's unusually bloodthirsty but because hunting is simply a required activity to survive in such places.

Though Artemis takes the lives of animals to keep a full belly, she's also a goddess of those very same creatures. In the *Iliad*, for instance, Homer calls her the "Mistress of

---

179. Budin, *Artemis*, 1.

180. Akrotiri was destroyed by a volcanic eruption in the sixteenth century BCE. The ash from the explosion preserved the village.

181. Budin, *Artemis*, 12–13.

182. Giesecke, *Classical Mythology A to Z*, 24.

Animals."[183] The youngest and most vulnerable animals of the forest were the ones most sacred to her, and much of Artemis's iconography benignly pictures her with a variety of creatures in benign settings. She is just as likely to be holding a fawn in her arms or feeding a swan as to be shown hunting them.[184] Artemis isn't just a goddess of hunting; she's a goddess of responsible hunting, not killing just for the sake of killing.

Artemis is rarely alone on her hunting expeditions. In both art and our imaginations, she's often surrounded by a retinue of perpetually young nymphs. Although there are no myths definitively stating Artemis's sexual preferences, a story involving Zeus and the nymph Callisto suggests Artemis was no stranger to same-sex encounters. In that particular tale, Zeus disguises himself as his daughter in order to seduce Callisto. Zeus's ruse is successful, suggesting that physical pleasure between Artemis and her nymphs was not uncommon.

One of the reasons for Artemis's perpetual virginity may have been her role as the Greek deity of transitions. Continually living on the cusp of full adulthood suggests a deity perpetually stuck in a moment of transformation. For many young women and adolescent men, Artemis was the goddess who presided over their rites of passage, facilitating the final steps into full adulthood. Despite having no children of her own, Artemis also presided over childbirth, and in one Roman story she was so proficient in this skill that she was the midwife for her mother, Leto, when her brother Apollo was born.[185] For this reason, Artemis is considered by many to be the goddess of midwives.

Another reason for Artemis's association with childbirth is due to her role as the goddess of transitions. To be considered an adult woman in Greek society, it was necessary to both be married and give birth. Artemis oversaw the transition from maiden (*parthenos*) to bride (*nymphê*). The final transition was to *gynê*, a word that means both wife and mother in Greek.[186] Due to her presiding over so many stages and transitions in a woman's life, it's no wonder that Artemis was thought of as the goddess of women by many in ancient Greece.

While Artemis governed a variety of beneficial realms, she was also capable of great cruelty. Like her brother Apollo, Artemis was a goddess of plagues, and in myth she often demanded human sacrifice to end such afflictions (though there's no evidence that anyone was ever actually sacrificed to the goddess). She was also the goddess of infant mortality,

---

183. Burkert, *Greek Religion*, 149.

184. Budin, *Artemis*, 54.

185. Budin, *Artemis*, 103.

186. Budin, *Artemis*, 92.

and it was believed her "gentle arrows" took the lives of both birthing mothers and their babies.[187]

Because of her connections to childbirth and wild spaces, the virginal Artemis was also an unlikely fertility goddess. The most famous expressions of Artemis as a fertility goddess are representations of her from Ephesus, most famous for the multitude of breasts the goddess appears to have in such images. But a closer look reveals that the many breasts of Artemis are not breasts at all, but rather leather bags known as *kursas*, which were filled with items to promote fertility and abundance.[188] As a goddess of the natural world, Artemis certainly had a role to play in the earth's fertility, but she was also not a wet nurse.

Over the centuries, Artemis absorbed a variety of elements from other goddesses. Due to her association with the Roman Diana (which means "bright one"),[189] Artemis became the goddess of the moon, replacing Selene in both art and poetry. Artemis is also some- times shown carrying a torch, a tool most associated with Hekate. Like Selene, Hekate was a lunar deity, but perhaps more importantly, she was also a goddess of Witchcraft, the underworld, and the spirits of the dead.[190]

Perhaps the greatest example of syncretism involving Artemis/Diana comes from the Roman writer Ovid (43 BCE–17/18 CE), who conflated Artemis with both Luna and Hek- ate. To Ovid, Diana was a triple goddess, though not the modern conception of a triple goddess being maiden, mother, and crone. Instead, Diana as a triple goddess represented the heavens (Luna, the moon), the earth (Diana/Artemis), and the land of the dead (Hek- ate). The Diana-Luna-Hekate combination also represented the three phases of the moon: Diana the crescent moon, Luna the full moon, and Hekate the new moon.

Many of our more modern interpretations of Artemis arise from the conflation of Diana, Selene, and Hekate.[191] Diana became the goddess of Witchcraft in the minds of many, an attribute that originally belonged to her Titan relative Hekate. Diana's connec- tion to Witchcraft was further reinforced by her being one of the very few Olympian dei- ties (and the only female one) mentioned in the Christian New Testament. (The other two deities mentioned there are her father Zeus and brother Hermes.) Because of this develop- ment, when Christian writers found themselves wanting to vilify a Pagan goddess, Diana

---

187. Budin, *Artemis*, 140.

188. Budin, *Artemis*, 21.

189. Giesecke, *Classical Mythology A to Z*, 39.

190. Tony Allan, *Titans and Olympians*, 79.

191. Tony Allan, *Titans and Olympians*, 79.

became the obvious (and to the ill-informed who had only the Bible as a resource) and only choice.

Beginning in the Renaissance, Artemis began to be pictured almost exclusively as a carefree goddess of the hunt and the moon. Certainly Artemis was a huntress, but the carefree smile on her face would have surprised the ancient Greeks. But if the gods have agency in this world, that also implies that they grow and change; and if Artemis is now thought of as a goddess of the moon and Witchcraft, maybe she is both of those things. Who are we to tell a deity that they must be preserved in amber just as they were 2,400 years ago in Athens?

ARADIA

Diana further cast her spell upon the world of Witchcraft in 1899 with the publication of *Aradia, or the Gospel of the Witches* by American folklorist Charles Godfrey Leland (1824–1903). *Aradia* is allegedly a collection of Witchcraft mythology and spells from a group of practicing Witches in Italy's Tuscany region. Leland claimed to have received the material in *Aradia* from his confidant Maddalena, who was one of the Tuscan Witches. There are many scholars who doubt the authenticity of *Aradia* (Maddalena's original material has never been recovered), but we believe that *Aradia* most likely represents some sort of long-lasting Italian magickal tradition.

The first line of the Witch gospel invokes the goddess Diana and tells of her falling in love with her brother Lucifer. The result of their love and coupling is Aradia, a messiah-like figure who is sent to Earth by her mother to liberate the Witches of Tuscany from their oppressors. The Witchcraft in *Aradia* is often quite aggressive, and when Aradia instructs her Witches on how to worship Diana, she adds that this must be done until the last of those Witches' "oppressors shall be dead."[192]

Though Aradia is thought by many to be the star of the book, with her name on the cover, it's Diana who feels like the more important deity in the text. It's Diana who makes "the stars and the rain" and is hailed as "Diana ... Queen of the Witches."[193] Most of the book's invocations are also in praise of Diana, and it's Diana who ensures good wine.[194]

The Diana of *Aradia* is unique in several ways. Not only does she marry, but she also (obviously) has a daughter. This is vastly different from portrayals of Diana or Artemis in Greek and Roman mythology. But *Aradia*'s Diana is also familiar. Though her brother/lover

---

192. Leland, *Aradia*, 7.

193. Leland, *Aradia*, 18, 20.

194. Leland, *Aradia*, 44.

Lucifer is listed as the god of the moon (and sun), it's impossible to read *Aradia* and not picture Diana under the light of a full moon. Her vindictiveness is also consistent with the Artemis/Diana of myth, and the imagery of Aradia as a youthful goddess is in line with how her mother was pictured in the ancient world.

Aradia announced the rebirth of Witchcraft in the modern world and is arguably the most influential text in the Modern Witchcraft Revival. The words allegedly first spoken by Aradia and then written down by Leland have become the backbone of many Witchcraft traditions and show up in such iconic passages as Doreen Valiente's (1922–1999) Charge of the Goddess. No matter how she's addressed—Artemis, Diana, or even Aradia—the goddess of the hunt will likely be forever associated with Modern Witchcraft.

PERSONAL INSIGHTS WITH ARTEMIS
by Winston Filipek

Four of the five Greek deities I work with have come to me in one form or another. Connecting with Artemis was different. I had to reach out to her. I had been out hiking, and I saw, not too far off the path, a deceased doe. After many weeks of visiting this trail, I felt I should procure the bones. Out of respect for the animal, I wanted to ask permission. The deity I thought of was Artemis, since the deer is one of her symbols. After some initial offerings to the area of the doe's body and waiting for nature to take what it wanted from the doe, I went to Artemis again, asking if it was time. After some divination with oracle cards and receiving the sign, it was time.

While walking on that trail, I noticed there were other people out as well. I asked Artemis, as the daughter of Zeus (with whom I also work with), if she could send rain just long enough so I could be alone on the trail. Coincidence or not, it started to rain in minutes, with no prior sign. I went to the doe's location. All I could see was her skull surrounded by vegetation. Everything else was completely covered. I gathered her and left one final offering of herbs. As soon as I was done, the rain finished and people started to reappear on the trail.

That is how I started to get to know Artemis. I set up an altar for her shortly after, and I began to go hiking more. Along the way, I would scavenge bones and feathers. In doing so, I learned that you must work for the rewards of the Huntress. Before I go hiking, I leave an offering of incense, usually pine, cedar, or mugwort, at her home altar and at the entrance of the forest where I hike. Then I say a prayer to Artemis to guide me.

When I hike and scavenge, I connect with Artemis. She is the goddess of the hunt, and while I am not hunting with bow and arrow, I am still hunting for the remains of the beasts of the forest. With these walks, I have been able to connect with her and find she even has a humorous side.

One day I had been hiking, and it came to the four-hour mark. I sat on a boulder and took a break. I had not found anything, and I decided that maybe I should head home. I walked to the forest entrance, but decided, for no real reason, to walk to the other entrance area. As I was walking, I noticed an oddly open section of trees. It would not have been out of the ordinary if I had not been on the same path multiple times before. I thought to myself, "Okay, Artemis, where should I be going?"

I walked down this section of the forest, which was clear. It was a strange feeling. Normally I had to duck under branches to get to my hiking area. As I walked farther along this path, I spotted the same boulder I had been sitting on moments before. Surrounding it were deer vertebrae and leg bones. I stood in awe and laughed to myself. When I had sat on that boulder earlier, there was nothing around it. This could not have been from animal scavengers, because these bones were bleached, weathered, and placed in a circle around the boulder, as clear as day. I have no doubt that Artemis led me back there and had fun in the process, almost like a friendly joke. After that I spent another hour or so hiking and finding more bones.

Artemis has almost blended into an older sister role with me. She will help when needed, but ultimately she wants you to grow up to be independent.

Winston Filipek is a Wisconsin-based eclectic Witch who has been working within the Greek pantheon for the last four years.

PERSONAL INSIGHTS WITH ARTEMIS
by Meg Rosenbriar

Artemis Rides Shotgun

The Artemis I know is shockingly modern and a quiver-ful of healing fun. She comes to me in current, fashionable dress, turning up the radio to 21 Pilots's "Tear in My Heart" and putting her feet up on the dash as I drive. Artemis sees me in need of a copilot. She sees my confusion of purpose and longing to do, go, and be. I move my purse over after I start the car's ignition and give her some room to lean back in my passenger seat.

Most days I'm on the back-'n'-forth preschool carpool circuit. I am shuffling kids here and trying to make time for magick there, but mostly worried about bills, Covid, my son's autism, and aging parents. You know—life.

I have one hour to myself most mornings, and I often use it to perform a cleansing bathing ritual to Artemis. Time is my most precious resource, so this ritual is my offering. I light a white candle out of respect for her pioneering right to bodily choice. This affirms that I am also the sovereign director of my own life choices. The candle is nestled in a sterling silver holder, reverberating her nurturing support to me. I burn a bit of *Artemisia vulgaris* to welcome her to my ritual.

Seated in the bath, I stretch my arms up to her moon in naked display of my earnest devotion. I dip my consecrated pitcher into the warm water and pour it over my face and hair three times.

Once, I lament, "Wise Artemis, calm the winds of war and bring me peace!"

Twice, I petition, "Hunter Artemis, guide my arrows, set my traps, and birth my purpose."

Thrice, I honor, "Fearless Artemis, may I dance wildly into the forest in ways that delight you."

I then rest, cleanse, recharge, and allow my troubles to wane in her tranquil light.

Eventually, Actaeon comes bursting through the bathroom door with unwelcome responsibilities and challenges to solve.[195] I grab my towel in modest annoyance and cover my longing for something more, something that would take shooting at the moon.

We return together to the car, heading out to the day's errands. Artemis's fingers dip out the window to the rhythm of the breeze and her hunter's eyes stay tuned to the road ahead. She sings loudly to the songs she loves. Her presence grows like a protective egg around my mundane worries. She enjoys the drive. She reminds me that the journey is the prize and the target is always moving, so we might as well join the hunt wholly, deeply, and without regret. And as she begins to belt out Dolly Parton's "9 to 5," I find my mind transformed and my magick full.

Meg Rosenbriar is a practicing Hegdewitch living with her family on the Connecticut shoreline. She is the co-founder of Witch With Me and the author of The Healing Power of Witchcraft: A New Witch's Guide to Spells and Rituals to Renew Yourself and Your World.

---

195. Actaeon was a Theban hero who discovered Artemis and her nymphs bathing. When he refused to avert his gaze, Artemis turned him into a stag and made his hounds hunt him.

MAGICK WITH ARTEMIS
by Astrea Taylor

In ancient Greece, Artemis protected women and girls from harm. In the modern age, many people believe Artemis assists all marginalized and/or vulnerable people, including women and girls, LGBTQIA+ folks, and BIPOC. In this way, she inspires rebellion against the norms, a shared sense of power, and community among outsiders.

REWILDING SPELL

Rewilding is a psychological concept that's loosely defined as spending time in nature to decompress the mind and connect with the spirit. This simple practice is thought to bring our mindset closer to an animistic state, in which everything in the whole world has a spirit, an intelligence, and an energy. Many anthropologists believe that early humans experienced this state of mind for several millennia. Rewilding can clear away some of the modern pressures, and sometimes we can encounter a sense of timelessness. After this practice, you may have more peace of mind, objectivity, and perspective on life.

Artemis is chosen for this spell because she's the goddess of wild places. This spell requires no materials except a wild space, such as a forest, the desert, or a shore. Ninety minutes is a good minimum aim for this practice, as that is the length of time that has been proven to have the most benefits.[196] It's best performed alone or with someone who can endure quiet moments of reflection. Artemis is perfect for this simple spell. As the goddess of the wilderness, she can help facilitate the right mental state.

Go to a wild area, turn off all your devices, and find a place to sit. Place your hands on the earth and whisper:

I release my burdens and attachments for this time. I ask Artemis, goddess of the wilderness, to help me remember my wild soul.

Take a deep inhalation and look around you with soft eyes. Breathe with a 6-6 rhythm: six seconds for each inhalation and six for each exhalation. Enjoy the warm feeling of the sun, the movement of plants in the wind, and the activity of animals and insects. Become one with the energy of the wild land. When it's time to go, give silent thanks.

---

196. Bekoff, "Your Brain and Health in Nature."

Ritual to Protect the Vulnerable

In the play *Iphigenia at Aulis* (c. 408 BCE), Euripides overturned the sacrifice of Iphigenia in the *Iliad* to have Artemis exchange the girl with a sacrificial deer. Artemis absconds with Iphigenia into the air and places her in a faraway temple, where she becomes a priestess.

This spell asks Artemis to protect those who are vulnerable in exchange for an animal's remains. It requires a wild place. A forest is best, but the edge of a park or an untended part of a yard may be used.

Materials
• An offering of untreated feathers, bones, horns, or hide of an animal
• A hand spade

Under a waxing crescent moon, carry your offering to a wild place. Walk until you find a quiet crossroads and you feel the presence of Artemis. Look for a place to bury the offering near the crossroads, while being careful not to harm any plants or wildlife. Dig a small hole and place the offering into it. Say:

> *Artemis, goddess of the wild places,*
> *Queen of the beasts and fowl, I call upon you now.*
> *I offer you the remains of one of your own,*
> *Returned to you with love and reverence*
> *In the hope that it might live again in your wilderness.*
> *Artemis, fierce guardian of independence,*
> *Soother of pain and troubles, at this very moment,*
> *There are women, girls, and other vulnerable people*
> *Who need your help and protection.*
> *With this offering, I plead for you to assist them—*
> *Protect them and show them the path to safety.*
> *Slaughter threats with your far-reaching arrows.*
> *Save them, protect them, give them strength.*
> *Watch over them and lead them to sanctuary.*

Send the energy you raised to those who need Artemis's protection. Bury the offering with soil. Cover it with debris to match the surrounding area. When you're ready to leave, give your heartfelt thanks to the goddess.

Flying Spell Tea with Artemis

In Italy around 900 CE, several women told church priests that they flew through the night skies with Diana.[197] This information may be one of the first mentions of the Witch's Sabbath, an astral journey where spirits met and congregated with the gods at sacred places. Eventually the lore became formative for some traditions' modern view of Diana as the Witch Queen.

Although there aren't historical records of Artemis assisting with astral projection, she was called upon in the Greek Magical Papyri for dream magick, and she is associated with mugwort (*Artemisia vulgaris*), a mildly psychoactive herb named after her that can cause lucid dreams and astral flight.

Materials
• Water
• Teakettle
• 2 teaspoons dried mugwort leaves or 1 tablespoon fresh leaves
• Tea strainer
• Teacup

Heat the water in the teakettle and place the mugwort in the tea strainer. As the water heats up, clear your mind and think of the transformation of water into steam. When the kettle boils, remove it from heat and pour the water over the tea strainer into the teacup. Allow the herb to infuse and breathe in the steamy vapors. After five minutes, remove the strainer. Place your hands over the steam and say:

Artemis, goddess of the wild and free,
I request your help with my entreaty.
Loosen my mind and set my spirit free
on a magical flight or a lucid dream.
Goddess divine, I drink to thee.

Repeat the spell a few times until it soaks into your subconscious mind. When the tea is cool enough, drink it all. Go to bed within thirty minutes and allow your mind and body to be still. Know that you have the freedom deep within you. The next morning, congratulate yourself on your experience, no matter what happened or what you remember. Astral projection and lucid dreaming may take practice to master. If it doesn't work out the first time, try the spell again without putting any pressure on yourself for specific results.

---

197. Regino of Prüm, "A Warning to Bishops, the Canon Episcopi."

Moon Pie Community Ritual

This delicious, modern ritual celebrates the members of your community. It's designed for two or more people, but it can be adapted for many more. It uses mugwort, a mildly psychoactive herb that was named after Artemis and considered sacred to her (*Artemisia vulgaris*). This ritual is so simple that even children can participate—just swap the mugwort for raw sugar. You'll need enough ingredients to make a moon pie for each person, as well as one for Artemis. This ritual is best performed outside on a night when the full moon is visible. If that's not possible, simply call upon the energies of the full moon light and wilderness. Designate one person to be the leader and one to be the maiden. If you have more than three people, use a table for the items, and either designate attendants to pass out each part of the cake or preassemble the cakes on a tray without the mugwort or sprinkles.

Materials
- A plate for each participant, plus one for Artemis
- Dried mugwort leaves (not powder)
- A mortar and pestle
- A small spoon for the mugwort
- Graham crackers
- Chocolate sauce or fudge sauce
- Whipped cream
- A large serving spoon
- Colorful sprinkles in a can
- Spoons for the participants

Collect all the materials and go outside. If you're in a group, form a circle (or concentric circles) around the leader. Pass out plates to each participant and place one for Artemis in the middle. The participants can walk or dance in a circle, if desired. The leader directs everyone to mimic the moon phases by raising their plates to catch the moonlight and lowering them to be in shadow, first in sync with the leader and then in waves through the circle. When energy has been raised, the leader says:

As we stop and settle ourselves beneath the light of the full moon, we take a deep breath and raise our plates high above our heads. We call upon the goddess Artemis, guardian and protectress of girls, women, and many others in our community. We ask for your presence in our ritual and for blessing—a blessing upon our bodies, our minds, our hearts, and our spirits. Wild one, huntress divine, we ask you to bless us with the magick of the wild places, the power to right wrongs, and the magick of true community. Empower us with your boldness. Empower our friendships just as we empower each other. And as we look into the eyes of the people in our community, may we always honor the spirit in every one of us. (Pause.) Tonight, each of us will transform your sacred herb, mugwort, from dried leaves into a fine powder. As we transform the herb, I ask you to transform us, refine us, and strengthen our community in your magickal moonlight.

The leader briefly grinds the mugwort with the mortar and pestle, then passes it to the next person to grind. When everyone has taken a turn grinding the herb, the leader and/or attendants dole out the layers of the moon cake, starting with graham crackers, then the chocolate sauce, and finally the whipped cream. The maiden picks up the can of sprinkles and joyously shakes some onto each person's plate. Finally, the leader takes the mugwort, stands before each person, and asks, "Do you wish to partake of mugwort, the herb of Artemis, knowing its mildly psychotropic effects?" If the person says yes, the leader sprinkles a tiny amount onto the pie. If the person says no, the leader does not. In either case, the leader says, "May Artemis bless you." The remainder of the mugwort is sprinkled onto the moon pie for Artemis.

The leader stands near the moon pie for Artemis and says:

These moon pies represent a celebration of our sweet and diverse community. We come together, as we are, to celebrate your magick, Artemis, and welcome it into our lives. We give you this offering in thanks for all you do for us, and for people all around the world. Now we feast upon your blessings!

Eat the moon pies and celebrate. Festive music can be played at this time, if desired. When nearly everyone is done, the leader says:

As we enjoy the last of your wonderful moon pie, we raise our plates high and thank you, sweet Artemis, for blessing us on this full moon night. May we know the meaning of true community all of our lives! We thank you and release you because we know we will carry your blessings with us wherever we may go.

End the ritual with the appropriate sayings for the group, such as "May it be so!" Continue dancing and celebrating community. When the ritual is winding down, take the moon pie for Artemis indoors. Place it on an altar overnight, out of the reach of any animals, and thank Artemis one last time.

APHRODITE
by Jason Mankey

The Pacific Ocean is cold and violent. The roar of the surf is always loud, but the Atlantic Ocean sounds quiet and meek compared to her sister sea. The Pacific Ocean can also be unpredictable. Dry shore, seemingly several yards away from the tide coming in, can turn wet in an instant, and almost always when your back is turned away from the sea, guaranteeing wet feet and (often) wet pants. When the ocean catches me unawares, I often joke that "Aphrodite has gotten me." In Greek, the white foam of the sea is *leukos aphros*, which is perhaps why I find quickly dissipating sea foam so magickal. If you look closely, you should be able to see some of Aphrodite in the word *aphros*.[198]

Most people think of Poseidon when they think of the ocean, but Aphrodite is also a goddess of the waters, and in some versions of her myth, she is the oldest of the Olympians. In Hesiod's *Theogony*, Aphrodite is born due to a conflict between Ouranos (the sky) and his wife Gaia, the earth. Repulsed by the looks of some of his children with Gaia,[199] Ouranos banished his unwanted progeny to Tartarus. Gaia was brokenhearted by the actions of Ouranos, so she fashioned a sickle out of flint and convinced her son Cronus to castrate his father.

The next time Ouranos descended from the sky to mate with Gaia, the sky god was pinned to the ground by the Titan brothers of Cronus. Then Cronus, using his sickle, removed his father's genitalia from his body and tossed them into the sea. The moment

---

198. Cyrino, *Aphrodite*, 13.

199. Gaia and Ouranos had three sets of children: Titans, Cyclopes, and the Hecatoncheires (who were said to each have one hundred hands and fifty heads). It's the latter two groups that were banished.

Ouranos's genitals touched the ocean, Aphrodite emerged from the sea and into the sky, forever straddling two worlds. Perhaps her ability to be a part of more than just the waters is why Aphrodite was especially favored by sailors and why she was known as "She of the Sea."[200]

Hesiod's tale of Aphrodite's origins is the most common one in mythology books, but Homer believed Aphrodite was the daughter of Zeus and the goddess Dione. Not much is known about Dione (linguistically her name seems to have much in common with that of Zeus), but Hesiod believed she was an oceanid, a daughter of the Titans Oceanus and Tethys.[201] If Hesiod was correct in his assumptions about Dione, then Aphrodite's parentage again represents the mingling of sea and sky.

Aphrodite is both a much-beloved and a much-maligned goddess. In popular fiction, she often comes across as a spoiled, narcissistic brat whose self-worth is governed strictly by how others see her. Aphrodite could be vain, but she also was a powerful goddess whose power held sway over even most of the Olympians. In the Homeric hymn to Aphrodite, the poet says nothing can escape Aphrodite, neither deity nor mortal, with the exceptions of the chaste Athena, Hestia, and Artemis (and I think a good argument can be made that Artemis too felt the sexual desire associated with Aphrodite—see page 89).

When people think of Aphrodite today, love and beauty are most often the first things that come to mind. Certainly those attributes apply to Aphrodite both today and in the past, but perhaps the most apt attribute of the goddess is *mixis*, or mingling.[202] Nearly every aspect of the Aphrodite story involves at least two outside forces mixing together. Sky and sea, both being sacred to the goddess, are but the first examples of Aphrodite's penchant for mingling.

Aphrodite is a Greek goddess with origins that likely lie far outside the country she came to call home. At the center of Aphrodite's story is the island of Cyprus, which is located south of Turkey, west of Syria and Lebanon, and about seven hundred miles from Athens. Cyprus was an important island in the ancient Mediterranean, and in addition to its native population, it was settled by people from the Middle East (most notably the Phoenicians) and mainland Greece. It was also the location where several different goddess traditions were combined to create Aphrodite, the goddess we know today.

---

200. Cyrino, *Aphrodite*, 108.

201. Cyrino, *Aphrodite*, 14

202. Cyrino, *Aphrodite*, 5.

Aphrodite is most likely the result of the mixing of the Middle Eastern goddesses Astarte and Ishtar with a native Cypriot bird goddess.[203] The native deity was a goddess of birds (an attribute Aphrodite would retain), while Astarte and Ishtar have long histories as love goddesses. This process can be clearly seen in the evolution of the worship site known as Paphos. Originally a sacred site dedicated to the Cypriot bird goddess, it eventually became the most sacred temple of Aphrodite in the ancient world. The deity that resulted from the mixing of these figures was worshipped by the Greeks who settled on Cyprus and then exported her back to the mainland.[204]

Aphrodite's connection to Ishtar and Astarte is supported by what some would say are unconventional depictions of those goddesses. There are bearded versions of both Ishtar and Aphrodite, and all three goddesses are featured with male equivalents, implying a certain amount of androgyny. Astarte and Aphrodite also share the use of the term *heavenly* as a descriptor. Astarte was the Queen of Heaven, while Aphrodite was often described as Heavenly Aphrodite.[205]

The idea of Aphrodite being a newcomer to the Greek pantheon is supported by her absence on the Linear B tablets. Sometime during the Greek Dark Ages, the goddess from Cyprus was adopted on the mainland, perhaps absorbing a more native goddess now lost to history. It's hard to say with certainty when Aphrodite entered the picture, though she features in both the *Iliad* and the *Odyssey*, with Homer assuming she was well known to his audience.

The mixing of cultures on Cyprus accounted for the rise of Aphrodite, and the realms she governs also contain a great deal of mingling. The most obvious one of those realms is sexual intimacy. Sex requires the mingling of two (or more) bodies, and even love requires two sets of feelings to sync up in order to achieve optimal results. As the goddess of love and intimacy, Aphrodite is about living one's sexual life on one's own terms. She never apologized for taking lovers (both mortal and divine) outside her marriage bed. Critical writers look at Aphrodite in such instances as promiscuous or adulterous, but a better word is *empowered*. Aphrodite owns her sexual identity and does so without coercing or forcing people into her bed.

While the mingling that occurs during sex and love is pleasurable, other instances of Aphrodite's mingling are far less pleasurable. The most notable is combat, and the wars that accompany it. Aphrodite was never a deity of war in the way that Ares and Athena

203. Giesecke, *Classical Mythology A to Z*, 18.

204. Cyrino, *Aphrodite*, 21–23.

205. Burkert, *Greek Religion*, 152–53.

watch over such realms, but she was no stranger to the battlefield. She participated in the Trojan War, and she took to the field of battle when it was appropriate. She was also depicted in some of her temples as armed, according to the travel writer Pausanias (110–180 CE).[206] As we will see later, the Roman goddess Venus was even more closely connected to war than was her Greek counterpart.

There are more statues and depictions of Aphrodite surviving from antiquity than any other Greek deity.[207] The beauty of Aphrodite and the art that was inspired by it are the most likely reasons for Aphrodite's prominence in art, but there's another reason that's often overlooked: Aphrodite was often portrayed naked. While nudity was not taboo in ancient Greece, portraying goddesses skyclad was not common. Aphrodite was an exception to this rule, and her nudity and sheer beauty without outside assistance was part of what made the goddess so revered in the ancient world.

The beauty of Aphrodite was such that she required no adornment, but many of the goddess's myths mention visits to her temple at Paphos before attempting to seduce gods and mortals. When it came to dressing up or applying makeup, Aphrodite knew spending time on one's appearance was a form of glamour magick. This is why she invested in fine jewelry, clothing, cosmetics, and perfume.

In the *Iliad* and the *Odyssey*, the word used most often to describe Aphrodite is *smiling*. There are a multitude of reasons why such a word might be applied to Aphrodite, but I can't help but think of her smiling seductively, knowing that she's in complete control of whatever situation she's in. Aphrodite had a mighty temper in myth, so it seems unlikely that she's smiling simply because she's happy. It's far more likely that she's smiling simply because she knows she's going to get what she wants eventually.

Conflated in the popular imagination with Aphrodite is the Roman goddess Venus. As was the case with the other deities of Rome, Venus absorbed most of Aphrodite's myths and legends, but the two goddesses could also be very different. The Romans associated Venus with flowering gardens, the earth's fertility, and the springtime, all attributes missing from the Greek Aphrodite. The Romans also honored Venus as Venus Genetrix (Mother), and they honored her as their divine mother.[208] According to myth, the people who would become the Romans were descended from the Trojan hero Aeneas, son of Aphrodite and

---

206. Cyrino, *Aphrodite*, 51.

207. Cyrino, *Aphrodite*, 78.

208. Cyrino, *Aphrodite*, 127–28.

the Trojan Prince Anchises. The Roman General Julius Caesar traced his lineage directly back to the son of Aeneas, Iulus, thereby incorporating Venus into his family tree.[209]

While Aphrodite was no stranger to war, Venus had a much more militaristic nature than her Greek counterpart. As the divine mother of the Roman Empire, Venus played a large role in ensuring the continued functioning of the state. To that end, she became a goddess of bureaucracy and a protector of civil servants.[210] It's difficult to imagine Aphrodite overseeing these functions.

In the popular imagination, the name Venus is much more ubiquitous than Aphrodite, while the names of the other Greek gods have regained much of their former stature. (How often does anyone refer to Jupiter instead of Zeus?) Perhaps Aphrodite is simply too long of a name, while Venus is a simple two syllables. As of this writing, songs named "Venus," odes to the goddess of love, have been at the top of the Billboard charts twice: one by the Dutch group Shocking Blue in 1970 and then another by the English trio Bananarama in 1986. We're still waiting for a song dedicated explicitly to Aphrodite to top the pop charts.

Even if the name Aphrodite hasn't quite recaptured the imagination of as many people as we might like, the goddess of love and beauty is an especially popular deity in Witchcraft. Both authors of this book have led rituals in honor of Aphrodite in public spaces, and they have strong relationships with the goddess. There are also a number of books, statues, and other materials targeted toward Witches and Pagans that are focused on Aphrodite.

That Aphrodite is popular with today's Witches shouldn't really be a surprise. Aphrodite has always loved mortals, often much more demonstrably than her Olympian peers. Her myth is full of sexual dalliances with humans, and all of those love affairs occur without shame or remorse. Aphrodite's embrace is also welcomed by her lovers, and not forced upon them—a clear difference between Aphrodite and most of the male gods who reside on Olympus.

Aphrodite is also intensely loyal to those who honor her and those she has sought out. During the Trojan War, she braved the battlefield to save Paris from certain death, magically transporting the Trojan prince to his bed and into the embrace of his lover Helen. Later in the *Iliad*, Aphrodite was actually wounded by the Greek warrior Diomedes when she attempted to intervene on behalf of her son Aeneas. Aphrodite may not have been the most attentive mother, but she clearly cares about those she's drawn to.

---

209. Cyrino, *Aphrodite*, 129.

210. Cyrino, *Aphrodite*, 129.

One of the most powerful ways Aphrodite connected to her followers in ancient Greece was at the Adonia, a festival held in memory of the mortal Adonis, one of Aphrodite's great loves. Held in July, the Adonia was both a celebration of the women of Athens and a lamentation for them. At the height of July's heat, women planted seeds in baskets (or pottery shards) and placed them on their roofs. In such a hot environment, the seedlings soon died, and when they did, the women of Athens climbed onto their roofs and cried in anguish together over the loss of Aphrodite's love.

The Adonia festival likely was more than just a commemoration of Adonis—it was also a chance for the women of Athens to purge whatever pain and suffering they had in their hearts. At the conclusion of the festival, the women joined together to feast and drink, celebrating the return of Adonis from the realm of the dead to Aphrodite's side. Few deities in Greece offered such personal and emotional rites, making this another example of Aphrodite's closer-than-usual ties with mortals.

While Aphrodite may not whisk us away to safety during every crisis, as she did with Paris and Aeneas, many of us still feel the goddess nearby with frequency. She can be felt when dealing with grief or experiencing the pleasures of the flesh. She is nearby when we work glamour magick, cast a love spell, or walk along the seashore. She assists with magick for self-love and emotional healing. May the goddess of love and beauty smile upon us often and reign eternally throughout our lives.

PERSONAL INSIGHTS WITH APHRODITE
by Jennifer Teixeira

On the jewelry box where my Aphrodite altar lives, her statue stands on a brilliant golden mirrored table, giving it height and allowing for special things to be placed under her for safekeeping. With her statue is the *Tarot des Femmes Erotiques* deck. Expensive floral perfumes and scented oils wait there too, ready for offering to the goddess, as well as shimmering body powder and gemstones in pink, gold, and sea-foam green colors. There are pink chiffon bags filled with baubles, beads, and seashells, gathered from beaches in distant parts of the world and laid out as offerings to her. There's rose water and an elixir for Aphrodite I made using honey, plums, strawberries, fresh rose petals and thorns, schisandra berries, damiana, hawthorn, cardamom, and vodka.

Every day I stand at her altar and make prayers to Aphrodite for guidance throughout the day. I ground myself and envision her in my mind. Her great beauty and charisma stand out to me as she takes her first steps out of the sea foam from which she was birthed.

I see her walking the Earth and guiding me to be my own version of love and beauty. I then ask her for guidance in my day, and what I should keep in mind for this new adventure, and I pull a tarot card from the deck at the foot of her statue. It's okay if I don't understand what the card means right away—it is simply something for me to keep in mind while I move forward throughout the day. I choose a beautiful floral perfume or rose water from the altar, and I apply it to the goddess and myself to connect our energies and share a special moment of olfactory goodness. I then offer her a drop of the elixir at the foot of her statue and, if I am looking for love in my own life, I will take a dropperful by mouth to help open the pathway to other children of Aphrodite.

There are several stones that have been placed on her altar to gather energy. Every day I take one with me before I leave home. Typically I keep the stone with me to gain favor in all situations. People will feel the energy of this beautiful goddess with you as you carry the stones that have been charging on her altar. In exchange for this stone, I will leave an offering to her of honey and chocolate, or a sensual fruit like apple or blackberries, or flowers such as honeysuckle or rose.

This working altar is cleaned on the dark of the moon, and new offerings are regularly left on the full moon for her to see in the moonlight. It is a wonderful start to the day and a great way to connect with this beautiful goddess of love.

Jennifer Teixeira is a Pan-Dianic High Priestess and healer living in the California Redwoods. Visit www.TheRootCutter.com to learn more about Jennifer, read her blog, or browse her handmade specialty products.

MAGICK WITH APHRODITE
by Astrea Taylor

Modern magick for Aphrodite deals with self-love, romance, beauty, attraction, lust, sex, and pleasure. For all outwardly directed magick in this arena, we advise open-ended goals, with no particular person in mind. It's far more ethical to cast a spell for a loving and attentive partner than for a specific person. We also recommend checking in with your partner(s) with every progressive sensual act. This ensures that boundaries are respected, and it also honors Aphrodite.

BEWITCHING APHRODITE PERFUME

Aphrodite was known for her intoxicating fragrance, as was Cyprus, the place of her birth. This perfume recipe is based on ancient texts, findings at a perfumery in Cyprus, and a recipe for a perfume blend that smells of the spring flowers, lush forests, and wet earth native to Cyprus.[211] It's magickally empowered by "the bewitching circle of dancing Graces" who attended Aphrodite whenever she donned her perfume.[212] Use this scent whenever you want to surround yourself with grace and beauty.

Cypriot perfumes were traditionally made with olive oil and essential oils.[213] The other ingredients mask the olive smell well, especially after a month or so. If you wish to use another oil in its place, try rose hip, almond, or jojoba. Don't use powdered cinnamon—it's too strong, and it could make the solution caustic.

Materials
- A small jar with a tight-fitting lid
- 1½ tablespoons olive oil
- ⅛ vanilla bean cut into eight pieces
- ¼ teaspoon crushed cinnamon sticks
- 3 drops neroli oil
- 2 drops diluted rose oil
- 2 drops ylang-ylang oil
- 4 drops diluted jasmine oil
- 4 drops cypress oil
- 2 drops pine oil
- 2 drops bergamot oil
- A marker

Measure the olive oil into the jar. Add the vanilla and cinnamon and swirl them together. Add the essential oils. Use the marker to draw a five-pointed star on the lid to represent the path of Venus in the sky. Draw a clockwise circle around the star to stand for the circle of Graces around Venus. Trace the star and the circle again and say:

> *Soft flowers, ripe fruit, hard wood, and sweet root.*
> *Graces, encircle me with all of the charms of Aphrodite.*

---

211. Eldridge, "Divinely Feminine Chypre Perfume Made with Essential Oils."
212. Homer, *The Odyssey*, book 18.
213. Hadjicostis, "More Than a Scent."

Cap the oil and store it in a dark, cool, dry place—on an Aphrodite altar, if possible—for at least a month to allow the cinnamon and vanilla to be extracted into the oil. From time to time over the next month, gently swirl the ingredients. After a month, test a small amount on your skin. Wash with soap and water if irritation occurs.

Whenever you wear Aphrodite's perfume, recite the spell and imagine the Muses dancing in a circle around you. The oil should last for about a year. For external use only.

Lady Mandrake Charm Bag for Sensuality

Mandrake roots are associated with magick for love and lust. The ancient Greeks wore them beneath their clothing to make themselves irresistibly attractive. Mandrakes are also connected with Aphrodite—one of her epithets is Madragoritis, or "She of the Mandrake."[214] This charm bag spell combines both of these aspects.

Materials
• Dried mandrake root (a 1-inch piece or a spoonful of chopped pieces)
• A small bowl
• A spoon
• 2 pieces of cloth, each about 4-by-4 inches
• Red string
• Scissors

Place the mandrake root in the bowl. Hold the bowl in one hand and stir it with a spoon. When you feel a connection with the spirit of the plant, whisper:

Love apple, lust charm, in my bag you will disarm. You make the willing so turned on!
Sweet love apple, sweet lust charm.

Repeat the spell as you spoon the mandrake into the two layers of cloth, tie the edges closed, and knot the string around them. Wear the charm bag around your neck so it hangs at your chest or around your waist. A note of caution: Mandrake is poisonous if ingested, and touching it is not recommended by many herbalists. Using it in a charm bag made of two layers of cloth limits the exposure but still allows proximity to its potent magick. If irritation occurs, wash your skin and discontinue use.

---

214. Weigle, *Spiders & Spinsters*, 83.

Mirror Spell to See One's Beauty

In ancient Greek art, Aphrodite is often portrayed as a beautiful woman gazing into a mirror. Our modern culture portrays anyone who spends time in front of a mirror as vain, but the Greeks didn't see it that way. To them, the mirror was a symbol of Aphrodite's transcendent grace and beauty.[215] It's likely that mirrors made them feel connected with Aphrodite and their own grace and beauty. This spell enchants mirrors to allow you to appreciate your positive features and your inner beauty too.

Materials
- A mirror
- A splash of rose water
- A soft cloth

Stand before your mirror and glance at your reflection. Wet your fingertips with the rose water and use them to cover the entire mirror. With the soft cloth, slowly wipe the mirror until it's dry as you focus on removing negativity, projections, and other blocks to seeing yourself as beautiful. Take a deep breath in, gaze into the mirror, and meet your eyes. Say three times:

I see Aphrodite in me. Grace and beauty, I welcome thee.

Anoint your face and your reflection with the rose water to seal in the energy.

Lust Potion

This sweet, spicy herbal concoction is made of aphrodisiacs for all genders, and it's strengthened by a magickal incantation. It makes a strong potion, which is good because drinking a lot isn't optimal for many sensual activities. It's smart and ethical to obtain the consent of anyone who imbibes this potion. Asking "Do you want to drink this magickal lust potion I made to have amazing sex?" is one of the best lines I've ever heard. Not only can it make your situation sexier and consensual, but it also guarantees you'll have the proper conversations about potential allergies and pharmaceutical interactions.

Materials
- 2 cups water
- A kettle

---

215. Fantham et al., *Women in the Classical World*, 83.

- A food-safe cauldron or large teapot
- 2 teaspoons each of horny goat weed, fenugreek, saw palmetto, damiana, and crushed cinnamon sticks
- ½ cup sugar or ¼ cup agave or honey (optional)
- 4 ounces vodka, rum, or brandy (optional)
- A fine-mesh strainer
- A funnel
- A clean bottle with a cap and a label

Boil the water in the kettle and then brew the tea in a cauldron or teapot. After ten minutes, add the sweetener (optional) a little at a time while stirring clockwise. Then, in your lustiest voice, say:

Lady Aphrodite, goddess sweet, imbue this potion with pleasure and desire.
Stir the loins! Bait the breath! Give good lust and deep satisfaction.

Add the alcohol if you wish, then taste it and make any adjustments while repeating the incantation. When you feel the concoction has been transformed into a lust potion, strain the tea and pour the liquid into the bottle. Label the bottle with a date, cap it, and chill it. It should last about 1–2 weeks.

SELF-LOVE BATH RITUAL

The Greeks viewed Aphrodite as a benevolent and helpful goddess. The Homeric hymns say that Aphrodite "gives sweet gifts to mortals."[216] She wasn't just a goddess for the most beloved people—she gave her presents to everyone. One of her epithets is Pandemos, which means "the one who embraces the whole people."[217] Over the millennia, many people have called upon Aphrodite for self-love. She knows the pleasure that self-love can bring. This ritual can help you feel the same way about yourself that Aphrodite feels about you.

There's an optional part of this ritual. Whenever Aphrodite wanted to regain her virginity, she would bathe in the sea at Paphos on the island of Cyprus. This act cleansed her of her history and opened the way for her to be with another love.[218] To the ancient Greeks, virginity was associated with being the sovereign of oneself and one's body and not sharing one's power.[219] Aphrodite wasn't the only goddess who did this—Hera also regained her virginity once a year by bathing in a spring at Kanathos.

---

216. Homer, "Homeric Hymn 10: To Aphrodite," in *Anthology of Classical Myth*, 204.

217. Burkert, *Greek Religion*, 155.

218. Homer, "Homeric Hymn 5: to Aphrodite," in *Anthology of Classical Myth*, 198–200.

219. Pomeroy, *Goddesses, Whores, Wives, and Slaves*, 6.

While this ritual won't restore virginity as it's defined in the modern era, it may ease some painful experiences and emotional attachments. For some people, it could even reinstate a sense of innocence. If you wish to include this part in your ritual, simply say the words that are marked as optional below.

This bath spell is a deep cleanse on many levels. The ingredients include beachy correspondences as well as floral bath oil and Rescue Remedy, a combination of flower essences from the Bach Company that is said to relieve emotional disturbance for some people. Rose incense is used because it's one of the flowers associated with Aphrodite and because it inspires feelings of pure love.

Materials
- A bathtub
- A recording of beach sounds
- Rose incense
- A lighter
- Seashells
- A handful of sea salt
- A handful of Epsom salt
- 1 tablespoon baking soda
- Floral bubble bath solution
- A few drops of floral essential oil diluted in carrier oil
- Rose petals (optional)
- 10 drops Rescue Remedy flower essence

Run a warm bath and play the beach sounds. Light the incense and place the seashells around the edges of the bathtub. Lovingly sprinkle the salts and baking soda into the water. Say:

With these salts, shells, and scents, I call upon the energy of the sea at Paphos, Cyprus.

When the bathtub is nearly full, add the bubble bath solution and the oil. Turn off the water and sit down. Sprinkle the rose petals (optional) into the bath. Place 4 drops of Rescue Remedy under your tongue and 6 drops in the bath. In a gentle voice, say:

I call upon Aphrodite, the lovely sea-foam-born goddess. I ask you to be with me in this ritual of self-love to inspire me to love every part of myself and to know your presence.

Optional:

I also ask you, Aphrodite, to renew my virginity, just as you renewed yours at Paphos whenever you wished to become whole unto yourself. Aphrodite, return my sovereignty to me. Return my power to me. Remove any energetic drains attached to me. With your love, I am made whole unto myself and filled with your loving, mystical purity.

Close your eyes and relax. Meditate on Aphrodite's energy. With each wave sound, imagine waves of Aphrodite's love entering your heart. Allow any blocks to fall away. Think about what your higher self feels like and align with that feeling. Say to yourself, "I love and accept myself just as I am," several times until you can say it without any tension in your body. Take as long as you need.

When you rise from the foamy waters, allow anything that you don't wish to take with you to stay in the bathtub—really feel that it's separate from you. Drain the water and watch it go away while maintaining the feeling of separation from that which you are leaving behind. When it has all drained, turn your back on it. You are cleansed and renewed! If you desire, you may shower off any excess soap or salt.

ATHENA
by *Astrea Taylor*

Athena is one of the most complex deities in ancient Greece. Her name means air, divine mind, and moon.[220] She was seen as the embodiment of cities as well as their protector, especially in Athens. She rules over civilization, wisdom, battle, peace, intelligence, and creativity. She's also the goddess of invention—she's credited with inventing chariots, bridles, carpentry and ships, wool production, plows, juries, clay pots, and flutes.

In Greek art, Athena was mostly characterized as a girl or a baby freshly born from the head of Zeus until about 440 BCE. After that time, she was more commonly portrayed as a fully grown woman.[221] Depending on the source, she has blue, green, or gray eyes. As a war goddess, she wore all kinds of battle gear, including armor, a spear, and a helmet with a horse-hair crest or a sphinx flanked by two griffins. Athena carries a shield that bears a circle of snakes and an image of Medusa's head, a *gorgoneion*. She sometimes carries a goatskin, which was a common sacrifice to her. Owls and snakes are her animals, and they may connect her with a group of ancient bird-snake goddesses. She's also associated with olive trees.

Athena is seen as a level-headed goddess of civilization. She is a goddess of all of the people in a city: those on the bottom who make things, those in the middle who go to war, and those at the top who make decisions. She assists them in the perfection of their crafts and the advancement of intelligence. Many of her domains are activities that can be improved with awareness and strategy. Her associations with ancient activities such as

---

220. Deacy and Villing, "Athena Past and Present," in *Athena in the Classical World*, 7.
221. Seltman, *The Twelve Olympians*, 56–57.

weaving cloth and war, as well as innovative ones, means that she united the gods with the Greeks as they evolved together, always with her insightful influence.[222]

Before Greece rose to power, several cultures revered a goddess with a similar name and likeness to Athena. In Crete, Atana was a shield-carrying "Goddess of the Palace" who was honored with processions. Mycenaeans also had a "Palace Goddess" named Atana who was the goddess of intuition and was associated with youth, a shield, a snake, olive trees, and a bird.[223] Libyans and Egyptians identified Athena as Neith, their temple warrior goddess who carried a shield. Plato believed the name Athena was a derivation of the Egyptian words *Ht Nt*, which translates to "temple of Neith."[224] Historians believe these myths were merged with the maiden warrior goddess who was the daughter of Zeus.[225]

According to Hesiod, Athena's mother was Metis, a Titan goddess of cunning wisdom, but she did not give birth to her. Athena's father, Zeus, swallowed the pregnant Metis after hearing a prophecy that their son would overthrow him. Afterward, Zeus got a headache so intense that Hephaestus had to split his head open with an ax. Athena emerged from Zeus's head fully grown, with shining armor, a shield, and a spear. She shouted a war cry and stomped a victorious war dance, which caused such a fright among the gods that Mount Olympus rocked, the earth roared, the sea turned purple, and its waves stopped. Even Helios, the sun, halted his horses.

When Athena set down her weapons and removed her armor, the gods saw she also embodied wisdom. The earth and Helios resumed their usual activities. Zeus welcomed her to Olympus, where she became his favorite daughter—she was the only one to whom he gave access to his powerful lightning bolt.

The Homeric hymn to Athena omits a mother, and Greek dramatists used Athena's "motherless" birth to promote a dominant male role in procreation.[226] However, this is the only instance of a male parthenogenesis,[227] so a goddess was likely to have been involved, even if she was hidden.

---

222. Deacy and Villing, "Athena Past and Present," in *Athena in the Classical World*, 10.

223. Seltman, *The Twelve Olympians*, 54.

224. Shearer, *Athene*, 41–43, 50.

225. Seltman, *The Twelve Olympians*, 54.

226. Mitchell-Boyask, *Aeschylus*, 118.

227. Park, "Parthenogenesis in Hesiod's *Theogony*," 261–83. The only other instance of male parthenogenesis could be Aphrodite, if parentage could be assigned to the severed genitals of Ouranus.

One of Athena's most famous myths is how she bested Poseidon to become the goddess of Athens. He caused seawater to rise into a pool on the Acropolis, from which the first horse leaped out. Athena grew an olive tree from the rocky soil. These hardy plants, which provided food, shade, oil, and building materials, were considered more useful to the Greeks, so she won the contest. To this day, olive branches are associated with peace and victory.

Athena was always a virgin goddess. She had no partners or children, but two myths depict her as motherly. After Prometheus formed the first humans from clay, Athena breathed the spirit of life into them and gave them souls. Yet another myth is the birth of Erichthonius, the first king of Athens, who is sometimes portrayed as a snake. He was created when Athena refused Hephaestus and he ejaculated on her thigh. Athena wiped it to the ground and a child appeared. She cared for him and taught him her wisdom.

In the Trojan War, Athena assisted the Achaean warriors and heroes against Troy, especially Ulysses. In the *Odyssey*, she demonstrates her support as his patron deity by protecting and guiding him. Although Athena interacted with powerful gods in myth, she often exceeded them in intelligence and insight. Her birth from Zeus's head was a unique way to join forces with him—perhaps even a cunning way to gain power. She and Zeus were both known for wisdom, but she shared hers with humanity. Poseidon ruled the sea and created horses, but Athena is credited with the creation of ships, bridles, and chariots to master those forces. Where Prometheus could only give form to humans, Athena gave life. In her denial of Hephaestus, she helped create a ruler who changed Athens. In the *Iliad*, Athena bests the god of war, Ares. Her measured actions contrast with Ares's fiery impulsiveness—she strategized to win not just the day's fight, but the entire war.

Athena's most famous temples are on the Acropolis, an elevated outcropping that stands over five hundred feet above the city of Athens. This is where a thirty-foot statue of Athena stood—it was so big, the sailors returning home from the sea could see it.[228] The Acropolis had eight temples, the largest of which was the Parthenon. Unlike many other temples, this one had an enormous inner sanctum, which may have been used for group gatherings or in rainy weather. An older temple to Athena held her most sacred and ancient image: a piece of olive wood in her image, which was said to have fallen from the sky and was known as the Palladion.

Men and women alike left offerings at Athena's temples all across Greece, most often the first fruits or their first pottery efforts. Women made many offerings to her—possibly

228. Shearer, *Athene*, 7.

more than to any other goddess.[229] Her temple received several votive offerings, which were buried on the Acropolis when the temple was cleaned.

Athena's festival, the Panathenaea, was a citywide unifying celebration held annually on her birthday late in the month of Hekatombaion after much preparation. On our calendars, the festival begins in mid-August. About two months before the event, noblewomen and priestesses cleaned and purified her temple. They undressed the olive wood image of Athena, veiled her, and carried her in a procession to the sea, with a sweet fig bread carried by the first in line. As Athena bathed in the sea, all city work ceased, to give her a break from overseeing city matters.

Weeks later, the priestess of Athena held a ritual to honor the girls who had been temple priestesses for the past year, and new priestesses were initiated into Athena's service. The ritual included carrying a mysterious veiled object from the temple into an underground passage. When the priestesses reached the sanctum below the earth, they picked up another mysterious veiled object and carried it to the temple. Athena's priestesses then attended the Eleusinian mysteries at the Skira festival.

The night before the Panathenaea, Athenians gathered in the forest nearby to hold a ritual and offer a sacrifice to Athena and Eros. At dawn, the fire from the ritual was brought to the city gates, where a procession began to wind through the city. Every Athenian attended—priests and priestesses, men, women, children, and militia on horses. Sacrificial oxen accompanied the people as they wove through the city, up to the Acropolis, and finally to Athena's temple. They carried water, wine, incense, food, chairs, and parasols. The oxen were sacrificed, and Athena's priestesses offered the olive wood Palladion a beautiful new dress embroidered with battle scenes. At the feast afterward, poets recited Homer's poems and there were musical contests, athletic contests, and dancing. The newly elected officials were also honored in ritual.

Every four years, a "greater" version of the Panathenaea festival occurred. The Palladion was given a great billowing dress that looked like a ship's sails. It was placed in a wooden ship and carried through the city. Even more festivities occurred, including chariot races and ship races.

Athena's influence was woven throughout people's lives. She was considered the mother of Athens and humanity. Apart from the annual Panathenaea, she presided over maturity rituals for boys and especially girls, which had dancing, singing, and tutoring from women.[230] She was also part of pre-marriage rituals for women to invoke protection

---

229. Fantham et al., *Women in the Classical World*, 34.

230. Fantham et al., *Women in the Classical World*, 12–13.

and conception.[231] Artists called upon Athena's intuition in creating art—potters even held a hand over their kilns and invoked her for a good fire. Weaver women invoked her skill to transform wool into fine clothing for their household. Warriors called upon Athena's fighting spirit and her close association with Nike for victory in battle. Alexander the Great made several offerings to her on his journeys and considered her assistance paramount to his success.[232] Politicians asked for Athena's blessings, protection, and wisdom about how the city should operate.

The Greeks invoked Athena in a couple of magickal rites. They called upon her aid in a land-dispute curse near Delphi in the early sixth century BCE to bring poverty and fruitless crops to anyone who tried to till the ground. The purpose of this was so it would remain an untaxed, freely accessible area for spiritual seekers to pass through. The result of the curse is unknown, but it's assumed that the threat alone would have intimidated anyone who tried to live there.[233] One person in an ancient Greek territory that is now modern-day Hungary wrote a curse tablet requesting Athena to pursue an unfaithful wife.[234] The Greek Magical Papyri, one of the best-known texts of the ancient Greek era, states that Athena bestows power upon magickal practitioners. In it, she is invoked to assist in love magick known as the Cup Spell.[235]

The Romans combined many of Athena's attributes with the Etruscan goddess Minerva, a warrior goddess with wings, a lightning bolt, and owls. Together, they formed the Roman goddess Minerva, the protector and embodiment of Rome. However, despite her shining armor, Minerva was not a battle goddess, but rather the goddess of commerce, housewives, artisans, teachers, and doctors.[236] The Romans also created the goddess Roma, a battle-hardy version of Minerva, with a horsehair helmet and a spear. When the Romans colonized Gaul and Celtic lands, they syncretized Minerva with many local goddesses. They combined Minerva with the Irish goddess Brigid, the Celtic goddess Brigantia, and the Gallic goddess Brigindo to create Britannia, the goddess embodiment of the land. She was often depicted as a young woman with a gorgoneion on her armored breastplate, a trident spear, a horsehair

---

231. Shearer, *Athene*, 27.

232. Graziosi, *The Gods of Olympus*, 101.

233. Faraone and Obbink, *Magika Hiera*, 37.

234. Stratton and Kalleres, *Daughters of Hecate*, 342.

235. Betz, *The Greek Magical Papyri in Translation*, 95, 136.

236. Shearer, *Athene*, 76–80.

helmet, and a shield. They also syncretized Minerva with Sulis, the Celtic solar goddess of healing. Hundreds of curse tablets were found at her temple in Bath.[237]

In the first century CE, the Roman poets Ovid and Virgil created new myths where Athena punished women, including turning Arachne into a spider and Medusa into a monster. These stories might be less about the Greek goddess Athena and more about the Roman goddess Minerva.

Athena was adapted into primitive Christianity as Sophia, the spirit of wisdom, creativity, and reason who assists humanity and sometimes appears as an avenging angel.[238] There wasn't a goddess named Sophia, and this transformation of Athena into Sophia was transparent. Sophia isn't far from *sophos*, the Greek word often associated with Athena that means divine wisdom, skill, knowledge, and cunning.[239] Around 500 CE, the church rededicated the Parthenon to Mary, another divine virgin mother.

In the late 1500s, Queen Elizabeth I used images of the goddess Britannia to unite soldiers to fight for Great Britain. Centuries later, Britannia had a daughter, Zealandia, the goddess and embodiment of New Zealand. Marianne and Columbia, revolutionary-era goddesses and the embodiments of France and the United States, respectively, also arose as reincarnations of Britannia and Libertas. They're depicted as battlefield goddesses leading the charge toward victory and reason.

Athena was one of the deities that inspired Theosophy, a wisdom-seeking religion that was a foundational part of the Spiritualist movement.[240] One of its founders described Theosophists as followers of Athena.[241] A later group, the Anthroposophical Society, called Sophia a "goddess of wisdom."[242]

Athens is one of the ten oldest cities in the world,[243] and twenty-seven other cities or villages are named Athena or Athens—twenty-four of which are in North America alone. Dozens of international companies use her name. These attest to Athena's broad and lasting influence on civilization and progress.

Witches have called upon Athena's assistance for decades. Doreen Valiente (1922–1999) included her in the Charge of the Goddess, and several other Witchcraft books invoke her in rituals and spells. Athena assists artists, craftspeople, lawyers, warriors, writers, sci-

---

237. Shearer, *Athene*, 84.

238. Harris, "Athena, Sophia and the Logos," 57–64.

239. Online Etymology Dictionary, "Sophia," accessed June 2022, https://www.etymonline.com/word/sophia.

240. Blavatsky, *A Modern Panarion*, 263.

241. Leadbeater, *Freemasonry and Its Ancient Mystic Rites*, 82.

242. Steiner, *The Goddess*, 40.

243. Hansen, "The World's Oldest Cities."

entists, scholars, activists, and modern-day heroes. Her resistance to binary gender roles inspires some people who identify as asexual or nonbinary, and some activists are inspired by her in their fight for equal rights.

PERSONAL INSIGHTS WITH ATHENA
by Astrea Taylor

For several years now, I have called upon Athena to help me weave my magick into the world. She's helpful with many different kinds of magick, but particularly magick that deals with the mind. She is one of the smartest gods, especially when it comes to arts and crafts. She has helped me learn whatever craft I have asked for assistance with, and she also helps with writing invocations and inventing rituals and spells that work.

I have an altar to Athena along the east wall of my ritual space. This location brings about her airy qualities. On it, there's an image of Athena holding a tiny owl, several pieces of clear quartz crystals, Herkimer diamonds, lepidolite, feathers, an incense holder, and a bell. Her favorite offerings are wine, olive oil, incense, and energy.

Athena seems to like being called upon in my rituals second, right after Hestia. I call upon Athena, as well as the element of air and the guardians of the east, to open that energetic pathway. Athena is also the second-to-last deity that I release from the ritual, right before Hestia. In my new moon and full moon rituals, I usually ask my chosen deities and spirits to assist with a boon. I let my mind grow still, and I ask each of them what they have to say about it. Athena is often enthusiastic about my goals. She blesses my magick with her energy and tells me we will get it done. Athena has told me that she is not just a goddess of war, but also a goddess of health, vitality, strength, inner fortitude, the old, the new, the now, and the always. She has said that she is the light, and her chosen people bring her light into the world. She has also told me that she protects those she mentors, the chosen few.

While I was researching Athena for this book, she appeared to me in a dream that I will never forget. In this dream, I was in the middle of a quest in a sprawling, utopian cityscape. All of a sudden, the scene was pulled to one side. It was as if the city before me had been printed on a velvet curtain, and it became two-dimensional and folded against itself. Then the veil dropped, and before me, in a dark room, was a girl. Her entire being shone with a mysterious milky light, which looked like a dozen full moons or electrified ether. She glowed with an inner brilliance that moved beneath the surface of her skin and emanated several feet from her head and body.

I didn't have to ask who it was. It was clear to me that this was Athena, the girl goddess who blesses artists. She smiled softly, as if amused. Her eyes remained serious and owlish, just as you'd expect the eyes of someone so old and wise to appear. I was dazzled by her amazing energy, which seemed so full of ability and love. For a long moment, we communicated without words while staring deep into each other's eyes. I knew she was examining my mind and soul deeply, and I allowed it. She seemed to be assessing me, weighing what she saw. Her smile shifted into one of satisfaction, as if she had accomplished what she had set out to learn. I felt an even greater connection with her, as well as love and support. She made me feel seen and wholly cherished. All too soon, Athena dropped the velvet curtain of my dreamscape back in place, and it snapped back into three dimensions of the same city, as if nothing had happened.

At the time, I didn't know that Athena was associated with the veil of the otherworld. I was surprised to learn that there are at least two historical associations of her with it. In Homer's *Iliad*, she told Diomedes that she'd lift the veil from his eyes that prevented him from seeing the gods in combat. Although Athena wasn't associated with wearing veils, she was one of the inspirations for the statue of a veiled goddess in ancient Egypt, along with Neith and Isis. This statue and its inscription inspired later philosophers to theorize about the veil-like separation between humans and nature or the divine.[244]

To me, Athena is the revealer of insights and the shining goddess of ability. She bestows unlimited amounts of energy, inspiration, intelligence, soul, wisdom, and logic, and the artist's eye. She lifts intelligent minds and helps creative people persevere in their projects. In doing so, Athena inspires even more art in the world. This is her legacy as well as our future.

MAGICK WITH ATHENA
by Jason Mankey

RITUAL FOR ATHENA, GUARDIAN OF THE CITIES

In both of the Homeric hymns dedicated to Athena, she is called "Guardian of the Cities."[245] Along with Ares, she is also mentioned as a destroyer of cities—she is a goddess of military tactics after all. Athena's connection to cities shouldn't be all that surprising. As a goddess of multiple handicrafts, Athena's influence on cities is profound. Without civiliza-

---

244. Armstrong, "The Veil of Isis," 51–57.
245. Homer, *The Homeric Hymns*, 36.

tion, laws, math, crafts, and wisdom, cities and towns would not exist. Within every city and town there are dozens of reminders of Athena's gifts.

Stunning architecture, courthouses, public transit and shipping centers, the highway system, public art, and even the local coffee shop (being a great barista is a skill!) all have Athena's fingerprints on them. Nature is certainly an important component in Witchcraft and Paganism, but for many of us, cities hold their own allure. This activity is a walking meditation designed to help us appreciate the gifts of Athena in the urban areas so many of us call home. It's an activity that can be done in conjunction with a trip into town, or it can be the entire focus of a day spent hiking in the urban jungle.

For this activity you'll need a small amount of birdseed, just a couple of ounces. We are using birdseed as our offering to Athena because owls were sacred to the goddess (and were often used to represent her), but also because sprinkling a little birdseed on the ground is mostly unnoticeable and won't result in anybody getting fined for littering. Because this activity is designed to be done while moving through a busy urban area, there aren't a whole lot of words to say out loud. If you are comfortable saying random bits of ritual for all the world to hear, have at it, but this can mostly be done silently.

The idea behind this ritual is to visit at least six sites that correspond to the attributes of Athena. Once in front of those spots, you are encouraged to take a few moments to contemplate the goddess's gifts and how they've made both your life and society better. Visit places that resonate with you, and avoid places that you dislike. Before beginning your journey with Athena, you might want to make a list of places to see, or at least plot a route through town. Alternatively, you can also just wander. You'll be surprised to see how many things important to the goddess will show up on your journey.

We realize that not everyone likes cities, but at one point or another, nearly all of us have to visit them. And even if you don't like cities, they have given us a great deal over the centuries. Cities are hubs of commerce, art, justice, and dozens of crafts and skills. All of these things are gifts from Athena.

Start your walk by taking a deep breath and thinking for a moment about Athena. Imagine her blessing ancient Athens, and her blessings extending from that city to many other corners of the world. Either with thoughts or words spoken aloud, invoke Athena and let her know your intentions:

Great Athena, daughter of Zeus, formidable goddess, be with me as I explore your many gifts to the world. May I see your power in the avenues I explore and grow closer to you through my journey. If it pleases thee, please walk with me. O goddess of Athens, hail and welcome!

At each of the six stops on your journey, take a few moments to contemplate how such places have transformed the world. In a few instances you may also want to consider how far we have to go as a species to realize everyone truly being able to receive Athena's gifts. Despite the best efforts of many, our world is still full of inequality, racism, homophobia, transphobia, and other ills, and all of these things are frowned upon by Athena. After observing each spot and reflecting on the goddess, leave a small offering of birdseed in an out-of-the-way place (preferably near a tree, where a bird is more likely to see it).

Any spot where a skill or craft is being practiced (or even distributed) is a fine place to honor Athena. Examples of this include artisanal markets, coffee shops, cocktail lounges, bookstores (a personal favorite!), craft stores, and even hair salons. Any place where someone is practicing a learned skill has been blessed in some way by Athena.

As a goddess of civilization and justice, Athena can be found at your local city hall, state capitol, or courthouse. While making offerings to Athena in these places, I also pray that justice will one day be available for everyone, not just the privileged. I'm also thankful for institutions such as hospitals and fire stations that allow us to have cities that aren't full of disease or constantly on fire.

Mathematics are the province of Athena, and the results of math can be seen in skyscrapers and other architectural wonders. I can't help but think of Athena every time I look at the Golden Gate Bridge or marvel at some of our local art institutions. Athena's devotion to learning and civilization can also be seen at schools. When passing a university or other institute of higher learning, I thank Athena and leave her an offering.

When your journey has come to an end, leave Athena the last of your birdseed and thank the goddess for walking with you:

Lovely Athena, goddess of wisdom and strength, thank you for your companionship today. Thank you for your gifts. Blessed be!

HEPHAESTUS
by Astrea Taylor

Hephaestus is the embodiment of fire, a magician, an artistic metalworker, and the patron god of potters, smiths, and inventors. Hephaestus means "fire," and he is associated with gaseous fires and crude oil fires naturally found in the mountains.[246] In the Bronze Age, pottery and metalwork were so rare that they were thought to be magickal and the work of the gods. His symbol is the metalworker's tongs.

Hephaestus is thought to be a Bronze Age fire god who arrived in Greece from Anatolia. In that era, smiths were connected with kings, and he was honored with over fifty shrines, far surpassing the popularity of Zeus.[247] However, esteem for smiths fell in the fourth century BCE, causing Hephaestus to decline in attention.[248] Hephaestus may have connections with other smith gods of magick, such as the Semitic god Kothar and the Egyptian god Ptah.[249] He may also be related to the Sicilian pre-Greek god of volcanos, Adranus.

In myth, Hera created Hephaestus without a father in response to Athena's emergence from Zeus's head. Either Hera or Zeus hurled Hephaestus from Olympus, which injured his feet and made him limp. However, it's believed that his injury gave him special powers.[250]

---

246. Seltman, *The Twelve Olympians*, 93–97.
247. Stratton-Kent, *Geosophia*, 193–95.
248. Seltman, *The Twelve Olympians*, 92.
249. Stratton-Kent, *Geosophia*, 195.
250. Burkert, *Greek Religion*, 168.

Hephaestus made several magickal inventions, including impenetrable armor for Achilles and a spelled chair for Hera, which trapped her in it as a punishment for abandoning him. She was freed only when Dionysus convinced Hephaestus to speak the magick words of a liberating spell.

Hephaestus married Aphrodite, which made sense because they were both popular in Anatolia in the Bronze Age.[251] This union may also have represented the marriage of craft and aesthetics. However, as time went on and Hephaestus's allure faded, the Greeks viewed the union as strange. He was considered the ugliest Olympian, and she was the fairest, so it had a Beauty and the Beast quality. As the Greeks began to favor warriors over smiths,[252] it's no surprise that Aphrodite became lovers with Ares. When Hephaestus learned about this, he fashioned a net made of magickal chains to catch them in bed and trap them there. It worked, and all the gods laughed at them until Hephaestus released them.

Hephaestus and Athena were the main ruling deities of Athens, and they bettered the crafts there. Athena refused Hephaestus's offers of mating and marriage, but in a way he helped create Erichthonius, the first king of Athens. The *Iliad* shows Hephaestus to be married to Charis, one of the Graces known for her charm, beauty, and creativity.

His city, Hephaistias, was the capital of the island of Lemnos, and it had a purification ritual where new fire was brought from the mountains to the smiths. Hephaestus also had a temple on the Acropolis in Athens, which still stands to this day. He was honored at many of the Athenian festivals along with Athena, including the smith festival Chalkeia.

Many Greeks were thought to have some kind of injury, especially after a war. They may not have been able to fight again, but smithing was a good occupation, so those injured from war were encouraged to take up the forge. In the winter, the smithery was a favorite place for unemployed men to visit because they could share camaraderie in a warm place.[253]

Hephaestus was thought of as a magician who could make the inanimate animate and trap both gods and mortals. He was invoked in binding spells, and several can be found in the Greek Magical Papyri. Gnostic magicians used the magickal symbol of his tongs on their forged gems, talismanic disks, and nails.[254] Hephaestus was also called upon for assis-

---

251. Stratton-Kent, *Geosophia*, 195.

252. Burkert, *Greek Religion*, 167.

253. Hesiod, *Theogony; Works and Days; Shield*, translated by Athanassakis, 99.

254. Stratton-Kent, *Geosophia*, 193.

tance with unbinding. Some craftspeople used magickal curses on their rivals to limit their success and productivity.

Smiths were thought to be among the most powerful magicians in ancient Greece. The Daktyloi spirits were smith brothers who invented things, sang songs with magickal words, danced, and worked metal magic. They created the magickal spells known as the Ephesian Letters. One of the spirits in particular was considered a master of medicinal herbs, spells, and mysteries.[255] Although their myth is separate from that of Hephaestus, it's strikingly similar and worth considering as a secret part of his smith lore.

Eventually the Romans syncretized Hephaestus with the Etruscan god Mulciber and local, pre-Greek volcano deities.[256] The result, Vulcanus, is an underground god associated with magma and volcanoes,[257] which makes sense considering the active volcanos and the lack of gaseous fires or crude oil fires in Italy. Poets such as Milton equated Hephaestus's descent from heavenly Olympus with that of Lucifer.[258]

Magicians and Witches of all kinds are inspired by Hephaestus's magickal abilities and eye for invention. He's a particularly smart patron deity for artists, metalworkers, potters, and other craftspeople.

MAGICK WITH HEPHAESTUS
by Jason Mankey

INGENIOUS RITUAL

Hephaestus might be the cleverest of all the Greek gods (with apologies, of course, to Hermes). Whether it's trapping his mother, Hera, in an ornate throne or fashioning a device to catch his wife Aphrodite in bed with Ares, Hephaestus was able to put his fellow Olympians in compromising positions by using his craftiness. Not all of us are destined to end up working a forge or crafting thunderbolts of lightning (which Hephaestus built for Zeus), but many of us need to fashion a bit of cleverness now and again. Matching that impulse up with the power of fire gives us an entryway into understanding the mysteries of Hephaestus.

---

255. Sandra Blakely, *Myth, Ritual, and Metallurgy in Ancient Greece and Recent Africa.*
256. Stratton-Kent, *Geosophia*, 197.
257. Seltman, *The Twelve Olympians*, 92, 98.
258. Seltman, *The Twelve Olympians*, 99.

You can participate in this exercise any time you want to connect with Hephaestus, but I think it works best when dealing with a problem that requires a bit of extra thinking. I find that having a need draws Hephaestus closer to those who wish to honor him.

Materials
• A candle (and a safe place to keep it)
• A lighter or matches
• A libation (such as wine)
• A libation bowl (optional)

Begin by lighting your candle and calling to Hephaestus:

God of fire, master smith, strong-handed Hephaestus, I call to you. Shine like the flame in front of me and help me to experience your mysteries. As you have done, show me how to overcome all obstacles in my way no matter my limitations. May I know success and prosperity as you do, O gracious god of the Art Divine. Hail and welcome!

If you are simply looking to commune with Hephaestus, look into the candle flame, let your eyes lose focus, and visualize the god in your head. As you gaze into the fire in front of you, visions of the god may appear in the flame. Whatever you see should be recorded at the conclusion of the rite so you can interpret it as needed later. In addition to the candle flame, you might hear the distant hammering of the god or catch the air from the bellows of his forge. Be aware and alert for whatever method the god might use to message you.

When dealing with a problem that requires cleverness, share that information with Hephaestus before looking into his flame. Speak truthfully and honestly to the god about your needs and desires. For example, you might say:

All-taming artist with flaming torrents bright, I seek your counsel and assistance this night. Show me how I might set a trap to trip up a work adversary so that the world may see how big a fool they truly are. Let me be as clever as you are, great god of the smith, and reveal to me in your flame what I need to know, if it pleases thee. Praise to you, O great Hephaestus!

Look into the candle flame and let your mind drift. Allow your eyes to lose focus and drift into that place between the waking and the unconscious mind. As the flame flickers, look within it for answers and ideas to the problem you are looking to solve. Let your mind wander, and journey within yourself to see if an answer lies there. Be aware of all your senses. Solutions might present themselves in a variety of ways.

No matter how inconsequential or silly it might seem, take note of anything you see or experience during this part of the rite, and write it down at the conclusion of your ritual. In the days ahead, what may seem like nonsense might be the solution you are looking for. If you don't experience Hephaestus during the rite or see any possible solutions, don't worry about it, and try again. Remember, you are building a relationship, and sometimes that takes time.

When you are done with the rite, thank Hephaestus for his presence:

Master craftsman, cunning god, I thank you for your presence this night. Help me to further understand and experience your mysteries in the days ahead. Shine brightly upon the path I walk. Praise to thee, O great Hephaestus!

Extinguish the candle and pour your libation to Hephaestus into a libation bowl or upon the earth. As you pour your offering, thank the god of the forge one last time for his presence and energy.

ARES
by Jason Mankey

Though Ares was an Olympian, in many ways he was a minor god among the Greeks. He does not show up in Greek art or mythology with much frequency, and when he does feature in myth, it's usually because another god (often Hephaestus) has gotten the better of him. Though a god of war, Ares's love of war does not guarantee that he will be the victor. For example, Ares backed the Trojans at Troy, but Athena helped lead the Greeks to victory. The amount of material on Ares is equally scarce in the modern era, as scholars devote very little space to him when writing about Greek religion and the gods.

One would think that Ares's pedigree would have given him a more prominent role on Mount Olympus. As the only son of Zeus and Hera, he seems like the logical candidate to be Zeus's favorite son and heir. But in the *Iliad*, Zeus admits to loathing his son, calling him hateful and both a whiner and a liar. If that wasn't bad enough, Zeus also tells Ares that had he been the son of a different god, he would have been kicked out of Olympus long ago.[259] That Ares does not hold Nike (victory) in his hand as his sister Athena does is a clear illustration of his reputation among both the Greeks and the rest of the gods.[260]

In myth, Ares most often gets the short end of the stick. Hephaestus especially seems to have the war god's number. The most famous example of this is a clever snare devised by the god of the forge to capture Ares and Aphrodite in the act of making love, trapping them in a golden net. In another tale Hephaestus fashions a beautiful and enchanted throne for his mother, Hera, trapping her in the chair the moment she sits upon it.

---

259. Homer, *The Iliad of Homer*, 152.
260. Burkert, *Greek Religion*, 169.

Enraged on behalf of his mother, Ares races into Hephaestus's forge in full battle regalia but is forced to retreat when the fire god shakes a bar of hot iron at him. Bards most obviously preferred the clever Hephaestus to the more hot-headed Ares.

As someone who believes in the gods as real beings, I find that writing negative things about Ares has me looking over my shoulder awaiting some sort of calamity, so let me take a moment to explain the role of Ares among the Greeks. Ares was the fighter, the peak of physical perfection, the machine you wanted fighting for you when squaring off against an opponent. But Ares was not the god of tactics or thinking things through. Ares was the god who would lead the charge into the breach and take delight in killing the enemy. He thrived on death. Athena, on the other hand, was the goddess of battle tactics, using her shrewdness to keep her soldiers alive and limit casualties.

Ares more than lives up to his name, which in Greek is connected to war and the most intense part of a battle.[261] The fearsomeness of Ares is backed up by the presence of his sons Phobos (fear) and Deimos (terror), whose energy entraps many a warrior on the field of battle. It stands to reason that Ares would honor courage and bravery in battle, but the poet Anacreon (c. 582–c. 485 BCE) wrote the following epitaph for a friend who fell during battle: "Timokritos fought well. This is his grave. For Ares spares the coward; not the brave."[262]

The frightening fierceness of Ares might not have been the only reason for his lack of popularity in many parts of Greece. Ares was almost always portrayed as a foreign deity. In myth, Ares called the land of Thrace home, a land the Greeks believed was filled with nothing but barbarians.[263] (Thrace was named after the Thracian tribes who lived there, and today comprises the far-eastern corner of modern Greece, much of Bulgaria, and western Turkey.) Most Greeks embraced foreign deities and foreign influences upon their own deities, but being Thracian invited a bit of contempt.

It's natural to assume that Ares was a more major god in the warlike city-state of Sparta, but even the Spartans eyed him warily. Worried that Ares might try to abandon them, the Spartans kept a statue of the god bound in chains near one of his temples in their city. By keeping his image in chains, the Spartans believed that he would never be able to run away from them.[264]

---

261. Burkert, *Greek Religion*, 169.

262. Seltman, *The Twelve Olympians*, 106.

263. Seltman, *The Twelve Olympians*, 106.

264. Seltman, *The Twelve Olympians*, 106.

Ares did have a special relationship with one particular city-state: Thebes. According to myth, the hero Kadmos (or Cadmus) slayed a mighty dragon favored by Ares (and in some myths the son of Ares) and then founded Thebes upon that spot. After Kadmos sowed the dragon's teeth into the ground (on the advice of Athena), an army of warriors arose from the earth looking for a fight. Kadmos threw a stone into their midst, causing them to do battle with one another until only five survived. Those remaining five then helped Kadmos build Thebes. Many of the most important families in ancient Thebes claimed those five fighters as ancestors.[265] After the city of Thebes had been founded, Ares punished Kadmos, keeping him as a servant for eight years and then offering his daughter Harmonia to Kadmos as a bride in the hero's servitude.

Because of Ares's special relationship with Thebes, his myth was slightly different in that city-state. In most Greek mythology, Ares was a bachelor, but in Thebes he was said to be married to Aphrodite. In other city-states, such as Athens, Ares and Aphrodite often resembled a married couple in both literature and art. The two were most certainly not thought of as wed outside of Thebes, but their (adulterous) relationship was noteworthy enough to be written about and depicted with frequency.[266]

The Roman version of Ares was the god Mars, and in Rome, Mars was no afterthought. Not only did they name the red planet after him, but his name can also be found in the third month of the year (March). In the Romance languages, Tuesday is named after Mars, so if you are ever especially angry on Tuesdays, that may be because of the influence of the god. Perhaps most importantly, Mars was the second most important god in the Roman Empire after Jupiter himself.

Mars had other functions in Rome as well. In addition to his duties as a war god, Mars was an agricultural deity and guarded both farmlands and livestock. In Roman myth, Ares was the father of the Trojans Romulus and Remus, making him an ancestor of Rome's original inhabitants and further cementing his importance in the Roman Empire. Rome was also home to the spear of Mars, which was kept in a building called the Regia and touched by Roman military commanders before going to war for good luck.[267]

When images of the gods returned during the Italian Renaissance, Ares was rarely among them. When the war god features in literature, it's generally as a villain or a supporting figure. Perhaps his most famous modern-day depiction is as a frequent enemy of the superhero Wonder Woman.

---

265. Burkert, *Greek Religion*, 169.

266. Seltman, *The Twelve Olympians*, 106.

267. Giesecke, *Classical Mythology A to Z*, 76.

Among Modern Witches, Ares and Mars are rarely invoked, and there is a reason we didn't include a "Personal Insights with Ares" section in this part of the book (we couldn't find anyone who works with Ares). Still, there are times when the god's presence is necessary. While most of us will never be heading out into a conventional war, there are still battles to fight and injustices to fix. In other words, there are times when we need the energy and power of Ares. Just be sure to pair it with the strategy of Athena.

MAGICK WITH ARES
by Astrea Taylor

ARES SPELL FOR COURAGE

We all face moments when our courage falters. Maybe we're tired or intimidated, or perhaps we're not used to standing up for what we believe in. Ares can inspire a burst of inner courage, which can help you find the right words and take action. This spell uses a warming effect to invoke Ares. It also has a cooling effect to release him before his energy becomes too intense or warlike. Try this spell out a few times so you can attune yourself to his energy before you need it and also so you can release him when you want. Although it calls for spices and herbs, you can use chewing gum if you prefer.

Materials
• A pinch of cinnamon
• Mint leaves (dried or fresh)

To call upon Ares for courage, take a pinch of cinnamon between your fingers. Imagine you can see its energy—it may look like a blazing hot fire. Say:

Cinnamon carries the courage of Ares.

Then sprinkle the cinnamon in your mouth. Chew it and feel its spicy, sweet heat. Envision yourself doing the courageous thing. See the best possible outcome. Do what you set out to do.

When you want to make the Ares energy calm down, eat the mint leaves. Say:

With cool mint leaves, I release Ares.

Let the refreshing taste of mint take over and erase all the heat in your body. Give thanks for Ares's inspiring courageousness.

HERMES
by Jason Mankey

The element mercury is named after the Roman god of the same name, who was known to the Greeks as Hermes. Mercury is a fascinating element, as it's the only metal that exists as a liquid at room temperature. Because of this unique property, alchemists believed mercury to be the original element, or first matter, and they frequently experimented with the metal, believing that the end result would be gold. Mercury the element is slippery, elusive (it's one of the rarest elements in the earth's crust), and incredibly magickal, and is a consummate shape-changer, assuming the form of whatever container it occupies. In other words, mercury is very much like the deity it is named after.

Images of the Greek gods were always variable, but that variance was taken to new extremes with Hermes. The earliest images of this god were of a bearded adult male, easily identifiable as Hermes because of the winged sandals on his feet. The other tell-tale sign of Hermes was his short staff, the caduceus. Even if you are unfamiliar with the term *caduceus*, it's likely that you've seen Hermes's staff. The caduceus, with two intertwined serpents and wings at the top, was carried by a variety of messenger gods in the ancient world but is most associated with Hermes.

The Hermes most of us picture today is not a bearded adult but rather a clean-shaven youth. How youthful varies by artist, but sometimes this version of Hermes appears to be in his late teens. Hermes was often depicted as a teenager because he was the last of the original Olympians (at least until Dionysus ascended to Mount Olympus). Like the older version of the god, the youthful Hermes also wore winged sandals and carried a caduceus. This version was also more likely to wear a winged helmet.

The oddest visual representation of Hermes, and the most popular one in ancient Greece, is of Hermes as a herm (or herma). Herms were originally human-assembled piles of rocks, with people adding a stone to the pile at each visit. Over time, these piles of rocks became boundary markers and, most likely, places of worship.[268] Early abstract versions of Hermes were worshipped at herms, with the god appearing as a wooden post held in place by a pile of stones.[269]

In the sixth century BCE, the herm became even more stylish and evolved from a pile of rocks into a stone pillar complete with the face of the bearded Hermes, the god's erect phallus, and wooden posts protruding from what would be the herm's shoulders. The wooden posts on the herms were probably used as places to set offerings, but the herms had a secondary and perhaps more practical purpose: they were mile markers indicating the distance between the herm and significant religious centers in Athens.[270] Stylized herms were not just replacements for more difficult-to-carve statues either; they were so popular that they also appeared on pottery.

It's logical to think that herms were named after Hermes, but most scholars believe that Hermes was named after the herms! The herms became places of devotion and eventually transformed into an Olympian deity.[271] Early Greek writers such as Homer used the term *herm* in their works to indicate a "stay, prop, support, or foundation."[272] Pillars certainly make solid foundations, but the god Hermes has very little in common with the definition of herm.

Today, Hermes is most often spoken and written about as a trickster god. Trickster gods are deities associated with mischief (sometimes malevolent), deceit, and disorder. At their worst, tricksters are responsible for death (such as the Norse Loki instigating the death of Baldur), and at their best, tricksters share secret knowledge with human beings. (The most famous trickster in Greek mythology is Prometheus, who steals fire from the gods and gives it to humans.) Hermes's status as a trickster deity mostly stems from his first adventures as a god as told in the Homeric hymn to Hermes.

Unlike the other Greek gods, Hermes rarely plays a starring role in myth and literature. Instead, he most often occupies a supporting position, accompanying and guiding his Olympian peers. But in the Homeric hymn to Hermes, the messenger god takes center stage, and

---

268. Burkert, *Greek Religion*, 156.

269. Arlene Allan, *Hermes*, 7.

270. Arlene Allan, *Hermes*, 7–8.

271. Burkert, *Greek Religion*, 156.

272. Arlene Allan, *Hermes*, 6.

he does so just a few hours after his birth. In the hymn to Hermes, the god establishes himself as perhaps the cleverest of all Olympians, and the one with the fastest tongue.

The story begins with a just-born Hermes leaving his cradle in search of his brother Apollo's cattle. On his way to find the cattle, Hermes chances upon a tortoise and uses the shell to create the first lyre. After this early distraction, the god reaches the cattle of Apollo and steals them, but in order to confuse his brother, Hermes has the cattle walk backward as he drives them away from their pasture. To further disguise his tracks, the baby Hermes also crafts a pair of sandals from brushwood to disguise his footfalls. With the cattle safely away from Apollo, Hermes sacrifices two cows to the gods, dedicating his sacrifice to the twelve Olympians. This means he includes a sacrifice to himself and has declared himself an Olympian without the consent of Zeus.

When Apollo eventually confronts his thieving brother over the theft of his cattle, Hermes pleads ignorance and reminds Apollo that he is just a baby. Hermes also tells his brother that he has no idea what cows even are, and that he cares only for sleep and breast milk. If this sounds absolutely hilarious, that's because it is. While lying to Apollo, Hermes raises his eyebrows, the ancient Greek equivalent of crossing one's fingers when making a promise. The two brothers meet before Zeus to resolve the situation, where Hermes repeats his inspired bullshit, driving Zeus to laughter. Eventually the two brothers settle their differences, with Hermes giving his lyre to Apollo as payment for the stolen cattle.

Because of this story, Hermes will be forever associated with thieves and liars, but it's also indicative of his role in business. Like the proverbial used car salesman and many of the merchants who likely hung out at the Agora in Athens, Hermes uses his shrewd tongue to manipulate and obfuscate. And in the end, he makes a fair trade by offering his lyre for the two cows given to the gods.

Hermes is often praised for his cleverness. In addition to stealing Apollo's cattle and creating the lyre, Hermes was also the first person (or god) to create fire on demand. Hermes as a clever god also lines up with his role as a god of thieves. The only kind of successful thief is a clever one!

Aside from being a thief and a liar, Hermes might be most famous for being the messenger of the gods. When Zeus needed to share a message in a hurry, he turned to his fleet-footed son, but Hermes as messenger is probably a later addition to his myth. In the *Iliad*, it is the goddess Iris who serves as Zeus's messenger, and Hermes functions more as a guide, escorting King Priam to Achilles, the Greek warrior (and slayer of Priam's son Hector), undetected. Not until the *Odyssey* does Hermes share messages from his father.

Though Hermes is generally thought of as a messenger, the proper term for his role is *herald*. Hermes doesn't just share messages from Zeus; he speaks for Zeus.[273] This is another reason that it's problematic to think of Hermes as just a trickster. Hermes, through his role as herald, shares the will of Zeus with the world. As an instrument of Zeus, Hermes is a part of an ordered universe. His ability to sweet-talk nearly anyone makes him the ultimate diplomat.

In addition to working for his father, Hermes also guides the souls of the deceased to the underworld. Hermes's role as a psychopomp places him in a unique position among the Olympians. As a messenger and guide, Hermes is actively working in our world, in addition to the realms of the gods and the dead. It also means that every mortal will eventually come into contact with Hermes. The son of Zeus and Maia was also the guide of the gods in and out of the underworld. Persephone cannot return to her mother without Hermes there to guide her out of Tartarus (nor can she reenter the land of the dead without him).

Though rarely thought of as a liminal deity, Hermes most certainly occupies that space. His ability to come and go from Olympus, the mortal world, and the realm of the dead makes him unique in his ability to cross boundaries, which also makes Hermes a god of individuals who regularly cross boundaries. Along with his son Pan, Hermes was a god of shepherds, individuals who lived in the space between the wild and civilization. As a god of thieves, Hermes protected those who crossed over society's boundaries. He was also the patron god of graves, a space between the living and the dead.[274] Not surprisingly, because of all the running around Hermes had to do, he became the god of travelers.

Though the Romans equated their deities with those of the Greeks and made Greek mythology their own, there were always differences in how the Olympians were worshipped and honored in each culture. In the Roman Empire, Mercury became a deity involved primarily with trade. If a Roman merchant was in any way involved, Mercury was likely to be present. The Romans also had no use for herms or for Mercury as a god of travelers. The writer Strabo actively mocks herms in his work.[275]

Two progenies of Mercury were a part of most Roman households in the form of the Lares. The Lares were twin household guardian spirits, and their images were hosted in a household niche called a lararium. According to myth, the Lares were fathered by Mercury when he accompanied the nymph (still living) Lara to the underworld. On the way

---

273. Arlene Allan, *Hermes*, 41.

274. Burkert, *Greek Religion*, 158.

275. Arlene Allan, *Hermes*, 124.

to visit his uncle, Mercury raped the nymph, and the twin Lares were the result. Morning prayers and offerings at the household lararium involved both Mercury and his children (and sometimes other favorite deities of the household).[276] It made sense to start each day with an offering to Mercury, a god of good luck. Since Mercury was also as a god of thieves, that offering served a secondary purpose: keeping thieves away. (What better way to stop a thief than to call in a thief?)

Farther afield from Greece, Mercury was embraced by the Celts of Gaul, who made Mercury one of their primary deities. As a god of commerce, Mercury was often in the company of the Gaulish Cernunnos, who also had associations with money. The Roman writer Tacitus included Mercury and Hercules in a list of the most popular deities among the Germans and saw parallels between Mercury and Odin. That association is most noticeable every Wednesday. In Germanic languages, the third day of the week is named after Odin, while in Romance languages it's named after Mercury.[277]

The most startling transformation involving Hermes occurred much farther east, in Egypt. There, Hermes was seen as the Greek equivalent of the ibis-headed Egyptian god Thoth, who was primarily a god of secret knowledge, wisdom, magick, and writing. Many of those gifts don't seem to parallel those of Hermes, but as the herald of Zeus, Hermes was thought to have access to a variety of secrets. Writing was also important to Hermes as a god of commerce—so important, in fact, that the god is credited with inventing the Greek alphabet. In addition, both Hermes and Thoth were often pictured holding the scales of justice used to weigh the souls of mortals.[278]

The union of Hermes and Thoth into the same deity gave birth to another legendary figure: Hermes Trismegistus ("Hermes thrice greatest"). Trismegistus is credited as the author of several philosophical, magickal, and astrological texts, many dating back to ancient Greece. The writings of Trismegistus were popular long after the victory of Christianity and were prized by both Christian and Muslim scholars. In order to "legitimize" Trismegistus and separate him from his origins, both Christians and Muslims sometimes claimed that he was the grandson of the Hebrew Moses! For several centuries and among many today, the name Hermes Trismegistus is intimately associated with magick.

---

276. Arlene Allan, *Hermes*, 123–24.

277. Arlene Allan, *Hermes*, 132.

278. Arlene Allan, *Hermes*, 135.

PERSONAL INSIGHTS WITH HERMES
by Adrian Castillo

A popular god among Neopagans, Hermes is the multifaceted trickster god of the Greek pantheon and the messenger of Mount Olympus. The traditional representation of him is a stack of rocks called a *herm*. In the old Greek folk religion, travelers would leave a rock at the crossroads, which demarcated boundaries. Considering that Hermes is also a phallic god, this makes sense when you think about marking territory. At these herms, a traveler might leave an offering, which might be picked up later by a poor traveler in need of food. Hermes is also a god of the poor. Later representations of the herm were as a stone column with a bearded man at the top and a phallus at the bottom. This older representation of Hermes is the teacher to humankind.

From reading Hermes's stories, we can develop a religious practice. If Hermes stole cattle and offered it to the Olympians, it's a safe bet to say that he likes beef. And he's a god of travel. A modern offering to him could be hamburgers or tacos, both traveler's food. If you choose to erect an altar for him, you might make a herm and leave a *kerykeion*, or a symbol of two intertwined snakes copulating, with wings at the top. If you choose to use a statue of Hermes, make sure that it's either painted or decorated somehow and that it looks taken care of.

The cornerstone of my magickal practice is my personal relationship with the deities, rather than treating them like abstract concepts. Here are some things you can do to improve your relationship with Hermes: learn his epithets, read his stories, make the occasional offering, talk to him, learn about rhetoric and things that are sacred to him, and make a herm. And while I'm not suggesting anyone go gambling, I have gambled a small amount of money as an offering to him. From the Orphic hymns, we also know that Hermes likes frankincense.

MAGICK WITH HERMES
by Adrian Castillo

CONSECRATING A HERM

I've seen different ways of consecrating a herm, and they're all valid. This is a simplified method to get started. Choose an epithet of Hermes that you'd like to work with. For this exercise, I've chosen Hermes Chthonios, or "Hermes of the underworld."

Materials

- Matches
- A bowl of water
- Red wine or juice
- An offering bowl
- Some rocks from a four-way crossroads (preferably long, phallic ones)
- A drawing or artwork of a kerykeion (optional)

Prepare the khernips (lustral water) by lighting a match and putting it in the bowl of water. Splash the water on yourself and the area you're working in. As you do so, say aloud:

May all that is profane be far from here.

Pour wine out first to Hestia in the offering bowl and say:

Drink, Hestia, to thine is always the first and the last.

Take a sip of the wine.
Now offer the wine to Hermes:

Drink, Hermes Chthonios, son of Zeus and Maia, messenger of the Olympians.

Sip some of the wine.
Invoke Hermes with one of his hymns, such as the Orphic hymn to Hermes. Now that he's in the space, cleanse the rocks with the khernips and invite the god to consecrate the herm:

Hermes, I ask thee to bless this herm and invite you to dwell within it if it is your will.

Chant "Hermes Chthonios" several times over the herm.
Place the herm in a nice container, and optionally, place a symbol such as the kerykeion near the herm. Offer red wine to your newly consecrated herm and thank Hermes. Prepare to close the ritual by offering wine to Hestia:

Hestia, to thine is always the first and the last, to Hestia, drink!

Pour out the offerings from the offering bowl either outside in a green area or at a crossroads if you can.

It's not practical to leave your herm at a crossroads in this day and age, so instead, you can draw a crossroads or even use tape to make a symbol of a crossroads and place the herm over it. One of Hermes's job descriptions is to be a psychopomp, which is a deity or entity that can take spirits to and from the land of the dead. If you've established a relationship with Hermes, you can ask him for help with unruly dead people and ask him to take away any unwanted spirits that are hanging around. It's always a good practice to demonstrate gratitude to Hermes and offer him some wine in return.

Adrian Castillo is a practicing Hellenist with an emphasis on Hekate and Hermes. He's also an Ifa initiate of the Yoruba tradition of West Africa and a third-degree Wiccan priest in the Waxing Moon Circle tradition, and on occasion he does piñata discordian rituals.

SHRINE FOR TRAVELERS
by Astrea Taylor

This magickal shrine calls upon Hermes as the protector of travelers. It was inspired by a small Mercury shrine someone set up in a New York subway station that had images of the god, a caduceus, the astrological symbols for Mercury as well as the symbols for Virgo and Gemini (the zodiac signs Mercury presides over), and the word *Traveler*. It also had a MetroCard, some dice, fake flowers, an LED candle, and a note that said "may all your trains be on time."[279] It was brilliant because the people using the subway needed to reach their destinations safely.

You could carry this shrine with you when you travel, or you could set it up in your car. You could take inspiration from the anonymous artist and erect it in a place of transit where other people can see it. The shrine could also be constructed at places where magickal people pass through, such as a Witch shop in a tourist city or at the crossroads at a festival. Dimes are suggested because Mercury's head was printed on them during the early to mid-1900s in the United States. However, you don't need dimes with his image for this spell.

Materials
• A small, empty box (such as a matchbox, a wooden box, or a shoebox)
• A pen

---

279. Owl, Russ (@russ_owl). "Was thinking that I really need the train to come quickly and then saw that someone has installed a little cardboard shrine to Mercury, god of transit (?) in my subway station," with two photos. Twitter, October 14, 2020, 1:21 p.m.

- Paper (optional)
- Several dimes or other silver-colored coins
- Other offerings (such as feathers, small stones, dice, flowers, or travel-related items)

Draw an image of Hermes and his caduceus on the inside lid of your box. Place the dimes inside, along with the other offerings. Tap the box three times and say:

I invoke Hermes, the guide, protector of travelers. Shield me on my journey and protect me from harm. Bless my paths and secure my transits.

Take the box with you when you travel. When you wish to have safe travels, leave a dime from Hermes's box as an offering to him. You can also leave several dimes if you need extra help. When you've reached your destination, add new dimes to the box and recharge it with the invocation.

Business Blessing Votive Charm

This votive charm was inspired by a spell in the Greek Magical Papyri that used a votive of Hermes Agoraios, or "Hermes of the marketplace."[280] Orange beeswax was the largest component of that spell, so for best results with this charm, check your local craft store for beeswax sheets. A candle was an important part of that spell, but the candle needed to be any color except red. (There's no explanation why this is.) One notable difference between that spell and this charm is the absence of sacrificing a rooster. Instead, chicken is the suggested food offering.

This charm also calls for juice of the "aeria" plant, which is commonly believed to be mistletoe. Use a special mortar and pestle for nonedible herbs due to the poisonous qualities of mistletoe when it's ingested. Be careful not to touch your face until after you wash your hands.

Materials
- Mistletoe and ivy (fresh or dried)
- A mortar and pestle for nonedible herbs
- A small amount of water (if using dried material)
- Cheesecloth
- A ceramic plate
- Orange beeswax

---

280. Betz, *The Greek Magical Papyri in Translation*, 81.

- A small piece of paper
- A pen
- A box
- A marker
- An offering of red wine or juice
- An offering of food, preferably chicken
- A chime candle (any color but red)
- A candleholder
- A lighter

Combine the mistletoe and ivy in the mortar and pestle and grind them together. If you're using dried material, add a small amount of water drop by drop until it forms a paste. Put the paste into a cheesecloth and press the juice out onto the ceramic plate.

Warm the beeswax by holding it in your hands. When it's pliable, combine it with the juice and knead it in, adding more juice if possible. Using most of the beeswax, form a figurine of Hermes with a hollow base by using your finger to form the votive. In his left hand, form a herald's wand, with wings at the top and two serpents intertwining from the bottom to the top. Make a small bag from the beeswax and place it in Hermes's right hand.

With the pen and paper, write, "Hermes Agoraios, give income and business to this place because we have made a home for you here." Roll up the paper and place it inside the hollow area of the votive. Close the hollow part with the remainder of the beeswax. Place the votive in a box. With the marker, draw a crown on the box, along with the words "Hermes Agoraios blesses this business." Place the box in the back of a closet at the place of business or somewhere in the business where it will not be bothered.

Set out an offering of food and red wine. Light the candle and say:

I invite you to partake of this feast, Hermes Agoraios. I thank you for your blessings and for granting great prosperity on this business, _____ (say the name and nature of the business), which is owned by _____ (say the owner's name).

Let the candle burn out completely if it can be watched the entire time. If not, extinguish it and light it again later with gratitude. Once a month or whenever you make a profit, give thanks to Hermes with offerings of more food and wine and a fresh non-red candle.

DIONYSUS
by Astrea Taylor

Wine played a role in nearly all ancient Greek rituals,[281] and where there was wine, there was Dionysus. The god of wine, enthusiasm, liberation, intoxicated ecstasy, madness, and drama was also the personification of those things. Some artists depicted him with horns, a full beard and mustache, and/or a headdress of grapevine and grapes. Dionysus was called the Frenzied One, and he was considered one of the favorite gods of women.[282] He may seem a little out of place in the ancient Greek world, which was seemingly obsessed with hierarchy and laws. However, his wild celebrations balanced the rigors of daily life and found a purpose in Greek society. He was adopted into the Olympian pantheon as a testament to the importance of wine and loosening the reins of the rule-oriented culture from time to time. His offerings were first fruits, his animal was the bull, and his plants were ivy and grapevine. He carried a wine cup and a sacred wand, which was topped with either ivy or pinecones.

Based on the etymology of his name, Dionysus could have been from several different places. The Greeks believed he arrived from Thrace, the northeast region of Greece also known as Phrygia.[283] While Dionysus's celebratory rituals are somewhat like those of Attis, the Phrygian god who experienced madness and danced to the music of flutes and drums with nymphs, their myths are very different. The earliest mentions of Dionysus are on Linear B tablets found at Pylos, a Greek city on the southwestern mainland, and on

281. Garland, *Daily Life of the Ancient Greeks*, 268.

282. Fantham et al., *Women in the Classical World*, 88.

283. Seltman, *The Twelve Olympians*, 162.

votive offerings from the fifteenth century BCE on the island of Keos, which indicates that the sanctuary they were found at is his.[284]

Dionysus's mother was Semele, a mortal woman whose name meant "earth."[285] When Semele and Zeus became lovers, Hera disguised herself as Semele's nurse and told her she should demand to see Zeus in his true form. Because Zeus was so powerful, Hera knew that his thunderbolts would consume Semele and her unborn child (Dionysus). When this happened, Zeus grasped the semi-divine fetus of Dionysus, opened his thigh, and sewed him into his flesh. Some stories say Dionysus was dead, but being embraced within Zeus revived him. Dionysus grew there until he was born. He was raised in Nysa by nymphs or maenads. Upon maturity, he traveled to the underworld to retrieve his mother, then deified her and renamed her Thyone, which means "ecstatic frenzy." Semele possessed some of the women who attended her son's festivals.[286]

Dionysus discovered the mortal princess Ariadne, the mistress of the labyrinth, crying. She had been abandoned by the hero Theseus, to whom she had given her thread so he could find his way out of the labyrinth. Dionysus and Ariadne quickly fell in love and married. She was deified as a goddess of paths and labyrinths. Their story may have been a parable for how Dionysian celebrations remove sadness, especially for women.

Dionysus had several celebrations and rituals, but the Agrionia is perhaps the most enigmatic. These nocturnal romps in the woods for women only were held by Dionysus's dedicated group of frenzied priests and priestesses. They all drank wine and danced to the primal music of drums and flutes (which sounded more like modern-day oboes). The energy would build up among the participants, with loud shouts and nonsense words, until everyone was ecstatic, or mad, or they merged with Dionysus.

The Greeks thought of ecstasy as being outside of one's usual mentality or personality. Madness was a step deeper. It was synonymous with frenzy, mania, and Dionysus's divine essence. The maenads, his women followers, were so frenzied that they were known for literally ripping animals apart. It's no wonder that these celebrations existed in a culture that had long wars, rigid rules and social classes, sexism, and repression. The Dionysian madness released pent-up emotions. It was considered therapeutic. The madness didn't last forever, though. The festivities occurred at the proper time and place, as did the return

---

284. Burkert, *Greek Religion,* 162.

285. Seltman, *The Twelve Olympians,* 171. The Orphics believed Persephone was Dionysus's mother, but they were in the minority.

286. Burkert, *Greek Religion,* 179. Possession also occurred with women who practiced ecstatic dance with the Phrygian goddess Meter Kybele.

to society. Ecstasy, madness, and everything that happened around those bonfires were not thought of as something to be sought out obsessively. They were not viewed as a way of life for the vast majority of people, and the experiences there weren't meant to inform one's life. Rather, Dionysian celebrations were a break from everyday life, or they were considered a part of life but not life itself. At the end of the festivities, a priest performed purification rites to lift the madness and restore sanity.[287] These rituals obviously had an honored place in society, which was made clear when Dionysus was elevated to the status of an Olympian god. The inclusion of Dionysus among the elite gods meant that Zeus permitted these wild rites—in other words, a little madness was necessary so that reason could reign supreme.

One of his myths, the story of the mad Minos princesses, was a cautionary tale for any woman who wouldn't take part in the festivities. The Minos princesses refused to celebrate the Agrionia, and they continued their weaving. Angered, Dionysus made snakes appear in their baskets, sent vines to curl around their looms, and made wine and milk rain down upon them. The princesses went mad and tore a child to pieces as a sacrifice to him. They then ran outside to join the festival, lest something else happen.[288] This tale is a simple parable about how we all need to break free every once in a while. An attitude of "all work and no play" leads to madness, especially for those Athenian women who were encouraged to stay indoors all the time. The madness of Dionysus would get to them one way or another, so they might as well succumb to it before anyone was harmed.

Masks were common at the Agrionia. Both his priests and his priestesses wore the mask of Dionysus. Some of the celebrants wore masks too—wearing them ensured secrecy and liberation from identifying with their worldly selves. Although it's possible that sex occurred at these celebrations, it appears that consent was respected. Euripides's play *The Bacchae* features the phrase "she who is naturally chaste will partake of Bacchic rites without being touched."[289]

Another great festival was the Rural Dionysia, where celebrations were held throughout the month of December to celebrate the birth of Dionysus. They featured joyful, drunken processions of men carrying cakes and giant phalluses through the streets. Some of the men dressed as women and sang songs about phalluses.[290]

---

287. Burkert, *Greek Religion*, 110.

288. Burkert, *Greek Religion*, 164.

289. Seltman, *The Twelve Olympians*, 171.

290. Kerényi, *Dionysos*, 296–97, 335.

The Great Dionysia (aka the City Dionysia) started in the sixth century BCE. Around the time of the Spring Equinox, people dipped a statue of Dionysus in the sea and processed from Eleutherae, the alleged birthplace of Dionysus, to his theater in Athens. For four days, people watched tragic plays. To break up the somber mood, satyr plays were also enacted, featuring actors in masks and costumes who acted drunk and wore comically large phalluses.

The Anthesteria festival, or the Older Dionysia, was held for three days in the spring. The festival started with a procession of people carrying last year's wine to the sanctuary of Dionysus in the marshes of Athens. At nightfall, the wine was opened and tasted. There were drinking competitions, offerings of first fruits, singing and dancing, and invocations to Dionysus as the Reveler and the Stormer.[291] During the festival, people used protective magick to repel ghosts and bad energy by painting their doors with resin, chewing buckthorn leaves, and winding ropes around sacred places.[292]

One of the stories told at the Anthesteria was the tragedy of Ikarios, the first man who ever made wine, whom Dionysus had taught. Ikarios shared it with his neighbors, but because they had not experienced intoxication before, they feared they had been poisoned, and they drowned Ikarios. His daughter, upon finding him, hanged herself in sadness. This story offers the reasoning for the ancient association between red wine and blood, both of which are used in sacrifices and offerings.[293] Anthesteria also marked a time when the community chose a "king," likely the master of a guild. The "king" absconded from the activities, much like Theseus, and left his wife, the "queen," alone. She would later meet Dionysus (which may have been the king in a mask), and together they would leave to have a sacred marriage or union. This short play recalls the meeting of Ariadne and Dionysus and their marriage. It's thought that the queen and Dionysus made sacred offerings that ensured success for the entire community.[294]

Dionysus presided over nocturnal Orgia festivals. These were originally secret parties for women only, which happened three or four times a year. They involved drinking, drugs, hunting animals, singing, and sexual initiations under a priestess of Dionysus.[295]

---

291. Burkert, *Greek Religion*, 237.

292. Burkert, *Greek Religion*, 238.

293. Burkert, *Greek Religion*, 164, 238.

294. Burkert, *Greek Religion*, 109, 241.

295. León, *The Joy of Sexus*, 130.

The festivities may have even involved eating raw flesh,[296] although that could have been a euphemism for sexual activities that took place.

In the third century BCE, a priestess of Dionysus invited men to the Orgia festivals. Around the same time, the celebrations spread to other parts of Greece. The festival also expanded into Italy, where the Etruscans called it the Bacchanalia, after Bacchus, their name for Dionysus. Dionysus was also associated with the Symposia, which were nights where a group of men drank together. These usually included discussions of philosophy and sometimes sexual activities with each other or a hired woman.[297]

Dionysus broke gender norms in many ways. He was depicted as either a young, naked, and effeminate man or an old, bearded man wearing a woman's garment. The fact that he had priests as well as priestesses went against the more common Greek practice.[298] He was depicted in rituals as male and female, as both his priests and his priestesses were allowed to wear his mask. When they did, they were considered living representations of Dionysus. He was renowned for having priests, priestesses, and followers who were gay. These aspects were acknowledged and celebrated.

In Dionysus's earliest states of godhood, he was seen as an agricultural deity who introduced vines to Greece and helped them grow. He was the god of wine, milk, honey, and all other natural fluids.[299] Dionysus was represented in art as a mask hanging from a post, usually with a phallus, which meant "the best of good luck." This ancient image of him was found in many places. These posts were eventually called herms and were attributed to Hermes, who had more stability and better associations with fertility, commerce, and protection.[300] Some Greeks associated Dionysus with death and Hades, the god of the underworld. Others believed Dionysus could assist the souls of the dead to the underworld.

The power to induce madness was frightening to some people. In at least one region of Greece, Dionysus's statue was kept hidden for the majority of the year due to the belief that seeing it could cause madness. It was brought out from its hiding place only on the night of his festival. In another area, people wrapped chains around one of his images or statues, which were unbound only for his ritual.[301]

---

296. Burkert, *Greek Religion*, 163, 291–92.

297. Pomeroy, *Goddesses, Whores, Wives, and Slaves*, 143.

298. Burkert, *Greek Religion*, 98.

299. Seltman, *The Twelve Olympians*, 156, 169.

300. Seltman, *The Twelve Olympians*, 67–68.

301. Burkert, *Greek Religion*, 90–92.

The mythical cause of Dionysus's madness was ascribed to Hera's infliction of it upon him. In culture, though, the two deities were merely at odds with each other, and it's clear to see why. Hera represents hierarchy, marriage, and order, while Dionysus's wild festivals featured many activities that could be seen as the antithesis of order.[302]

Dionysus masks inspired Greek theater, specifically tragedy, a word that translates to "goat song."[303] Actors often wore masks and took on other qualities, just like participants in Dionysus's rituals. Both were thought to be outside of themselves, too. Although the actors were not likely experiencing the ecstasy of the ritual, they were experiencing something larger than themselves.

In the Greek Magical Papyri, Dionysus was invoked in a love spell. The magician wrote his plea to him on a piece of tin.[304] Dionysus was also invoked in a curse tablet as "the biter," as one of the gods who could make a spirit bind the horses of the magician's competitors.

By 186 BCE, the Bacchanalia celebrations in Rome had grown to enormous gatherings where the focus was to defile new, young initiates, often against their consent. Anyone who refused was tortured and sometimes even murdered.[305] The people who led the rituals or participated in the abusive behavior were either imprisoned or executed (about five thousand people). That same year, the Roman Senate issued the Bacchanal Decree, which said that celebrations were limited to no more than three women and two men. This likely slowed the festivities, but they did not stop. It's clear that Bacchanalia celebrations were held in Pompeii around 79 CE when Mount Vesuvius covered the city in ash. The largest mansion there was dedicated to Dionysus, and it was called the Villa of the Mysteries.[306] There are still records of Romans being initiated into the secret Bacchanalia rites even into the late fourth century CE, when Christianity was becoming far more dominant.[307]

Bacchus eventually became conflated with the Christian figure known as the devil. This is no surprise due to his associations with loosening morals, dancing, liberated women, drinking, and sex. The depictions of Bacchus with a circle of people dancing in the woods is synonymous with both of their celebrations. Later, poets wrote about Bacchus, including

---

302. Burkert, *Greek Religion*, 165.

303. Sabin, *Classical Myths That Live Today*, 39.

304. Betz, *The Greek Magical Papyri in Translation*, 130 (PGM VII. 459–61).

305. León, *The Joy of Sexus*, 132.

306. León, *The Joy of Sexus*, 133.

307. Bowden, *Mystery Cults of the Ancient World*, 198–99.

Milton, Keats, Emerson, and Hunt. In the early 1960s, Robert Cochrane, the founder of Traditional Witchcraft, compared his Horned God with a young Dionysus.[308]

These days, science supports the belief that dancing and mania dispel stress. In the wilderness, animals tremble and shake to release their stress, but it's not something we humans do. If anything, most people bury their feelings and continue about their daily lives. The consequence is that the reptilian part of the human brain remains stuck in a state of high alert, creating conditions such as chronic stress and post-traumatic stress disorder.[309] Dancing is comparable to trembling, especially when there are loud drums involved. There's evidence that dance can heal the mind and integrate the body, even in people with severe conditions like dementia, which is marked by a lack of memory.[310] It appears the Greeks made this connection long ago. Both the Greek word *mania* and Mnemosyne, the Greek goddess of memory and the mother of the Muses, come from the same root word, *men-*, which is about states of mind or thought.[311]

Dionysus remains one of the most popular Greek gods. Magickal practitioners who are actors are inspired by his way of dissolving the self and taking on a whole new persona in a performance. Some Witches invoke him in ecstatic trances and work magick from that mental state. Dionysus can remove blocks and impediments, and he is also called upon in special occasion celebrations, particularly to mark a liberation from repression.

PERSONAL INSIGHTS WITH DIONYSUS
by Astrea Taylor

I read about Dionysus for years before experiencing him. Although there's evidence of children as young as three years old drinking at his festivals,[312] that doesn't happen so much these days. But even when I was old enough to drink, I was burdened with a heavy class load in college. When I finally managed to break free, I barely knew how to dance. At the time, I felt I didn't reside much in my body—I entertained the notion that my body was merely a vehicle for my mind. In truth, I felt dismembered by a society that only seemed to value certain types of bodies, which I didn't have.

---

308. Cochrane, with Jones, *The Robert Cochrane Letters*, 165.

309. Shaw, "When Trauma Gets Stuck in the Body: How Do We Heal?"

310. Hornthal, "Dance/Movement Therapy"; Klimova, Valis, and Kuca, "Dancing as an Intervention Tool for People with Dementia."

311. Online Etymology Dictionary, "men," accessed June 2022, https://www.etymonline.com/word/men.

312. Burkert, *Greek Religion*, 237.

All of that changed when I went to my first rave. There was something overwhelming about the sheer volume of the music. It was so loud that the beats resounded in my body and overpowered my mind. I began to move to the music, and to my astonishment, I found that my body knew how to dance. My body knew how to interpret the music through me without my having to think whatsoever. I danced for hours, years of repression melting away as I felt the joy of movement without anyone's judgment. I didn't know it at the time, but this was Dionysus showing me a taste of liberation.

Eventually I finished college, and my real studies began. I read countless books on the Greek gods, and my experience in dance made sense in the context of Dionysus's gifts. I found him again on the dance floor, then again at a bonfire drum circle at a Pagan gathering, and then again in several other places. Calling out to him in those places gave me a rush of ecstasy. I sought out Dionysus in order to lose myself. The next day, I felt that my mind was better organized than it had been the night before. I had mental space where I hadn't before. It was like someone had defragged my mind, making it faster and more capable.

Through many years of working with Dionysus, I know that he is the dance, the flow, and the mindless state of trance. Dionysus is intoxication—the hidden realm that lies beyond our current states. He is freedom and the rapture of the present moment. When his dance and trance come over me, I'm connected with him as well as something ancient, primal, and deeply true. Letting loose into that expansive realm is such an amazing experience, and for me, it alleviates deep chronic stress.

I've glimpsed Dionysus from the corners of my eyes around ecstatic campfire dances that lasted all night. I've seen him the morning after, dancing in the grassy edges of the forest to drumbeats audible only to us. He's always dancing or swaying, always moving in a blissful trance state. I've felt his presence in dance clubs too, though they don't seem to be his favorite place to visit.

In my morning divination, I know I'll experience Dionysus when I draw the Devil tarot card. It's an indicator to let loose of my regular life, work, and responsibilities. Inevitably, that night I'll imbibe, play music, dance, and revel in being alive.

I call upon Dionysus in my magick often. Dancing with him activates my more magickal self. Sometimes I dance with him to cleanse my body's energy before a ritual (which is just as important as cleansing the outside of the body, in my opinion). He's helpful in removing blocks and obstacles that stand in the way of my magickal intentions. I've danced with him to cast a magick circle by calling upon the elemental energies in my body. Often I dance with him in ritual to raise my energy to a peak just before I release my intentions into the world. And whenever I feel trapped by a society I don't always fit into, I dance with him to transcend it all. Dionysus reminds me to shake off the world and remember my true spirit, and for that I'm eternally grateful.

MAGICK WITH DIONYSUS
by Jason Mankey

WINE MAGICK

Modern depictions of Dionysus often reduce the god to a few major attributes, especially wine and theater. While those two associations are an important part of his myth and legacy, Dionysus has always been far more complicated. Though it's rarely mentioned by writers and scholars, Dionysus has a long history inhabiting the prophetic center of Delphi.[313]

For nine months each year, Apollo and his Pythia shared prophecies with the ancient world, but from mid-November through mid-February, Dionysus and his followers ruled over Delphi. In the cold of winter, the followers of Dionysus would sing, dance, make love, and drink wine. Beneath the snowy shadow of Mount Parnassus, they celebrated the joys of being alive. Ancient accounts of Dionysus at Delphi don't mention the god's followers actively engaged in prophecy, but it's not out of the question; the energy of Delphi lends itself to glimpses of the future.

This ritual calls for wine (I think the title gives it away!), but grape juice may be used if wine isn't your thing. If you have a chalice or glass dedicated to your Witchcraft work, I suggest using it to hold your wine. Wine comes in a variety of colors, the most common of course being red and white (and increasingly pink in the form of a rosé). When I'm dealing with an especially vexing situation or find myself in a bad place, I always use red wine. On those days when my mood is lighter and I feel like I'm on top of the world and just want to be with "D," I'll go with a sparkling white.

This exercise serves a variety of purposes. In its simplest form, it can be used to draw closer to Dionysus and feel his presence in your life. I sometimes use it as a pick-me-up when dealing with a bad or difficult situation. Dionysus wants us to be happy, and his blessings (in moderation) assist with that. This exercise can also be used to catch a glimpse of the future if you need some insight into a situation.

---

313. Broad, *The Oracle*, 40–41.

Materials

• A glass of wine or grape juice

To begin, find a quiet place with at least a little bit of light, enough so that you can peer into your glass. Pick up your chalice of wine (or juice) and hold it out in front of you, as if offering it to Dionysus. Ask the god to be a part of your rite:

> *Great Dionysus, son of Zeus and Semele, I call to thee. In this glass of wine, may I experience your power and ecstasy. Through its sacred waters, may I grow ever closer to you. Cherished are your gifts, O bearer of the vines. Hail and welcome!*

Close your eyes for a moment, then lift the chalice to your lips, letting the wine spill over your tongue. As you sip the wine, let the power of Dionysus fill your being. You should feel a comforting warmth, one that is much more than just the effect of the alcohol in the wine. Take a second sip of the wine and know that Dionysus wants you to be happy and fulfilled. As you swallow the wine, imagine it burning through all your unwanted emotions and fears.

On nights when I simply need to feel the presence of Dionysus, I do little more than this, feeling the power of the god in every drink of wine. When I cradle my chalice of wine in my hands, I often feel the embrace of the wine god himself coming to offer comfort and solace. When I seek to rid myself of anger and sadness, I drink the wine while visualizing the juice of the grapes cleansing me of all that I wish to be rid of.

I often find myself speaking directly to Dionysus in these moments, and while I've never heard his voice reply to me, his energy is always response enough. I sometimes feel his warmth wash over me or his energy calming me or providing personal power. We might not have traditional conversations, but I know that he is most definitely present.

When dealing with an especially difficult problem, you can use the wine poured in honor of Dionysus to scry and reveal your potential future. When scrying with the wine, I always begin by calling to him again:

> *Great Dionysus, benevolent god and giver unto mortals, I ask that I might catch a glimpse of what is to come in your most sacred of waters. Reveal to me what might be so that I may resolve the difficulties that lie in front of me. Thanks to you, O son of Zeus, for your gifts!*

Clear your head and let your eyes lose focus as you peer into the wine swimming in your chalice. I find that it helps to move the wine a bit as you look into it. You can do this by slowly rotating the cup or by swirling the waters (in a clockwise direction) by moving the glass or using your finger or an athame or wand. (For best results, I recommend using an athame. As an instrument of your true will, the athame will add your truest intentions to the wine.) As you gaze into the chalice, the answer might reveal itself to you in the moving sea of wine, or perhaps a vision will manifest in your mind. Whatever you see, make a note of it or commit it to memory.

At the end of your time with Dionysus, be sure to thank the god for his presence:

Immortal god of divine madness, I thank you for your companionship tonight and your presence in my life! May I honor you in all I do. For you, son of Semele, I leave this offering as a gift and a show of my gratitude. Hail Dionysus!

If you're outside, pour a small libation on the ground. If you're inside, place your chalice (with a healthy drink of wine remaining in it) in an honored space as a gift to the god or pour it into a libation bowl. Before setting down the chalice, say, "For thee, Dionysus," so the god knows the wine is for him.

HESTIA
By Astrea Taylor

Hestia, the virginal goddess of the hearth, was a crucial part of Greek life. It was nearly impossible to create a sacred space or make sacrifices without her transformative and soulful fire. She had sacred fires in every Greek city, and she presided over the hearths in every home and temple as well. She is thought of as the hearth, as fire, and as a virginal goddess who guards homes and grounds spiritual energy into the material world. Her fires burn brightly as the light of Olympus.

The Greeks held Hestia in the highest regard. She is called the chief of all goddesses of humankind in the Homeric hymn to Aphrodite. Plato believed that she is the most ancient goddess, the essence of all things, reality, and that which is (or being-ness).[314] Hesiod called her the source of all things and the ground of being.

Hestia is known as the first and last of the Olympians because she was the first child born to Cronos and Rhea—a very auspicious position. However, as the firstborn, she was also the first deity Cronos swallowed in his terror about the prophecy that one of his children would overthrow him. When Hestia's younger brother Zeus made Cronos vomit up all his children, she was the last to emerge. This is where her association with being "the first and last" arose. Hestia's pre-Greek origins are unclear, but at least two cities in Crete had hearth houses, or community places where her fires were kept burning at all times, which are similar to those found in ancient Greek art.[315] She may have emerged from the animistic reverence for fire, the hearth, and home.

---

314. Plato, *Plato in Twelve Volumes*, 401.
315. Burkert, *Greek Religion*, 61.

Every Greek city had a central hearth house dedicated to Hestia, which was thought to be tended by unwed widows. Whenever Hestia's flame went out in a home, someone from the household retrieved fire from the community hearth. Making a fire from scratch was considered a difficult task, so this amenity was a gift. If the fire ever went out at a hearth house, a sacred fire was created using the rays of the sun and mirrors or polished glass.

Likewise, Hestia was among the first of the Greek gods to be honored in newly colonized lands. Settlers transported her fire from the hearth houses of their founding cities, and upon arrival, they constructed a hearth house and dedicated it to her.[316]

In ritual, the hearth was synonymous with the altar, or the place of offerings for the gods. Hearths were composed of brick or stone. They sat just outside temples in the open air (except for the hearth at the Temple of Apollo at Delphi, which was located inside). Ritual fires were started with great ceremony, and aromatic wood was burned on the hearth as incense.[317] This first offering to Hestia purified the attendees, cleansed the space, and delineated the sacred space.[318]

Later in the ritual, an animal was sacrificed and its blood was splashed upon the altar with great decorum. If the fire leaped up, it was a sign that the gods were present.[319] The hearth was then used to cook the sacrificed animals to provide food for the banquet. The bones, fur, and/or feathers of the animal were burned, presumably as the last offering to Hestia.

These acts appear to portray Hestia as a facilitator of the sacred to humanity. She grounds the sacred energy for ritual, creates boundaries for the ritual space, maintains the energy throughout the ceremony, transforms sacrifices into food, and blesses the ritual with the consumption of the final offering.

Hestia has also been interpreted as sacred energy itself. Torchlit processions were a significant part of many important rituals, including the Panathenaea, marriages, funerals, Dionysian festivals, and the Eleusinian mysteries. These processions may have been symbolic of people carrying Hestia's soulful spirit to another location. Hestia is also seen as the one who grounds the sacredness and soul into a place. When the fire went out in a home, it was analogous to the spirit of the home withdrawing. Fresh fire from the hearth was sought as soon as possible. Likewise, when someone passed away at home, the hearth

---

316. Garland, *Daily Life of the Ancient Greeks*, 18.

317. Burkert, *Greek Religion*, 61–62.

318. Vernant, *Myth and Thought Among the Greeks*, 127–75.

319. Burkert, *Greek Religion*, 61.

fire was extinguished to represent the spirit leaving the body, and new fire from the community hearth was obtained only after a period of mourning.[320]

The Noumenia was a household celebration of the gods of the home, and it was held the day after the new moon. It honored Hestia as well as the other home gods. People gave special offerings to her on this sacred day in exchange for blessings upon the home and its inhabitants.

The Greek words for heart and hearth are identical: *kardia*.[321] Just as a heart is located in the center of every body, a hearth was built in the center of every Greek home. It follows that Hestia is associated with the center of family life and domestic happiness. This connection is also clear in the Homeric hymn to Hestia, which says that she tends the sacred fire at the Temple of Delphi, the center of the ancient Greek world.[322] The hearth was in the middle of the temple, thus making Hestia the very center of Greece.

Hestia influenced home life greatly. In houses with only one room, Hestia (the hearth) was the first thing one would see upon waking and the last thing seen before sleep. At every meal, a small offering was made to the hearth, such as food, oil, or libations of wine. Because children were born at home, Hestia was also the first deity they met. Likewise, she was also the last deity seen by those who died at home. Families blessed their new household members with Hestia's protection by tossing figs and nuts at them, which were symbols of nourishment and wealth.[323] Fathers ran five-day-old babes around the hearth to formally introduce them to Hestia and place them under her protection.[324]

The important task of ensuring that Hestia's home fire never went out fell to unmarried women and girls.[325] Her constant flame could be an allegory for what was considered "women's work." Little was recorded about household rituals and whether Hestia was invoked for magickal purposes. However, some assumptions can be made. Hestia must have kept women company through the cleaning and cooking chores that happened during the daytime as well as those in the night, such as calming a crying baby. She may have been an emotionally reassuring companion to women who felt lonely from time to time. She may have played a role in domestic creativity too, such as cooking, making art, and decorating. Singing or the recitation of poems may also have been favored by her. The

---

320. Burkert, *Greek Religion*, 61.

321. Fry, *Mythos*, 75.

322. Burkert, *Greek Religion*, 170.

323. Garland, *Daily Life of the Ancient Greeks*, 109.

324. Garland, *Daily Life of the Ancient Greeks*, 89.

325. Seltman, *The Twelve Olympians*, 40.

Homeric hymn to Hestia asks her to "lend grace to this song," which indicates some creative generosity. Hestia's fire could be seen as a metaphor for maintaining one's sacred center and balance—not burning too brightly nor too dimly. A balanced but steady approach gives warmth, love, and nourishment.

In their theories of the universe, Neoplatonists expanded upon Plato's philosophy of Hestia being the central essence around which all things revolved. They theorized that she was also the center of the earth and the smallest indivisible part of us.

The Roman goddess Vesta was similar to Hestia, but her position was more elevated.[326] Vesta had beautiful temples for her flame in every city, which were much larger and far more beautiful than the homely Greek hearth houses. Several dedicated virgin priestesses tended the flame, and they were held in the highest honor.[327] The everlasting flame had a role in protecting the city, so if it ever went out, punishments were severe.[328]

Since 1936, the flame for the Olympic Games has been created by priestesses at Olympus by using a parabolic mirror and the sun's rays, just as it was in the ancient world. The arrival of the sacred fire to the games marks the beginning of the ceremonies, and the flame endures until it is extinguished as part of the closing ceremonies.[329]

In 1955, Robert Graves, an English historian, published *The Greek Myths*, which popularized a theory that Hestia gave up her Olympian status to Dionysus. However, this has not been substantiated in ancient texts, and the concept and names of the twelve Olympians appear to have been regional.

Among some modern practitioners, Hestia is called upon in magickal practices for the home, family, love, creativity, prosperity, nourishment, protection, centering, community building, and activism. She opens the gateway to magick and facilitates its energy. Her altar is no longer relegated to the hearth. These days you can find her image on stoves, kitchen altars, fireplaces, and fire altars and in ritual rooms. She is sometimes worked with as a sole deity, especially among house Witches. Many invoke her "first and last" qualities by calling upon her before a circle is cast and afterward, extinguishing her fire last. One great way to start a magickal relationship with Hestia is to light candles on the Noumenia and make offerings of incense, wine, and oil. Connect with her and feel how her connections open you up to many other aspects of magickal practice. Allow her fiery energy to initiate new phases in your craft.

---

326. Burkert, *Greek Religion*, 170.

327. Sabin, *Classical Myths That Live Today*, 195.

328. Bulfinch, *Bulfinch's Greek and Roman Mythology*, 8.

329. Olympic Games, "Tokyo 2020: The Torch."

PERSONAL INSIGHTS WITH HESTIA
By Raechel Henderson

On a practical level, I work with Hestia in all my magickal and mundane tasks. When I refresh the protective spells around my house, I invoke Hestia's powers. I ask her to keep my home and all who dwell in it safe. I use my anointing oil—made with rosemary and olive oil and consecrated in Hestia's name—to bless my home and the items within. I bless my dishes so that all meals are eaten in harmony, the furniture so that all who sit are gathered peacefully, and even the beds so that my family may know rest. I make space for Hestia's presence when I am mixing incense for full moon rituals as well as when I am making a DIY tub cleaner. Including her in all aspects of my life creates a solid foundation for a safe home.

But Hestia isn't just the goddess of the hearth and home, and here is where my work with her expands beyond household chores and meal planning. She is the goddess of the state, the underpinning for the structure of the government and city. And it's that aspect of her that informs much of my interaction with the larger world. The idea of "as above, so below" is very much in effect here, as government regulations have a direct impact on the family and home. I see, then, in my work with Hestia on the home front and in grassroots movements a way to influence the state through that connection.

I invoke Hestia in all of my spellwork targeting the government, politicians, and social justice issues. I call on her to protect protestors, to remind those running the government that they serve the people, and to bring aid and comfort to those suffering due to homelessness, food insecurity, and bigotry. And I support my Witchcraft with donations to organizations that address those issues. The work I have put into better understanding Hestia has been rewarding on so many levels. It has enhanced my magick and home life, providing meaning and depth that wasn't there before.

Raechel Henderson is a dual class seamstress/shieldmaiden and the author of Sew Witchy: Tools, Techniques & Projects for Sewing Magick *as well as* The Scent of Lemon & Rosemary: Working Domestic Magick with Hestia. *You can find her on Instagram and Patreon or at her blog at idiorhythmic.com, where she writes about magick, creativity, living by one's own life patterns, her family, and books.*

MAGICK WITH HESTIA
By Jason Mankey

Home Connection Spell

As an author, I often find myself away from home for weeks at a time presenting workshops and rituals. As much as I love doing those things, I sometimes find myself missing my hearth and home. On those days when the homesickness gets to be a little too much to bear, I call upon Hestia, who helps me reconnect with my house and the loved ones inside of it. This spell/activity can be used for business travel, when visiting relatives, or even when you are on vacation. You will need an anointing oil that reminds you of home—I usually pick rose or jasmine. Depending on where you are traveling, you may not be able to light an actual candle (especially true of hotel rooms). If that's the case, an electric candle will work just fine. And remember, never leave a burning candle unattended.

Materials
- 2 candles (one for home and one for travel)
- Candleholders (if necessary)
- An anointing oil that reminds you of home
- A libation (such as wine)

Begin by deciding which of the two candles you will be keeping at home. I generally use a larger candle for my home candle and travel with a smaller one. Over time I may go through several small travel candles before my large candle has burned away. Once you have decided which of your two candles will be kept at home, place that candle in a prominent spot in your home or in a place with particular meaning to you. (Make sure this is a safe place to light a candle!) Place your candle in that spot and call upon Hestia:

Sweet Hestia, she who is both first and last, I dedicate this space to you so you might dwell in our home if it pleases thee. Bless this place with your wisdom and strength. So mote it be!

Anoint your two candles with whatever oil you have chosen. Begin with the house candle. As you anoint your candles, think of everything you love about your home. Pour that love into your candles as you prepare them with oil. Once the candles have been anointed, light the larger candle and invoke Hestia:

Hestia, eternal queen, sacred and divine goddess, I light this candle in honor of you. May this flame ever lead my spirit homeward!

Pick up your second candle and light it from the candle that is already lit. As you light it, say:

From Hestia's flame, I light this candle. May its luminescence bring my spirit home no matter how far I travel. Let the blessings of Hestia and this home she dwells in stay connected to this candle no matter where this mortal may roam. So mote it be!

Let your candles burn for a few moments while taking some time to reflect on both Hestia and the place you call home. If you've chosen a much larger candle for your home candle, I find it helps to strengthen the connection between the two candles by lighting the home candle periodically and calling upon Hestia as you do so. When not traveling, I keep my travel candle near the home candle to further link them. After blessing and prepping your candles, pour a libation for Hestia to thank her for her presence.

If you find yourself using an electric candle as your traveling light, that's fine. Simply symbolically light it by bringing it close to the first candle's flame and flick on the electric candle at that moment.

When you're traveling, light your travel candle and call upon Hestia. Ask for her blessings and to connect you with your home. After you do so, the energy that comes from the candle should feel familiar, like home. I often let my mind drift as I look into the candle flame. This always conjures up images of my house and the people and things I love there. When you're finished, extinguish the candle. Thank Hestia, offer her a libation, and enjoy sweet dreams of home.

OTHER
MAJOR DEITIES

HADES
by Astrea Taylor

Hades is the dark-haired Olympian son of Cronos and Rhea. After the battle with the Titans, he was given the realm of the underworld, where he rules over the dead. He and the underworld are called Hades, Aides, and Erebus. He has other names as well, including Aidoneus, Klymenos, Ploutos, and sometimes Plouton. Hades presides over funeral rites and burial customs, and he carries a scepter with a perched bird at the top. His golden chariot is drawn by immortal black horses, and he also has a cap of invisibility. He uses these to burst from the earth, snatch the living, and take them with him to the underworld. The realm of Hades is described as a misty gloom and a dark place of terrors and anguish.[330]

Hades means "unseen" in Greek, but it's not exactly clear where he originated. There's no Mesopotamian fertility connection to his role. In Mycenae, similar temple structures to the dead were found,[331] which makes some historians believe he was an indigenous deity of Greece.[332] He has similarities to another Indo-European concealed god of the dead who bestows wealth, the Hindu Kubera.[333]

The name Hades was seldom used because it was considered unlucky and saying his name might summon him. It was also believed that Hades didn't answer any prayers under

---

330. Hesiod, *Theogony; Works and Days; Shield*, translated by Athanassakis, 51.

331. Burkert, *Greek Religion*, 196.

332. Penglase, *Greek Myths and Mesopotamia*, 149.

333. Taunton, *The Path of Shadows*, 12.

that name.[334] Hades was called the most loathsome, disliked god because he roars in terror and has no mercy for humankind. The Olympian gods hated the House of Hades—they almost never attended funerals, and their priests and priestesses were not permitted to attend any funeral or viewing.[335] Likewise, Hades and Persephone never went to Olympus due to their underworld natures.[336] It appears that farmers appealed to Hades so he would not destroy the crops with disease or rot.[337]

Like Persephone and Kore, Hades had another name: Ploutos, the giver of wealth. This name was likely derived from Plouton, the god of wealth and rich soil and the son of Demeter and Iasion. Hades and Plouton soon became conflated because they were both associated with being underground.[338] Ploutos was more associated with wealth in agriculture[339] and the mining of metals. He is sometimes depicted with a cornucopia or a sheaf of wheat.[340]

Hades is also called Infernal Zeus, Underground Zeus, and Chthonic Zeus because of his rulership below the earth. Farmers petitioned the name Chthonic Zeus along with Demeter as they planted seeds to make the crops grow. At Corinth, pairs of statues of the Heavenly Zeus and the Underground Zeus were found together, which may have reflected a belief that the two gods or the two worlds balanced each other.[341]

Hades and Pluto have only a few myths. Hades is most known for his abduction of Kore to the underworld. He once loved a nymph named Menthe. When Menthe complained about Persephone (Hades's new wife), Persephone stepped on Menthe and relegated her to the fragrant plant mint that grows near the entrance to Hades. Cerberus, the three-headed dog who guards the gate of the underworld realm, was his companion. Hades was in close contact with the Erinyes, also known as the Furies. These winged goddesses of vengeance punished the wicked and facilitated the restless dead to take revenge against those who wronged them.

The Greeks were very familiar with death—so much so that some might call them morbid by today's standards.[342] This makes sense considering that in the ancient age, death

---

334. Burton, "Worshipping Hades," 211.

335. Burkert, *Greek Religion*, 202; Garland, *Daily Life of the Ancient Greeks*, 176–77.

336. Graziosi, *The Gods of Olympus*, 9.

337. Burton, "Worshipping Hades," 216–17.

338. Seltman, *The Twelve Olympians*, 149.

339. Burton, "Worshipping Hades," 221.

340. Bowden, *Mystery Cults of the Ancient World*, 81.

341. Burkert, *Greek Religion*, 200–2.

342. Garland, *Daily Life of the Ancient Greeks*, 174.

was a common occurrence. No one was immune to Hades, and sooner or later every-one must be taken away in his invisible chariot. Hades ensured the right procedures were undertaken so the dead were respected and people could grieve. Funerals were treated with the utmost importance, because death carried a *miasma*, a spiritual pollution of sorts, as well as health hazards.[343]

Greek funerals had three acts. Upon death, women cared for the body and facilitated the visitation of loved ones. After a couple of days, the second step ensued: a funeral pro-cession started from the house. Either the body was transported in a cart or men carried it atop a ladder to the hollow gravesite.[344] In the third act, the dominant male household figure invoked Hades and carried out a stylish and mournful ritual. Little is known about the ceremony itself, but it's clear the mourners demonstrated their grief with a dramatic flair—it was believed the dead appreciated it.[345] Some were cremated, and their ashes placed into urns. Finally, the burial occurred, and a gravestone was erected. These acts meant the soul would have a place in Hades and the family could move on.[346]

Hades was not honored very often, as it was thought that he couldn't offer much to the living.[347] An entrance to Hades was part of the sanctuary at Eleusis, but his sole temple was at Elis. It was opened only once a year, and only his priest could enter.[348] Temples to Pluto were slightly more common, but they were located only in places where noxious gases emitted from the ground, such as the Ploutonion at Hierapolis.[349]

The Oracle of the Dead at Ephyra was associated with Hades. It was a dark, partially subterranean temple with several rooms, where petitioners underwent a ritual that would last for days. They'd sacrifice an animal, sing to the underworld gods, consume food (pos-sibly hallucinogens), be purified, and toss a stone into a dark room.[350] Some of these rituals may have been for protection.[351] The participants walked through an underground laby-rinth and through the three gates of Hades. Eventually they arrived at a vaulted under-ground chamber—one of the entrances to Hades. There, they could contact the spirits of their beloved dead to commune with them or ask about the future. Before leaving, the

---

343. Garland, *Daily Life of the Ancient Greeks*, 177.

344. Garland, *Daily Life of the Ancient Greeks*, 174–75.

345. Garland, *Daily Life of the Ancient Greeks*, 176–79.

346. Garland, *Daily Life of the Ancient Greeks*, 179.

347. Burton, "Worshipping Hades," 212.

348. Burton, "Worshipping Hades," 221.

349. Matyszak, *Ancient Magic*, 28–29.

350. Burkert, *Greek Religion*, 114–15.

351. Altas Obscura, "Necromanteion of Ephyra."

participants swore an oath to never speak about their experiences upon threat of death from Hades himself.[352]

Similar to this temple was the Oracle of Trophonius at Lebadeia, where people took an underworld journey and slept in a dark, vaulted chamber. The next day, priests assisted in dream interpretation.[353]

It was believed that the living could travel to Hades in their dreams to communicate with their loved ones, and Hades was sometimes invoked for necromancy. He was also called upon in the most sinister curse tablets. Supplicants struck the earth and requested him to punish their foes in many ways, asking for even sterility and death.[354] Hades was called upon to enact revenge upon the souls of the dead and to bind the wicked until their death.[355] The Greeks also used him to enforce punishments if an oath was broken. Some of the curse tablets requested both him and the Erinyes to act against the cursed. In the Greek Magical Papyri, Hades was invoked to assist with a dream oracle.[356]

The Romans renamed him Pluto and Dis Pater, which translates to "rich father." Hades remained the god of the underworld. By 167 BCE, the Oracle of the Dead was destroyed, and in the 1700s a temple was constructed there to St. John the Baptist.[357] Later, Christians associated Hades and his bird-topped staff with Satan and a pitchfork.[358]

Although Hades/Ploutos is not the most popular Greek deity by far, modern Witches and magickal practitioners work with him. He is invoked magickally for necromancy and in curses. Ploutos (not Hades) is called upon for wealth and success.

PERSONAL INSIGHTS WITH HADES
by Debbie Lewis

I have been a devotee of Hades for the last year and a half. This is how I came to worship the Father of Souls. During the pandemic, I noticed that within my spiritual path, I was lacking something. I had been a devotee of Hekate for over eighteen years, and I never had a male counterpart. One night before bed, I asked for a sign as to who I need to work

---

352. Altas Obscura, "Necromanteion of Ephyra."

353. Burkert, *Greek Religion*, 115.

354. Graziosi, *The Gods of Olympus*, 63–64.

355. Faraone and Obbink, *Magika Hiera*, 26, 46.

356. Betz, *The Greek Magical Papyri in Translation*, 261–62.

357. Altas Obscura, "Necromanteion of Ephyra."

358. Stratton-Kent, *Geosophia*, 115.

with to better my spiritual path. Once I had fallen asleep, I found myself within a darkened room. Whenever I tried to get off the floor, it felt as if I was cemented to it. At first I wanted to panic, as anyone in this situation would. Instead, I observed what I could by moving my head. When I looked around, the room was pitch black until I saw the glow of the torches ahead of me, which allowed me to see who was in front of me. Before me were stone steps that led to a platform with a chair placed upon it. In the chair was a man with jet black hair and an expression that I could only describe as hardened. His eyes shifted from black to a yellow glow. During this time, I experienced something I never have had happen to me—I had the sensation of coming in and out of consciousness, yet instead of returning to my warm bed, I always came back to the same spot. It was as if my soul was trying to leave, but it was unable to. After I realized what was happening, I focused on the man's words.

When I finally woke up from that dream, it stuck with me for weeks. I racked my mind trying to figure out who it was and what had happened. Eventually, a series of dreams started coming for months on end that picked up right where I had left off. It wasn't long before I realized I was roaming the underworld. When I had this realization, only one God came to mind: Hades.

Before initiating a journey with Hades, I searched for all the resources I could about him. I found very little about how he was worshiped. When it came to the myths, it was a little more informative. One of the most famous stories or myths was how Hades became the god of the underworld. The next one was the kidnapping of Persephone, which some pagans and witches today have come to believe was a consensual elopement rather than an abduction.

Recently, I went to Hades's altar and confessed that I felt I wasn't doing enough in his name. I said that if he would guide me, I would do whatever he placed before me. Two days later, I was asked to give my representation of the father of the underworld, Hades, for this book. Things like this let me know I am on the right path.

When it comes to offerings, I go more on feelings than what is usually associated with Hades. One of the offering requests I received from him while in an astral state was a white, milky soup. I came to find out this was lemon soup, which, by the way, is amazing. A few other offerings I suggest are skulls, cigars, red wine (dry), crafted items made of bone, mint, honey, obsidian, bloodstone, pomegranate seeds, harvested foods (corn, squash, apples), raw red meat, and blood.

When it comes to working with Hades, you see the world in a different way. Along with realizing the benefits of working with Hades in ritual, here are a few suggestions on what types of work you can do with Hades:

- *Death rituals:* These are normally performed on the sixth day after a loved one has passed away.
- *Monetary gain rituals:* One of the associations Hades has is with precious minerals and gems within the earth.
- *Harvest rituals:* When we think of the harvest, one of the first thoughts that comes to mind is death, knowing that the season has come to an end and all things return to the earth. If we look at the tale of Persephone, we see this as a theme within the harvest season.
- *Rebirth rituals:* These types of rituals are to be used to help let certain aspects die and allow us to come anew. When you invoke Hades during these rites, you are allowing yourself to be reborn from the fires of the underworld.
- *Spirit work:* This is a term I'm using to describe a broad spectrum of practices with ancestors, elementals, and other spirits. When doing any type of spirit work, I highly suggest calling upon Hades to aid in your endeavor.

Debbie Lewis (Middletown, Ohio) is an active ordained Pagan Priestess and the founder of the Devine Witch. She can be found on social media platforms such as YouTube, where she shares her knowledge.

MAGICK WITH PLOUTON (HADES)
by Jason Mankey

RITUAL TO LIFT THE VEIL

Most mythology paints Hades as a grim figure and not the type of god to grant favors to humanity. However, the characterization of Hades in the Orphic hymns is quite positive. The hymn to Plouton refers to Hades as having "kindness in your heart" and says that he gives "support to mortal kind."[359] This suggests a figure willing to be involved in our lives as a positive force.

---

359. Dunn, *The Orphic Hymns*, 79.

Hades is most famous for governing the realm of the dead, but he (along with his brothers) also rules over the earth. Hades has long been praised as one of the gods whose powers contribute to the turn of the Wheel of the Year, which is not surprising given that most fields reflect the yearly cycle of life, death, and rebirth. This implies that Hades exists not only in the realm that bears his name but also as a part of this world. This is important because it means that Hades can hear our pleas on the mortal plane while still ruling over the lands of death.

This activity is designed to help you tap into the power of Hades and reunite with loved ones who have crossed over the veil into his realm. Hades, as a god of the dead, has the power to lift the veil whenever he chooses. Reuniting with our beloved dead does not have to be reserved strictly for Samhain, but can be done whenever you want to feel a stronger connection with them. For this ritual, choose an incense that sets the mood for the work—whatever suggests the realm of the dead to you. This ritual is best performed in a dark room, under a night sky, or as the sun sets.

Materials

- An altar
- Incense that sets the mood for the work (whatever suggests the realm of the dead to you)
- A candle (and holder, if necessary)
- 1 coin for each dead soul you wish to connect with
- A small offering bowl
- A physical memento for each dead soul you wish to connect with (such as a picture of them)
- Something that each dead soul you wish to connect with has touched (or their name written down on paper)
- A trowel (if finishing the ritual outside) or a bowl of earth (if finishing the ritual indoors)

Set up your altar and materials and begin the rite by lighting your incense and taking a moment to steady yourself. Breathe deeply and think of your lost loved ones. As you picture them, imagine them in the land of the dead as Hades looks on. Light your candle and say:

Great Plouton, lord of the dead and ruler beyond the veil, I light this candle in your honor so it might serve to guide the souls of my beloved dead back to me for a short time.

Look into the candle flame and envision the barriers between this world and that of the dead melting away, and your candle acting as a beacon to those you have loved and lost.

Pick up a coin and hold it tightly in your dominant hand. Infuse a bit of your own energy into it so that the ruler of the dead and his ferryman will know where to send the souls of your beloved dead. Place the coin for this member of your beloved dead in the offering bowl while saying:

> *To the god of wealth and the underground, I give this coin. From your domain it emerged and to your domain now it shall return. Charon, ferryman, accept this as the toll that will ferry my beloved dead back to me. Mighty Plouton, accept this coin as my offering to you.*

Add a new coin to the bowl for every soul you wish to be reunited with.

Once the coins have been placed in the bowl, look at the items representing each individual soul. Look at their pictures, say their names aloud, and let your mind reflect on their memories. Hear their laughter, see their faces, and remind yourself of their touch. Lose yourself for a moment in their memories before saying:

> *Plouton, he who rules over the realms of death, I beseech you to loosen my loved one(s),*
> *_____ (insert the names of your beloved dead here), from your care and to allow them to briefly visit with me once more. Great lord of mysteries, I beseech you to allow me this boon. So mote it be!*

If you can finish the ritual outdoors, extinguish your candle, pick up your bowl of coins and your trowel, and find a quiet spot to dig into the earth. Notice the soil in your hands. It's the soil of Hades, who rules what lies below the earth's surface. Once you've dug a couple inches into the ground, place your coins in the ground and say:

> *Plouton, guardian of souls, I give this offering to you. May I be reunited with those I love through your power and your grace.*

Cover the coins with the dirt taken from the ground, close your eyes, and let your senses extend around you. If Hades (and Charon) have accepted your offering, you should feel those you've lost near to you once again. You might feel an emotion you associate with them, or perhaps a scent or a brief vision. Cherish whatever is given to you.

If you are inside, simply dig into your pot of earth, place your coins there, and proceed with the ritual as written above. Be sure to thank Hades (as Plouton) for the gift he has given you and to blow out your candle at the conclusion of the ritual.

PERSEPHONE
by Astrea Taylor

Persephone, who was originally known as Kore, the maiden, is the goddess of flowers. She became the queen of the underworld and the messenger of springtime and rebirth. Persephone had a key role in the Eleusinian mysteries as well as many other agricultural rituals. She is credited with removing the fear of dying among her initiates.[360] She had several names, including Savior Girl,[361] the torchbearer, and Dread Persephone. Persephone is one of the most enigmatic deities of the era, as she embodies many complex dualities.

Persephone is thought to have arrived in Greece with Demeter and Poseidon, her original parents, along with the Indo-European people.[362] There may be an ancient connection between Persephone and the Mesopotamian and Sumerian goddess Inanna (sometimes called Ishtar). In that seasonal myth, Inanna descends into the underworld, receives powers over life and death, and returns to the world, but her husband must return to the underworld seasonally.[363] Persephone is also similar to Ereshkigal, the Mesopotamian goddess of the underworld, specifically in her terrifying aspects noted by Homer.[364]

The Homeric hymn to Demeter is Persephone's best-known myth, but regional differences are evident in her myth. Eleusis and Locri were both part of the Greek world, and they both had sanctuaries and rituals dedicated to Persephone. However, in Locri, the artwork in

---

360. Burkert, *Greek Religion*, 200.

361. Seltman, *The Twelve Olympians*, 155.

362. Seltman, *The Twelve Olympians*, 146.

363. Penglase, *Greek Myths and Mesopotamia*, 18–23.

364. Penglase, *Greek Myths and Mesopotamia*, 154.

Persephone's sanctuary didn't depict Demeter. Instead, Persephone is shown preparing for her wedding and sitting alongside Hades receiving offerings. Scholars theorize that it was a place for women to focus on marriage and fertility rather than the mysteries or death.[365]

Some scholars believe this break in continuity showed that Demeter held the initial importance in the rites in the matriarchal and agricultural eras, and Persephone held more importance as the tide shifted into patriarchal times.[366] This shift toward an alliance with the newer power is evident in the fact that Persephone is married at the end of the myth, while Demeter is not. In many ways, Demeter represents the old ways of living and Persephone the new.

Persephone's myth may have also reinforced the need for people, especially women, to use caution when outdoors. Kidnapping was a common occurrence. It also alludes to the fact that many marriages were arranged without the knowledge or approval of the bride and her mother—only fathers held the power to make decisions.

Persephone's role as queen of the underworld was very important. She welcomed the dead to the underworld and decided where they would go, based on their lives and initiations. One of the big secrets of the Eleusinian rites was that the initiated were told they would have a nice afterlife, where they would be happy.[367] Knowing they would live beyond this life made people more at ease with death. The concept of a rich afterlife likely bound the initiated together because they knew they would see each other there. It also incentivized people to urge their non-initiated loved ones to take the rites so their place in the afterlife would be secured. However, if Persephone judged a soul to be bad, they went to a place described as cold and dark, with a pervasive gloom, where everything was evil.

Persephone determined the length of time that souls would spend in the underworld before they could be reborn. Souls could bargain with her to make amends for their wrongdoings or ask her to enact vengeance upon the people who caused their injuries. Homer called her Dread Persephone likely because she inflicted punishment on the souls of the dead. Many of the curse tablets found in Greek tombs asked for her and Hades to enact revenge. They included requests for destruction of the wrongdoer, to receive the same treatment as the deceased received, and justice. Persephone was also called upon to bind people for various reasons.[368] For all her authority, she was also forgiving. She cured

---

365. Bowden, *Mystery Cults of the Ancient World*, 80–85.

366. Donovan, *After the Fall*, 33–34.

367. Mylonas, *Eleusis and the Eleusinian Mysteries*, 281–85.

368. Faraone and Obbink, *Magika Hiera*, 4.

people who had been damned by the gods, and she allowed a queen who died for her husband to go back to the land of the living, as well as the wife of Orpheus.

Persephone is also highly relatable in many ways for a Greek goddess, and the Eleusinian rites made her more so. Just as Persephone didn't die when she was taken to Hades, initiates learned that their souls wouldn't die either. They would be with Persephone, who also lived, flourished, and died. With her wisdom about cycles and spirits, the souls of the dead would await the right season, like seeds stored below the earth. At their deathbeds, initiates had faith in her judgment and the season of their return from beneath the earth, just as she returned every year. If the Homeric hymn to Demeter is any clue, Zeus decrees the time of death and rebirth, and Hekate escorts souls back to the land of the living.

The Lesser Mysteries, also known as Persephone's mysteries, were held in early spring on the banks of a river and at a temple to Demeter in Athens. These mysteries were instructive and preparative for the Greater Mysteries, but they were not mandatory. Demeter attended. There was purification, fasting, bathing, sprinkling of water, singing, dancing, venerating, stories of Persephone through actors, and sacrifices. Demeter, her priestesses, and the hierophant attended. This ritual may have cleansed anyone who had spilled blood with the "fleece of Zeus" so they could attend the Greater Mysteries.[369]

In the Homeric hymn to Demeter, Hades tells Persephone that she will be offered the best rites and sacrifices. It's thought that these offerings were linked to caring for a person's body just before and after death. Greek women cared for the sick and dying, and upon death, they prepared bodies for the funeral.[370] Their rites consisted of cleansing and purifying the bodies, anointing them with oil, and singing prayers. They also held an open house for visitors to view them, because it was believed the dead needed attention from the living.[371] Women sang and cried at the funeral with the same loud cries consistent with sacrificial rituals. It was only through these strenuous efforts and the funerary rites associated with Hades that souls could pass into the realm of the dead.[372]

Another part of Persephone's offerings is veneration of the dead. Women especially visited graves often to give offerings of perfumed oil, bands of fabric, and herbal wreaths.[373] Some people were buried with golden tablets inscribed to Persephone.[374]

---

369. Mylonas, *Eleusis and the Eleusinian Mysteries*, 232, 236.

370. Garland, *Daily Life of the Ancient Greeks*, 80.

371. Garland, *Daily Life of the Ancient Greeks*, 175.

372. Garland, *Daily Life of the Ancient Greeks*, 175.

373. Fantham et al., *Women in the Classical World*, 96–97.

374. Bowden, *Mystery Cults of the Ancient World*, 81.

Like Hekate, Persephone was associated with Witches.[375] She was called upon in many ancient curses, which shows her ability to punish the wicked. She was also invoked along with Ereshkigal in a love spell for attraction and binding, and in a multipurpose spell with Selene in the Greek Magical Papyri.[376]

In Rome, Persephone became Proserpina, and along with Hekate, she was associated with raising the dead. Eventually, Christians built a chapel on Eleusis for Mesosporitissa, the Lady Within the Kernel of Grain, and to this day, villagers offer her loaves of bread and first fruits.[377]

Many modern Witches and magickal practitioners ask Persephone to assist with magick for recovering from change, the loss or death of a loved one, depression, and trauma.[378] Her underworld aspects hold space for these shadowy emotions, and they allow for our cycles to progress and transform rather than stagnate. Persephone gives grace to our cycles of life, death, and rebirth, both large and small. She helps with transformations and becoming one's truest self, no matter what. She inspires us to own our powers and rule our own realm with the strength of a queen. Persephone is welcomed back to the earth in some Beltane rituals, when flowers fill the air.

THE RAPTURE OF KORE / PERSEPHONE
This topic may be a trigger to some people, so if you'd like to skip ahead, go to page 178.

The Homeric hymn to Demeter is generally thought of as a seasonal parable about agriculture. The fertile fields (Demeter) produce flowers and daughter products (seeds, Kore). The farmer (a reaper of living crops, Hades) harvests the seeds and removes them from the gardens (the rapture) to be stored in pots underground (the realm of Hades) for several months. The seeds remain underground in storage until they are needed for consumption (eating the seeds) or it is time to plant them in the springtime (the return of Kore). The storage practice ensured nourishment through the winter months.

Although there is no indication that the ancient Greeks took this myth literally, kidnapping people for servitude was a reality, especially for women. The issue of consent is present in this myth now just as much as it was then. However, it's unclear how the ancient Greeks felt about it.

---

375. Luck, *Arcana Mundi*, 57.

376. Betz, *The Greek Magical Papyri in Translation*, 44, 90–91.

377. Ruck, *Sacred Mushrooms of the Goddess and the Secrets of Eleusis*, 186.

378. Downing, *The Goddess*, 42.

This issue is complicated by the English word *rape* to describe the abduction; however, the original Greek meaning does not appear to have sexual connotations. The Greek word *harpazō* described Kore's abduction in the Homeric hymn to Demeter and in Hesiod's *Theogony*. This word was used in the Bible to describe the actions taken by the Christian God upon humans.[379] It's defined as to "catch up, take by force, catch away, pluck, catch, [or] pull,"[380] such as what the Christian God would do to human souls on Judgment Day. Harpazō has the same root word as *harpies* (*hárpyia*), the birds with women's faces who carried wicked people to the Erinyes.

As language progressed and texts were translated into Latin, harpazō was translated into the Latin word *rapiō*, from the root word *rapere*, which means "to seize prey, carry off by force, abduct … [and] sexually violate, but only very rarely," because there was another word for sexual violation, *stuprare*.[381] Several centuries later, in Medieval Latin, a second definition was added to *rapiō* to include sexual violation. This is the root of the Old French word *rapir* and the Anglo-French word *raper*, which both mean "to seize, abduct." The Middle English words *rapture* and *rape* were first documented in the late 1300s, primarily as "[to] seize prey, abduct, take and carry by force." Starting in the 1400s, the English definition included a secondary definition: the act of abducting a woman, or sexual violation, or both.[382] When the Greek myths were translated into English in the 1700s, the words *rape* and *rapture* still carried the primary abduction meaning, and both were used synonymously in Greek texts and artwork. However, in modern times, the meaning of the word has changed to mean a sexual violation only. It appears that sexual violation was not part of the original text. Critics of this argument say there are insinuations in the abduction that are not stated outright. This is especially true for men who abducted women to "marry" them. The nonconsensual nature of abducting someone without their consent is a disturbing reality of history. Considering that powerful men wrote the narrative, this omission appears to smooth over any injury because it may not have mattered to them.

The second detail modern people bring up is that Kore cried out as Hades took her. Scholars agree that her scream is an expression of her unwillingness to go with him. Some view the scream as an expression of concern about a future violation. Looking at it from an anthropomorphic viewpoint, it could also have been the sound of one who believed she

---

379. History.com, "The Bible." This word was used in New Testament of the Bible, originally written in Greek around 50 CE.

380. Bible Study Tools, "Harpazo," accessed June 2022, https://www.biblestudytools.com/lexicons/greek/kjv/harpazo.html.

381. Online Etymology Dictionary, "rape," accessed June 2022, https://www.etymonline.com/word/rape.

382. Online Etymology Dictionary, "rape," accessed June 2022, https://www.etymonline.com/word/rape.

was dying. Kore would have known about Hades's method of capturing souls by chariot to take them to the underworld. The scream echoes the action taken by Greek women when an animal was ritually slaughtered as an offering.[383] It's also strikingly similar to that of the Mesopotamian goddess Geshtinanna, who cried out when Dumuzi was slain and was taken to the underworld.[384] Many things about Kore appear to have Mesopotamian roots.

Alternately, several parts of the myth mirror Greek marriage from a man's point of view. Kore's scream may have been a stand against marrying Hades. According to Plutarch, there was a custom in Sparta, at least, of "marriage by capture," where a man in a chariot took a woman for marriage. This practice continues in some parts of the world today as a marriage custom, sometimes as a consensual traditional practice and other times nonconsensual, with rape and even murder.

Although marriage was not initially discussed in the Homeric hymn as the reason for the kidnapping, it is later revealed that marriage was Hades's intention. Marriage appears to be insinuated in the myth. It was a custom for a bride and groom to travel in a chariot to the groom's home after a wedding. Some believe Kore's capture and detainment in the underworld is a parable for what happens to women in a Greek marriage. The myth could have been a hint at what to expect in marriage.[385] It's similar to how *Beauty and the Beast* was a tale invented to introduce Victorian women to a marriage that was likely arranged by their fathers. The hymn may have set a cultural norm to establish both a husband's and a father's power over a girl's life.

The hymn to Demeter skips ahead several months to when Hermes visits the underworld to assist in Kore's release. Hermes finds Hades sitting in bed and Kore sullen and reluctant. Some view this as proof that Hades abused her. However, at this time in the myth, Kore is called "chaste," and she is still Kore, the maiden. She is not yet called Persephone, the queen of the underworld. Both of these suggest that a wedding and a union had not yet taken place.

Hermes informs the couple of Zeus's order for Persephone to return to the world and her mother. Hades encourages Kore to go to her mother and assures her that he will be a good husband. He also says she will rule over the underworld and she will be offered the best rites and sacrifices, which elevates her to his equal. At this point, Kore leaps for joy, then Hades looks around stealthily and gives her pomegranate seeds to eat. It's unclear

383. Burkert, *Greek Religion*, 74.

384. Penglase, *Greek Myths and Mesopotamia*, 141.

385. Garland, *Daily Life of the Ancient Greeks*, 75.

if Hades is being stealthy toward Kore, as some people argue, or if he is trying to hide his actions from Hermes.

Pomegranates symbolized marriage, sex, and the loss of chastity, and they were sacred to Hera and Aphrodite.[386] They were used in love charms, and the mere presence of the seeds leads some to believe that the hymn to Demeter is a love story.[387] The question of consent arises, and whether Kore was given a choice to eat them. Some people posit that Kore did not know the meaning of the pomegranate seeds, but others believe that as an agricultural deity, she must have known the meaning. Could she have spat the seeds out? Perhaps. Or maybe Hades made sure she ate them by threat of force. However, the continued use of her original name (Kore: maiden), the word *chaste*, and the timing of the seeds after the offer may indicate that Kore and Hades were not yet married (Hera) or sexually involved (Aphrodite) until that moment.

The myth gets more confusing when Kore returns to Demeter and says Hades stealthily compelled her to eat the pomegranate seeds against her will. However, as you may have noticed, Kore's awareness of consuming the seeds goes against the stealth she speaks about. Regardless, this account demonstrates that she believes she was forced into marriage and union.

There is some evidence that points to positive perspectives of ancient people about the marriage between Kore and Hades.[388] The sanctuary to Persephone at Locri had a plaque that showed Kore joyfully packing a wedding trousseau[389] and preparing a bed.[390] However, these scenes were not found at Eleusis. Another positive view of the relationship is the fact that Greek girls who died before they were married were commonly called *Kore* on their graves and were said to marry Hades when they reached the underworld.[391]

Although there are several Greek myths with sexual coercion, those deities don't remain partnered together, they don't get married, and they aren't celebrated together. It's also important to consider that both the Greater and the Lesser Mysteries reproduced the acts of the Homeric hymn to Demeter as a play, and the Greeks viewed rape as a *miasma*, or a pollution, which was highly incompatible with a ritual setting. These positive aspects

---

386. Penglase, *Greek Myths and Mesopotamia*, 144.

387. Penglase, *Greek Myths and Mesopotamia*, 158.

388. Mackin, "Girls Playing Persephone (in Marriage and Death)," *Mnemosyne*, 1–20.

389. Fantham et al., *Women in the Classical World*, 32.

390. Bowden, *Mystery Cults of the Ancient World*, 80.

391. Fantham et al., *Women in the Classical World*, 7.

are incompatible with the theory that Kore was harmed, unless the harm is covered over so seamlessly that there is no trace except for hints in the vague language.

The fact that many women suffered in this way in history is undeniable and condemnable, but it's impossible to know the intricate details of this specific ancient story with absolute certainty. Until a definitive source is found, the ambiguities and valid points on both sides will remain.

PERSONAL INSIGHTS WITH PERSEPHONE
by Aria Vargas

The beginning of my relationship with Persephone started just after an invocatory ritual at ConVocation, a Pagan and Witch gathering in Michigan. The ritual invoked four Greek gods, and her husband, Hades, was among them. He told me, "My wife wants you to work with her." In that moment, I didn't know how to respond other than to be honored and surprised that the Lady of the Underworld had asked her husband to pass along that message.

The never-ending cycle of life, death, and rebirth is an integral part of working with Persephone. In each season I've worked with her, there has been something that follows that cycle, whether it has been shadow work or the passing of a beloved animal or loved one. It's a lesson that is always being learned.

There are many different ways I give Persephone offerings, but the main way I show her my devotion is by giving my time to do works in honor of her in my garden or elsewhere. If I'm giving a physical offering to her, it's typically either pomegranate tea or pomegranate seeds covered in dark chocolate. These are the types of offerings that she prefers with me and my practice.

Persephone has been a major factor in me being able to accept who I am and where I came from. I come from a background with a lot of trauma, and through her mythos and guidance, she has helped me to get to where I am today.

Aria Vargas is an aspiring fiction writer and artist. Being able to share her path and art with others is a privilege and honor.

PERSONAL INSIGHTS WITH PERSEPHONE
by Jason Mankey

There are six deities whose portraits hang in our coven's ritual room, and four of them are Hellenic. Those who know my wife and me are not surprised to see Dionysus, Aphrodite, and Pan on our walls, but Persephone often comes as a surprise. In some ways she was a surprise to me too, but upon further reflection, I realize that she's always been with me in my journey, often quietly but always present.

When I lived in Michigan, Beltane was the highlight of our ritual year. It was always the first sabbat to be completely free of winter's cold hand, making it especially welcome. Many of our rituals revolved around the idea of the Goddess of Spring returning from her exile and bringing warmth and new life in her wake. During those rituals, the goddess we called was never referred to by a specific name, but I see now that it was most certainly Persephone.

Often drawn down or invoked at our Beltane rites, our Goddess of the Spring was mesmerizing to watch as she interacted with those around her. Her tone was always full of joy, and her exchanges with others playful, but behind her eyes there was a fierce power that seemed to contradict her smile. For many Witches, the idea of a maiden goddess suggests passiveness or naivety, that was not our Spring Goddess. Instead, we witnessed a goddess with a steely determination and inner strength who seemed to inhabit two worlds at once.[392]

Only later, years after many of those initial rituals, did I realize it was Persephone who had come to us. As we began calling the goddess Persephone by name at our house, it slowly dawned on me that I had felt our lady's energy long before, at our earliest Beltane rites. Demeter's daughter chose to be a presence in my life long before I called to her by name.

Many years later I was asked to write a Samhain ritual for a local Pagan group after moving to California. I was told that the ritual could not feature any specific deities, so the words I wrote were centered on a nameless Goddess of Death. Upon reading what I had written, my wife smiled at me and simply said, "Persephone." Again, I may not have known Persephone was with me, but she was still whispering in my ear. One part of that larger ritual is now included in every Samhain rite that our coven enacts. We call it the Charge of the Lady of Death.

---

392. Like so much of the art in the Mankey house, the deity portraits that hang in our ritual space were painted by Laura Tempest Zakroff.

THE CHARGE OF THE LADY OF DEATH

I am she who is feared yet she who would bring comfort. I am the end of all things and the beginning of all else. I would give you peace, freedom, and reunion with those who have gone before you. My gifts are rarely sought, yet freely I offer them. I am she who embraces every woman and every man. None shall escape my touch, but fear it not, for I hold the Cauldron of Life within my hands, the power of immortality for all those who would be reborn in your world.

I am feared, yet I am the balance in this world without end. Without me, thou would not live again. I am the end of suffering, the release from all pain. I gather the spirits who have left your world and offer them a place in it once more. I am the mystery of the end and the wonder of beginnings.

When Persephone is mentioned in ritual and song, her mother's name is often spoken alongside hers. For a period of time, it was popular to imagine that Persephone, Demeter, and Hekate were one goddess in three different aspects: maiden, mother, and crone. But when Persephone is seen as simply one part of a larger whole, something is lost. Persephone is her own deity, with her own agency and power. Persephone is not just a daughter; she is also a mother.

The picture of Persephone that adorns our ritual room speaks of Persephone's balance and how she inhabits two places at once. Her face appears under the ground, deep within the earth, holding court with the deceased. The center of her being is a sliced-open pomegranate, a fruit of the dead yet very much a treat for the living. Where her legs should be, a tree pushes up through the soil to bask in the light of day. This is Persephone, operating in two places at once. She is not simply the grim wife of Hades who sits upon a throne in the land of the dead, nor is she just a blushing spring maiden.

Persephone is a goddess for all seasons. In the autumn she is the power that brings in the harvest. In the winter she is the still, calm, and reassuring voice of death. Persephone shares the promise of an afterlife as winter's cold prepares the world for what is to come. In the spring she's the promise of life emerging anew from the cold, and in the summer she's the quickening of the fields, completely in charge of her own power. Persephone is not wedded to a particular time or circumstance nor stuck in only one world; she inhabits every space her Witches occupy.

MAGICK WITH PERSEPHONE
by Nicki Ojeda (Tatiara)

RITUAL FOR RECLAIMING THE LOST PARTS OF THE SELF

As sensitive and magickal beings, we are attuned to imbalances within ourselves and in the outer world. Sometimes it seems nearly impossible to remain unaffected by them. Seeking balance, you feel the power of life's natural cycles calling to you. Your own whole and holy nature demands that you honor the Wheel of Life. A trip to the underworld is in order.

Persephone knows this mysterious world well. By working with her and braving the underworld, you access your own depths and all the mysteries underlying our waking reality. You are enabled to reclaim what has been lost and to bring in healing and profound change.

Persephone does not sacrifice her identity to live below. She is still the radiant goddess of spring, yet she rules the underworld with Hades. She knows the heights and the depths. She shows you how to bring that verdant energy up from your own depths and use it to nourish your day-to-day life and world. The trials of the sacred dark teach wholeness and bring soulful revelations and awakenings.

Your deep self reaches out to you, calling you to live a soul-filled life, beckoning you to go beyond the borders of your known world. It's better to make the trip to the hidden realm of your own volition, rather than being dragged there against your will, because once you are there, it's often difficult to know what to do. This ritual is meant to bring clarity so you can trust the journey and understand what is trying to be revealed.

Materials/Offerings
- Roses or hibiscus flowers
- Dark chocolate
- Dark red wine, pomegranate juice, or hibiscus tea
- Pomegranate seeds
- Obsidian
- Amethyst
- Spring flowers
- Black or maroon candles
- Matches

On the autumn equinox or during the dark time of a cycle, meditate and attune to the depths contained within your own body. Go deep within and do not run away from frightening or intense emotions. Ask them what they have to teach. Really dig for the hidden treasure.

Set out your offerings for Persephone and light the candles. Set the mood to bring her into your consciousness. Close your eyes and visualize her as Kore, the innocent maiden. Allow her to walk right into you. Become her—your gender is irrelevant here, as we all contain these energies.

Visualize a balmy, sunny spring day and inhale the scent of the flowers you've offered her. Allow yourself to surrender to the mysterious force that wants to take you down, down into the depths and beyond. Fully feel any fear that may arise. This isn't easy, as you are calling up what has been hidden. Out of the darkness, Persephone appears to you. She is a sovereign queen who knows the mysteries of above and below. Let her touch your heart, sending her wisdom into your core. If tears come, let them. Ask for her guidance in reclaiming the lost parts of yourself. Trust fully.

Eat the chocolate and drink the wine as you stare into the candle flame. The more emotion you can muster, the better. Use hand movements and intuition to call back hidden parts of yourself. Trust to do what feels right to you. Don't think. Feel.

Let gratitude flow as you feel the fullness of your true identity washing over you. Know that the sacred darkness has opened a portal within, and a new cycle beckons. Expect new perspectives, growth, and healing.

Stare at the flowers as you thank Persephone and slowly return to normal consciousness. Be sure to extinguish your candles at the conclusion of the ritual. Follow up on your just-completed time with Persephone by writing about your experience in a journal or book of shadows to ground it into being.

Nicki Ojeda (Tatiara) has been practicing Witchcraft for over thirty years. A former Renaissance Festival performer, she gives tarot and past-life readings online and creates custom essential oil blends. Tatiara is passionate about bringing magick to cooking, playing piano, and studying mythology and archetypal psychology.

HERACLES
by Astrea Taylor

Heracles was a son of Zeus who lived in the Age of Heroes (thought by most Greeks to be what we today call the Mycenaean period). Although he was a mortal, he was a giant among men.[393] He was known as the repeller of evil and the demigod of justice. Like a modern-day superhero, he battled chthonic creatures and wrongdoers with the goal of attaining peace in the land. Heracles is depicted as an athletic youth who wore a magickally impermeable lion skin and carried a club or sword.[394] He was known as the greatest of all warriors, and to some Greeks he represented the possibility of what every person could achieve, regardless of birth.[395] His hero worship was documented in an epic poem lost to the ages.

Many of Heracles's adventures are similar to those of the Sumerian deity Ninurta, or Ningirsu, but Heracles is thought to harken all the way back to the era of hunters.[396] Heracles was conceived when his mother, Queen Alcmene, lay on the same night with both her husband, King Amphitryon, and Zeus, who was magickally disguised as her husband. The result was a set of fraternal twins: Heracles from Zeus and Iphicles from her mortal husband, both of whom grew up as Mycenaean princes.

---

393. Garland, *Daily Life of the Ancient Greeks*, 51.

394. Graziosi, *The Gods of Olympus*, 149.

395. Garland, *Daily Life of the Ancient Greeks*, 299.

396. Burkert, *Greek Religion*, 209.

Heracles means "Hera's glory,"[397] but it's an ironic title because Hera magickally cursed him with insanity. She was angry about yet another child of Zeus who was not hers. Mad, Heracles killed his wife and children. Afterward, he regained his sanity and visited the Oracle of Delphi to seek atonement. She told him to accomplish twelve feats. Hera attempted to thwart him again by choosing tasks that would be impossible to accomplish. Nonetheless, Heracles accomplished them. With a love of adventure, he killed several indestructible beasts, such as the Stymphalian birds, the Nemean lion, and the Hydra. He captured the swift Stag of Artemis and obtained a girdle from the deadly Amazons. He even traveled to the underworld and retrieved Cerberus, the three-headed dog that guards the gates of Hades.

After the feats, Heracles accidentally killed a man. In penance for the murder, he became a slave under Queen Omphale, who made him wear women's clothes and do women's work. He went on to accomplish other great feats that served to further humanity and the gods, including freeing Prometheus, killing murderers and rapists, driving the centaurs away, protecting Apollo's sanctuary, and even defeating Thanatos, the god of death.

However, Heracles's other wife, Deianira, became jealous of his many affairs, much like Hera with Zeus. She gave him a garment coated with magickal poison that burned his skin. Heracles leapt into a fire and perished, but he rose on the flames to Mount Olympus.[398]

Heracles had many temples and statues, one of which was kissed so much that its mouth and chin were worn away.[399] He was celebrated in the Heracleia festival in late summer with a great bonfire. On Mount Oeta, the place where he reportedly died, a fire was lit every four years and oxen were sacrificed. Major and minor celebrations were held for him in Attica, and both had banquets of meat. This could have inspired a certain mindset for sacrifice at all rituals. In Kos, his priest made sacrifices while wearing women's clothing to account for the penance he served.

The legendary tales of Heracles were an inspiration to Alexander the Great, leading to Alexander's Greek Empire,[400] a conquest that has had a lasting impact to this day. Heracles was offered first fruits, often on rural altars. He was thought of as an example of a divinely

---

397. Seltman, *The Twelve Olympians*, 174.

398. Burkert, *Greek Religion*, 209–10.

399. Laing, *Survivals of Roman Religion*, 157.

400. Graziosi, *The Gods of Olympus*, 101.

ordained ruler, which set a precedent for rulers to come.[401] The Greeks used "Heracles!" as an interjection for all kinds of things, which is secondary only to "Jesus!" to this day.[402] Although one of Heracles's epithets is Misogynous, it's unknown whether his singing about hating women was part of a comedic play or not.[403]

Heracles was also considered a constant companion and an omnipotent helper, and he was called upon for nearly every occasion. He not only invented altars but also perfected sacrifice to appease the gods, and he was known for his great sacrifices for humankind.[404] Most ancient Greek homes had an inscription with Heracles's name above their doors to prevent evil from entering, and they used his image in amulets as protective talismans. He is also thought to be associated with primitive hunting magick and Roman love knots.[405]

You may know Heracles better by his Roman name, Hercules, where he continued to be memorialized.[406] Many high-ranking people compared themselves to him, including the Roman general Marcus Antonius and the Carthage general Hannibal. The Romans offered tithes to Hercules, which may have facilitated the tithes eventually offered to the church.[407] Indeed, Heracles's widespread acclaim and his return trip to the underworld, sacrifices, and ascent to the heavens may have assisted in the eventual appeal of Jesus. Some scholars believe the two vertical lines in some monetary symbols such as the dollar and the pound are the twin pillars of Hercules, the location of his farthest travels.[408]

Heracles's popularity isn't what it used to be, but there are still some modern magickal practitioners who work with him. Among them, Hercules is used for strength, to avert evil, and to protect loved ones.

---

401. Burkert, *Greek Religion*, 211.

402. Burkert, *Greek Religion*, 75.

403. Broad, *The Oracle*, 12–13.

404. Burkert, *Greek Religion*, 211.

405. Burkert, *Greek Religion*, 209; Laing, *Survivals of Roman Religion*, 218.

406. Graziosi, *The Gods of Olympus*, 128–29, 149.

407. Laing, *Survivals of Roman Religion*, 103–4.

408. Sabin, *Classical Myths That Live Today*, 227.

MAGICK WITH HERACLES
by Jason Mankey

HERACLES AS PROTECTOR RITUAL

There are more stories involving Heracles than any other Greek hero or deity. Though mostly an afterthought among Witches, Heracles was hugely popular in antiquity and much closer to humanity than many of the other gods. He was a source of protection for us mere mortals and was a bridge between humanity and the gods. Heracles is the one figure in Greek mythology who is unquestionably both a hero and a full-fledged god. Other humans were deified in Greek myth, but rarely were they treated as full-fledged deities.

This activity calls upon Heracles as a protector and as a bridge between worlds. Most of the major Greek gods have origin stories on Earth, but after reaching adolescence they generally make their home on Mount Olympus or in a distant realm on the border between myth and our reality. Heracles was different. He was born in this world and traveled extensively upon it (and to the underworld as a human), and near death he was snatched from his funeral pyre by his father, Zeus, who took him to Mount Olympus (according to the Homeric hymns), where he married the goddess of youth, Hebe.

This rite is designed to be used as a blessing to consecrate an indoor ritual space. It can also be used to bless any other living space, provided you are comfortable having the gods around in such places. The rite doesn't require much in the way of materials, but in addition to a room to bless, you'll need a largish libation bowl and offerings to Heracles. I recommend wine and meat, in that order. If you are avoiding alcohol, grape juice is fine, as is any other drink you value. (A seven-month-old can of soda you were never planning on drinking is not acceptable.)

I recommend meat as the second offering because Heracles was known as a large consumer of it. Feasting and gluttony are often associated with the god, so why not give him what he wants? Lamb and beef are fine offerings, and I suggest cooking them before giving them as offerings. If you are a vegetarian or vegan, honey or dessert cakes are fine alternatives.

Materials

• A libation bowl

• Wine

• Meat (or substitutes)

Start the rite by invoking Heracles:

Heracles the lion-hearted, I call to thee! Great son of Zeus, be with me in this place as I con-
secrate it as a space between the worlds where mortal and Mighty One might exist together.
I ask for your power to protect this space from any who might seek to interrupt or limit my
practice of the Art Magickal. To great Heracles, I say hail and welcome!

Move toward the east in your space and place your hands over your head (the classical
Greek stance for prayer).[409] Take a steadying breath and call to Heracles once more:

Heracles, slayer of the Hydra and the Stymphalian birds, I ask for your blessings in the
east, from where the gods arise. Just as you once walked upon the earth, let this temple be a
space where both mortals and gods might tread. May this space exist between the worlds in
time of ritual and rite so I might experience the mysteries of you and your brethren. For this
blessing, I offer you this wine.

Pour a drink of wine into your libation bowl as a token of thanks and move toward the
south. Raise your hands above your head with palms toward the sky once more and say:

Heracles, slayer of the Erymanthian boar, abductor of the Cretan Bull, I ask for your
protection here in the south. May words uttered in malice and contempt against those in
this space be ignored and discarded. May any magickal attacks be driven away as if swat-
ted away by your mighty club. Let this temple be a refuge of safety and solace for any who
gather here. For this blessing, I offer you this gift of flesh.

Place a generous handful of meat into your libation bowl and turn toward the west.
Place your hands over your head and visualize the gates between mortal and deity. As you
picture those gates, imagine them opening up and call once more to Heracles:

Visitor of Hades in the land of the dead and guest of Hippolyta, the queen of the Amazons,
I ask that you lower the boundaries between this world and the realm of the gods, great
Heracles. Let this temple be a liminal space where the souls of the dead feel welcome and the
denizens of mighty Olympus feel honored. May the gates be open when rituals are done in
honor of you, O mighty Heracles, and in honor of your peers. For this blessing, I offer you
the gift of the vine.

Pour a measure of wine into your libation bowl and move toward the north. Reach
upward with your palms toward the sky and call upon Heracles one last time:

---

409. Burkert, *Greek Religion*, 75. Note: If you are addressing a prayer to a sea deity you should extend your
arms toward the sea and turn your palms toward the water. If calling upon a deity of death, don't raise
your arms.

Slayer of the lion of Nemea, capturer of the Ceryneian hind, god of myth, legend, and present-day reality, strong Hercules, I ask one final boon of you. Let this space be one where only welcomed people and entities gather. Bar from entry those who are unwelcome or unwanted. May it be a space of perfect love and perfect trust. Let all who would defy that ideal fail to find purchase here. This I ask of you, son of Zeus and protector of humanity! For this blessing, I offer you the gift of flesh.

Place your meat in the libation bowl and return to the center of the room. Hold the libation bowl up above your head and say:

Mighty Heracles, always be welcome in this space! Mighty Heracles, may your gifts and protection be with us here between the worlds. Accept these gifts for your generosity. Praise be to heroic Heracles!

When your rite is done, take the contents of your libation bowl and place them in a compost pile or an out-of-the-way space outside. As you pour the contents out, thank Heracles one final time.

HEKATE
by Jason Mankey

Hekate might be the most popular goddess in Modern Witchcraft. Over the last fifteen years, there have been numerous books written by Witches (for Witches) that focus exclusively on her. Hekate is so popular that there are many Witches who refer to themselves as Hekatean Witches, making her the only deity I'm aware of that Modern Witches gravitate toward in such a way.[410] Many Witches are devoted to certain deities, but you don't see terms like Dionysian Witches or Athenian Witches being used with frequency as identifiers.

Because so much has been written about Hekate recently, probing her past can be challenging. Scholars of ancient Greek religion and mythology aren't silent on the subject of Hekate, but they most often write about her as occupying a secondary position in the ancient past.[411] Yet despite the short shrift given to her by some scholars, Hekate is given a large role and accorded a variety of honors and attributes in many influential Greek works from the Classical period.

In Hesiod's *Theogony*, Hekate is the daughter of the second-generation Titans Perses and Asteria. When Zeus began his war against the Titans, Hekate had the good sense to side with Zeus and his siblings, and that apparently paid off. According to Hesiod, Hekate's wisdom resulted in being honored by Zeus "above all others," and she was given certain privileges.

---

410. The goddess Diana shows up in the term Dianic Witchcraft, but Dianics are focused on the larger Goddess archetype, not just Diana specifically.

411. In Walter Burkert's *Greek Religion*, Hekate is given one exclusive paragraph. The other greater gods all get at least a couple of pages.

Hesiod wrote that Hekate was given "a share both of the earth and of the undraining sea. From the starry heaven too she has a portion of honour, and she is the most honored by the immortal gods."[412]

Hesiod then describes the power Hekate has over the earth and its inhabitants, adding that if Hekate likes a follower and finds them sincere, "favor readily attends him … and she grants him prosperity, for she has the power to do so."[413] Her powers are not limited to providing wealth. She can also stand in judgment, watch over warriors and athletes, increase livestock, and choose who wins and loses battles.[414] Hesiod makes Hekate nearly an equal to Zeus, and he spends more time detailing the powers and attributes of Hekate than those of almost any other deity in *Theogony*.

The Hekate of Hesiod is also actively involved in human affairs. She listens to those who call to her and rewards (or punishes) them appropriately. Ares loves war for the sake of war, but Hekate protects those who go to war and takes sides in battles. According to Hesiod, Hekate is also in charge of fostering newborns, which gives her a direct link to all of us at birth.[415]

Hesiod's overt reverence and awe of Hekate might have been the result of his family's personal devotion to the goddess.[416] Much like there are Hekatean Witches today, Hesiod was most likely a Hekatean Hellenic. An alternative theory suggests that the many lines dedicated to Hekate were added later by someone other than Hesiod.[417] Despite Hesiod's eloquence, later writers focused on other aspects of Hekate, which are the more familiar aspects of her today: magick, Witchcraft, ghosts, and an association with the dead and the underworld. Hekate was the goddess of the liminal, which is why she was the goddess of the crossroads and transitions.[418] Such attributes make it easy to see why Hekate is so revered today among modern Witches.

Associations with the dead and magick led Hekate to be perceived as a goddess of the night. In art, she's often pictured with a torch, which would have been necessary for nighttime travel. She carried the torch when searching for Persephone with the goddess Demeter. As a goddess on the move at night, Hekate's retinue included the spirits of the

---

412. Hesiod, *Theogony & Works and Days*, 15.

413. Hesiod, *Theogony & Works and Days*, 15.

414. Hesiod, *Theogony & Works and Days*, 16.

415. Lefkowitz, *Women in Greek Myth*, 22.

416. Burkert, *Greek Religion*, 171.

417. Lefkowitz, *Women in Greek Myth*, 20.

418. Giesecke, *Classical Mythology A to Z*, 58.

dead and dogs.[419] Dogs were especially sacred to the goddess, and they were sacrificed to Hekate at her temples.[420] As a goddess of the night, Hekate was also associated with the moon, and she was often syncretized with the moon goddess Selene (and later, the Roman Diana).

The origins of Hekate are difficult to pinpoint. Unlike most of the major deities, she does not seem to appear in the Linear B tablets of the Mycenaean era, and she's also absent from the *Iliad*. The earliest reference to Hekate comes from the sixth century BCE in the city of Miletus in southwestern Asia Minor (modern-day Turkey). There, the name Hekate is written on an altar dedicated to Apollo. If this is the birthplace of Hekate, it would make her Anatolian and an import into the pantheon of the Greeks.[421] In her iconography, Hekate is often pictured with lions, a motif that was common among goddesses from the Middle East.[422] An origin in Anatolia would also allow Hekate to absorb a wide range of influences.

Over the centuries. Hekate was equated with a number of different goddesses, including Demeter, Persephone, the previously noted Selene, and most notably Artemis. By the fifth century BCE, images of Artemis and Hekate were nearly identical, and in many places the goddesses had merged completely. Hekate, like Artemis, was generally portrayed as a maiden, with the only distinctions between them being Artemis's bow and Hekate's torches. And later, even this distinction began to fade and blur, with Artemis eventually picking up Hekate's torch. In both inscriptions and literature from the fifth century BCE, there are numerous references to Artemis-Hekate, further blurring the lines between the two goddesses.[423]

In both the ancient world and Modern Witchcraft, Hekate is often syncretized with the goddesses Demeter and Persephone. Like the harvest goddess Demeter, Hekate was also a goddess of abundance and had links to agriculture. But Hekate's links to Persephone are even more secure. Like Persephone, Hekate was a maiden goddess, and both shared the company of the dead. There were very few deities who might be referred to as Queen of the Dead, and Hekate was one of them. Like Persephone, Hekate often resided in the underworld, and in some myths she was portrayed as an attendant of Persephone (though it's really hard for me to imagine Hekate in such a secondary role).

---

419. Burkert, *Women in Greek Myth*, 171.

420. D'Este, *Circle for Hekate*, 24.

421. Budin, *Artemis*, 123.

422. D'Este and Rankine, *Hekate: Liminal Rites*, 23.

423. Budin, *Artemis*, 123.

Hekate was often depicted in triplicate, most notably with three heads, in a wide range of images. Hekate's portrayal as a triple goddess most likely evolved out of three masks of Hekate being left at the meeting place of three different roads.[424] This custom evolved into Hekate being identified as a "three-bodied" or "three-formed" goddess.[425] In the Roman world, Hekate went by the name of Trivia, "Goddess of the Three Ways."[426]

Hekate plays a major role in the story of Persephone's abduction by Hades. In that tale, Persephone's abduction is overheard by Hekate, who then leads Demeter to the abode of Helios, where the sun god reveals the location of Persephone. Due to the popularity of the maiden-mother-crone myth of the Great Goddess in many Pagan traditions, the tale of Persephone's abduction has been used in modern times to argue that Persephone, Demeter, and Hekate are the same goddess. When people erroneously make this argument, Persephone becomes the maiden, Demeter the mother, and Hekate the crone.[427]

This has led to some Modern Witches believing that Hekate is a crone goddess, with an abundance of art and other materials suggesting such a thing. Certainly Hekate is legitimately old, but in the ancient world she was never depicted as a crone or even an older woman. The story of Demeter, Persephone, and Hekate is not a clever allusion to the idea of maiden, mother, and crone in the ancient world.

Hekate was most often depicted as a young woman, and an unwed and virgin one at that, though there are exceptions. Because of Hekate's connection to the realms of the dead, she was a frequent companion of Hermes, who, along with Iris, was the only other god able to move freely between the lands of the living and the dead. The Witches Circe and Medea are sometimes said to be the daughters of Hekate, but these references are just as likely to be symbolic as truly motherly. Since Hekate is a goddess of Witchcraft, it could be argued that any Witch who honors her is her child. Thessaly (or Aeolia in Homer) was well known for its Witches, which made Hekate a frequent visitor to those lands.

Despite the syncretic nature of Hekate in Greek and Roman religion, the goddess always maintained a devoted following of people who honored her as a separate and distinct being. In the Orphic hymns (composed between 0 and 400 CE), Hekate is honored as

---

424. Burkert, *Women in Greek Myth*, 171.

425. D'Este, *Circle for Hekate*, 60.

426. Giesecke, *Classical Mythology A to Z*, 58.

427. The maiden-mother-crone idea posits that the Great Goddess is represented in triplicate, and the facets represent aspects of a woman's life. Many people (including the authors of this book) find this idea problematic for a variety of reasons. Because those terms/roles are limiting, some people don't identify with them. There are many more aspects of life to experience apart from those roles, and not everyone who identifies as a woman follows that trajectory.

the first deity sung to. In the Orphic hymn to Hekate, she's very different from the goddess written about by Hesiod. To the Orphics, Hekate was a goddess of extraordinary power and influence, but also a goddess of the night and the dead.[428] The Orphics also give her domain over the earth, sea, and heavens, with the last most likely being an allusion to a realm beyond this one.

Hekate was also a major force in the Chaldean Oracles, a Neoplatonist text popular near the end of the Roman Empire. In the Oracles, Hekate is a mediator between our world and the power that created the universe. Much like in the Orphic hymns, Hekate is given a grand role in the Chaldean Oracles and is called both Savior and the Soul of Nature.[429] During this late Pagan period, Hekate retained her domain over magick and Witchcraft, and her name was invoked in a wide variety of spells.

The name Hekate shows up in both Greco-Roman curse tablets and the Greek Magical Papyri. Curse tablets were used to curse individuals and most often invoked the names of deities associated with the dead. The magick in the papyri was far more variable and included a wide variety of deities and figures from various pantheons (Jewish and Christian figures even make appearances), but no goddess is mentioned more often in those documents than Hekate.[430]

Not surprisingly, mentions of Hekate nearly disappear after the Christianization of the Roman Empire, but the goddess would come roaring back at the end of the European Renaissance. From that period forward, allusions to Witchcraft and magick often included Hekate. In Heinrich Cornelius Agrippa's (1486–1535) *Three Books of Occult Philosophy* (published in 1531–1533), the author lists Hekate on a number of occasions, especially when dealing with the spirits of the dead.[431] Grimoires such as Agrippa's would go on to have a huge influence on modern magickal practices (including Witchcraft), and Hekate's inclusion in such volumes would serve as an introduction to her for many magickal practitioners.

Hekate's most celebrated appearances in the early modern period are in the plays of William Shakespeare (1564–1616).[432] Hekate was never a major character in Shakespeare's plays, but she shows up in *Macbeth* (1606) as the goddess of the Witches and a keen judge

---

428. Dunn, *The Orphic Hymns*, 41.

429. D'Este, *Circle for Hekate*, 129.

430. D'Este, *Circle for Hekate*, 29

431. Agrippa, *Three Books of Occult Philosophy*, 564, 567.

432. Jason is a committed Oxfordian who believes that Sir Edward de Vere (1550–1604), the 17th Earl of Oxford, was the true author of the plays attributed to Shakespeare. Sorry for the conspiracy theory–related footnote.

of human character. Shakespeare also wrote often of Hekate being a triple goddess, calling her the "triple Hecate" in *A Midsummer Night's Dream* (a reference to the moon), and in *Hamlet*, Hekate is the goddess of plants and poisons.

When discussing the Greek gods in the modern era, it's hard to escape the idea of agency. When a goddess makes herself known, and loudly so, there must be a reason. Hekate as a goddess of Witchcraft and magick speaks to modern Witches like few other deities. With her ability to traverse the realms of both the living and the dead, she's one of the few deities able to facilitate reunions with those we've lost. She's also empowering, living and doing everything on her own terms. So although the Greek world was highly patriarchal and Zeus held sway over nearly all the gods, even he honored Hekate above all others.

PERSONAL INSIGHTS WITH HEKATE
by Brianne Ravenwolf

Hekate came roaring into my life. She probably was trying to garner my attention way before that, but I wasn't listening to her clues. I definitely wasn't following my intuition back then. At first, my personal practice with her was a bit fractured. Six months later, with several crossroads in my life traversed, I was able to settle into what I now call my normal practice with her.

Personally, I have found Hekate to be a very understanding and compassionate goddess. When I wandered from the path that she chose for me, she would gently move me forward again. If I ignored what was best for me, like a strict parent, she would make sure I got her message.

During one of my meditations, a feeling came over me to sign up for a Modern Witchcraft class focused on Hekate. That led me to start a daily practice with Hekate, which I have followed ever since. Do I miss a day here and there? Yes, but again, Hekate kept and still keeps pushing me forward when I forget. Very seldom is it more than one or two days. Do I always do a dark or new moon working or ritual for Hekate? No, not always. I do a full moon ritual every month, though. My practice isn't set in stone with the calendar that way. My practice is mine and no one else's. Hekate will usually let me know if it offends her, and I will humbly apologize for that.

In Samhain and in November, I honor my ancestors with Hekate and spend time in the underworld with her: Hekate Nykhia, the Night Wanderer, Stalker, Goddess of the Underworld, Chthonia. It calms me knowing that when it's my time to cross over, Hekate Lampadios will guide me with her torches blazing across the bridge over the river of the dead.

In November, the dark moon closest to November 16 is the Night of Hekate. It begins at sunset. That's a very important time of the year for me to do a ritual honoring Hekate, with a supper and offerings that will be left at a nearby crossroads. That night, I release all that no longer serves me. I give Hekate gratitude for the gifts and blessings she has given me as well.

In my daily practice, the most important thing for me to do is to give Hekate humble thanks and gratitude for all that she has blessed me with. Before I get out of bed in the morning, I give her thanks for watching over me all night and letting me have another day with her. During the day, no matter what I'm doing, I get the feeling that Hekate is always with me.

I try to walk by myself early every morning outside in nature with Hekate. During that time of quiet solitude, I connect with her. It is there and in my meditations that I receive her clues, usually just a word or two, or a feeling. Call it intuition if you like, but that's what comes to me. At night before I go to bed, I give her thanks for all she has given me during the day. Hekate is on my mind all the time that way.

Another part of my personal practice with Hekate is a daily tarot draw. I always ask her for advice before I shuffle the deck. I learn a lot that way, and it gives me direction. Sometimes I get a card and I go, "Whoa, what's that about?" Usually it's when I have strayed a bit from my path with her. She applies the correction through the cards and lets me know what I need to do.

I am so blessed that Hekate came into my life when she did. She gave me the tools I needed at various crossroads I was at. When I didn't know which path or road to take, she showed me. She led me to where I am today. She chose me, and then she chose me to be her priestess. For that, I will be eternally grateful. She is my guardian. She guides me on my path with her, and she will open the gate to the underworld when it's my time to enter. Hail Hekate!

Brianne Ravenwolf follows a Hekatean Witchcraft spiritual path and is an active member of Circle Sanctuary. She writes the Patheos Pagan blog Between Two Worlds.

PERSONAL INSIGHTS WITH HEKATE
by Alexia Moon

For me, Hekate is a very hands-on deity, and she is not subtle at all in her messages. I have had several experiences in which she clearly wanted me to do something, and she does not hesitate to make sure I know that she wants me to act, whether by constant signs through mentions of her name in the most uncanny situations, such as the same card jumping out of the oracle at every reading, no matter how much I mix them. She is also a kind goddess, from my experience. She is not a maternal deity—far from it—but she is nonetheless kind, and she wants the very best for her devotees.

There is a specific episode in which Hekate all but saved my life. I was in an abusive relationship some years ago, growing more and more miserable but lacking the strength to break away from the cycle of harm and save myself. Hekate was very present at the time, even though my daily practice had been faltering. On one occasion in the middle of a forest, she "showed" me which paths I could choose from: I could remain as I was and keep heading to a very unhappy ending, or I could stand up, dust myself off, and begin striding toward the new, less traveled road, finally placing my own wellbeing in my own hands, far away from my abusers.

A couple months later, having made my decision, I left and regained control of my life, making my way back to freedom of choice. It ended up leading me to amazing communities like the Covenant of Hekate, the Fellowship of Isis, and others. This allowed me to finally fulfill a promise I made to Hekate when I was only a teenager. As a teen, I had promised the goddess that once I was of age and allowed into priesthood training, I would devote myself to her service, but on the path I was on then, that was not likely to happen. So not only did she rescue me, but she also made sure I would fulfill that promise. And that I did. Hekate is a very important deity in my magickal and devotional path, and I can't imagine my life without her. It is my sincere hope that I can continue to honor, worship, and serve her for all the years to come!

Alexia Moon is a Priestess of Hekate and Persephone through the Fellowship of Isis and a practicing Witch and Pagan for over fifteen years. She lives in Portugal with her four cats and is the founder of the Iseum do Caminho da Terra and the website Sob o Luar.

MAGICK WITH HEKATE
by Astrea Taylor

SPELL FOR PROTECTION FROM EVIL SPIRITS

Hekate provided protection from malicious spirits for people, homes, businesses, and even entire cities.[433] If you feel the need for safety, she can be called upon in her Apotropaia and Aurobore roles as the Averter of Dangers and the Devourer of Ghosts. This spell can be repeated whenever needed or on the new moon. If possible, start the spell at a liminal place, such as a doorway or a beach.

Materials
- A medium-size bowl
- Water
- A small piece of black tourmaline
- A stalk of mugwort, lavender, or dandelion

Fill the bowl with water and place the black tourmaline inside. Place your hand over the water and say:

Hekate, be with me now.

Dip the plant in the water and gently fling the water upon anything in need of protection. Say:

Hekate, hear my plea. Banish malicious entities.

When you are done, give thanks and dispose of the water and the plant—if possible, at a liminal place outside.

KEYS TO WITCHCRAFT RITUAL

Hekate was called upon by Greeks who wanted her help in crafting spells.[434] This ritual uses several of her correspondences to help you spend time with her energy to deepen your magick. It's designed to be repeated several times, preferably at midnight, a liminal time between one day and the next.

---

433. Johnston, *Restless Dead*, 206–10.

434. Johnston, *Restless Dead*, 204.

Materials

• A black altar cloth
• A ceramic plate
• A black candle (a thick taper or pillar)
• Matches
• A metal pin
• A metal key

At midnight, just before or after a new moon, set up your altar with the cloth and then the plate. Place the candle in the middle of the plate. Light and candle and say:

Hekate, with this key and torch, I call upon you and I ask you to be with me.

Gently push the sharp part of the pin into the middle of the candle, being sure to leave enough room to hang a key on it. Hang the key on the candle and say:

In your name, Hekate, I ask for greater Witchcraft wisdom. I ask for deepening.

If there's anything specific you wish to ask for, do so now. Sit before the altar and stare at the flame. Allow Hekate to come through to you in her role of the key-keeper of the universe. Hear her voice, if possible. Blow out the candle when you can no longer sit with her, and light it whenever you wish to commune more with her wisdom. When the key falls from the candle, it is Hekate giving you the key to deeper Witchcraft. Give thanks and carry it with you as a reminder of your growing awareness. Continue the spell until the candle burns down completely.

A Tablet Spell for Curses, Hexes, or Blessings

Many people in ancient Greece created curse tablets. These often took the form of markings on a small, thin sheet of lead or other metal. These tablets have been found in temples, pools, and gravesites across the ancient world. While some curse tablets requested serious injury or death, others were more like hexes, especially the ones used to make their opponents fail in court or in the arena. Some tablets were created for retribution or protection. There are even tablets to bind someone in love with the creator and tablets used for blessings. People who crafted the tablets commonly invoked Hades, Persephone, or Hekate to assist them in their requests. The chthonic powers and liminal nature of these deities meant they were accessible for this kind of work.

To make your own tablet, procure a piece of lead or tin. These can be found at a craft store or garden supply store in the label section. Alternatively, you could cut open a soda can (with caution, as the edges can be very sharp) and use that. If those options aren't available, you could try to scratch any metallic surface.

Materials
- Incense
- Matches
- A thin strip of metal
- A writing/etching implement
- A hammer and a nail (optional for curses only)
- A spade

On the waning moon, light the incense. Say:

I call upon Hekate, goddess of sorcery and Witchcraft. Please be with me, liminal one.

Get in touch with your emotions and speak your desire aloud. Write it on the strip of metal. Release your intention into the world and say:

By your will, Hekate, it is done. Thank you.

At this point, you can carefully roll up the metal, or fold it, or strike a nail through it. Find a place to dig a hole a few inches deep where no one will step on it or move it. Use the spade to dig a hole, place the tablet inside, and bury it. Walk away without looking back.

NECROMANCY RITUAL

Hekate is called the magician's goddess because she helps people interact with the souls of the deceased.[435] There are several records that indicate that ancient Greek people saw ghosts and interacted with them with no fear or surprise whatsoever.[436] They called upon the spirits of the dead in their rituals and to assist with their magickal workings. This necromancy ritual can help you strengthen your communication with someone on the other side. Preferably you'll call upon someone who will be open to working magick with you. If you wish, the ritual can be done at an actual crossroads or in a graveyard, as long as it's

---

435. Johnston, *Restless Dead*, 204.

436. Johnston, *Restless Dead*, ix.

possible to be discreet and respectful to anyone who may be in mourning. If that's not possible, it can also be performed at home by your shrine for your beloved dead.

Necromancy should never be done with anyone who is disrespectful of spirits or overly fearful of ghosts. Spirits are real, and angering one could have serious repercussions. Open-ended necromancy, with no particular spirit called upon, should be performed only by people who can banish malicious entities, as that may be a possibility.

Materials
- A photo of the deceased you wish to speak with
- Their favorite food and beverage (or a piece of cake and a glass of water)
- A black pillar candle (and holder, if needed)
- A pin
- Matches
- Your book of shadows and a pen

After cleansing yourself and your space, set the photo, food, beverage, and candle on an altar and say:

> *I call upon the spirits of the east, the powers of air. I call upon the spirits of the south and the powers of fire. I call upon the spirits of the west and the powers of water. I call upon the spirits of the north and the powers of earth. Hekate, a circle is cast in your ethereal crossroads.*

With the pin, mark an X on the candle to represent the crossroads. Then say:

> *Hekate, guardian of the gate, she who shows the way, I ask you to protect this ritual and open the roads for me. Part the veil between this world and the world of spirits. Bring _____ (full name of the deceased) and only _____ (name) to this circle.*

Light the candle and stare at the photo of the deceased. Allow your second set of senses to stretch out around you. Feel the otherworldly energy and the essence of the spirit in the circle. Imagine you can see the spirit of the deceased before you. Take in their facial expression and their body language. Pick up on any other details, such as their clothing. Say:

> *I want to speak with you. I want to hear your voice. I wish to see your form. I want to feel your embrace. I want to sense your thoughts. Will you talk to me?*

Take a moment to breathe and really feel the connection between the two of you. You may close your eyes if it helps you to feel the energy of the deceased. When you feel a link with the spirit, ask them questions and listen for the answers. Write their words down in your book of shadows. Repeat this for as long as you can sustain the energy.

When the connection wanes or your energy fades, say:

Thank you for spending this time with me. I look forward to speaking with you again soon. When I want to call upon you in the future, I'll light this candle. Hekate, thank you for assisting with this ritual. I ask you to keep these roads open between us.

Take three deep breaths to refresh yourself. Say:

Hekate, goddess of Witchcraft and key-keeper of the universe, I thank you and I release you and your ethereal crossroads. I release the spirits of the north and earth, the spirits of the west and water, the spirits of the south and fire, and the spirits of the east and air. I release the magick circle.

Feel your energy shrink back to the size and shape of your body. Wiggle your toes and roll your shoulders. Stretch. Do whatever feels right to ground your spirit back into your body. You may need to eat or drink. Extinguish the candles. Leave the offerings out for a couple of days, then dispose of them with gratitude.

For best results, do this ritual often to facilitate communication with the spirit. Once you're familiar with their energy and you're certain they wish to work with you, include them in your rituals and spells. You can also light their candle and simply meditate with them, knowing they are nearby.

PAN
by Astrea Taylor

Pan is the half-goat god of carnal lust and wild places. He's depicted as a young man from the waist up, with the hindquarters of a goat. Horns adorn his head, as well as long hair and a beard. He's the patron god of shepherds, hunters, and flocks of grazing animals. He's called the Lord of Every Mountaintop, the Terrifying One, and Crooked. He is often portrayed as aroused and playing the double-reed flute or the panpipes, which he invented. His home area was Arcadia, a region with mountains, glades, and pasturelands. He was honored there second only to Zeus.[437]

The ancient Greeks thought Pan was older than the Titans and even stronger than Zeus.[438] His name appears to be Indo-European in origin due to the root word *peh*, meaning "to guard or watch over," or the word *pa*, meaning "shepherd or pasturer." The actual deity could be much older—some of Pan's caves and grotto sanctuaries are thought to be ancient.

According to the Homeric hymn to Pan, his parents were Hermes and a nymph. His mother abandoned him after birth due to his irregular form, but Hermes scooped him up and brought him to Olympus. Because all the Olympian gods loved him, they called him Pan, which means "all" in Greek.

---

437. Borgeaud, *The Cult of Pan in Ancient Greece*, 6.
438. Borgeaud, *The Cult of Pan in Ancient Greece*, 173.

Pan was considered a liminal deity for many reasons. He was half-animal and half-man, with the urges and powers of both. At night he slept in caves beneath the earth, and by day he wandered the wild areas and danced with nymphs. His identity was not always male. He was sometimes portrayed as more traditionally feminine.[439] He was not viewed as a singular deity—there were several pans in the wild areas as well as Pan the god.[440] He resided in the places where civilization and wilderness met, on the fringes of society. He may have even acted as an intermediary between the human world and the otherworld, bringing a little of each into the other.

Pan has a long history of lusting after all kinds of living beings. Once he tried to capture the nymph Syrinx, but she turned into reeds. He fashioned the reeds together to create his panpipes. With them, he crafted songs that rivaled even those of Apollo.[441] Pan sought the nymph Echo and inadvertently caused panic in shepherds nearby, who tore her apart. In sympathy, Gaia gave Echo the voice of other people. Pan seduced Selene, and they remained a favorite couple in some parts of Greece. However, as was the case with most of the ancient deities, Pan never married.

Pan could terrorize people if he chose to. The root word of *panic* comes from Pan and the feelings some people felt in his wild areas. He used this power successfully in warfare. In the Battle of Marathon, he spread crippling fear through the invading Persian army. For this, he was credited with helping the Greeks win the war. Pan also turned an army against themselves due to confusing echoes on the wind. The Greeks described panic as an overwhelming sense of danger, which they felt in the wilderness at noon. However, it's believed that Pan induced panic only in people who didn't honor him.[442]

With the exception of a cave on the side of the Acropolis, Pan's altars were in the country. People gave him offerings of honey, milk, and cheese.[443] He also had a few temples and sanctuaries on mountaintops, where he resided to watch over his flocks.

Most of Pan's celebrations were held in caves or grottoes (cave-like structures). They involved incense, flute music, singing, wine, ecstatic dancing, and sacrifices of goats and cakes.[444] Intermixed with the music were the sharp cries of women, similar to the sounds made when sacrifices occur. It's unknown what they sounded like exactly, but the purpose

---

439. Mankey, *The Horned God of the Witches*, 56.

440. Burkert, *Greek Religion*, 173.

441. Sabin, *Classical Myths That Live Today*, 153.

442. Mankey, *The Horned God of the Witches*, 50.

443. Sabin, *Classical Myths That Live Today*, 151.

444. Burkert, *Greek Religion*, 172.

of screaming might have been to release pent-up emotions and allow them to be more present, or it might have been to stun the senses and bring about a shocked, magickal mindset. It's believed that Pan's festivities started during the day and ended at dawn. Many historians think they included nudity and sexual activities, and Pan's sexual pairing with Selene may have alluded to those activities.

Pan may also have had a role in the Eleusinian mysteries. In some versions of the myth, he encouraged Demeter to return fertility to the earth. A sanctuary to him was found near one of the mystery sites.[445] This agricultural aspect may have been hinted at in the Orphic hymns (written in the late Hellenistic period or the early Roman period), which calls Pan "all-growing god" and the "father of all." They go one to elevate him as "the ruler of the cosmos" and the "horned Zeus."[446] To these people at least, Pan was seen as an earthly and cosmic deity with fertility powers. He was also connected with the worship of the Great Mother. At night, girls sang songs to her and Pan.[447]

The Greeks were fascinated by Pan and his disinclination to be civilized.[448] His celebrations were attractive to all kinds of people for many different reasons. Pan was particularly important to shepherds. They called upon him often to bring their flocks home or to rescue lost animals. They made routine offerings to him to ensure the health and fertility of the flock.[449]

There is little known about Pan in Greek magick, probably because there are fewer records about what happened in the country. Pan was known to give signs to those who asked for them, usually from the natural world. He is mentioned in the Greek Magical Papyri as the "master of all," where he's called upon for spells of popularity, luck, and bringing someone closer.[450]

The Romans recast Pan as Faunus and celebrated him on Lupercalia on February 15, which is thought to be the predecessor of Valentine's Day. At the festival, young men wore goat skins and took part in the sacrifice of goats, a dog, and cakes made by the Vestals. Afterward, the men ran around the city while striking women whom they fancied with a leather strip.[451]

---

445. Mankey, *The Horned God of the Witches*, 53.

446. Dunn, *The Orphic Hymns*, 63.

447. Bowden, *Mystery Cults of the Ancient World*, 87.

448. Burkert, *Greek Religion*, 172.

449. Sabin, *Classical Myths That Live Today*, 151.

450. Betz, *The Greek Magical Papyri in Translation*, 76–78 (PGM IV. 2145–240).

451. Laing, *Survivals of Roman Religion*, 38–39.

Pan is said to have "died" a few decades after the turn of the millennia. It started when someone on Greek land shouted the news to a ship carrying a large group of people traveling to Rome. The rumor spread like wildfire, causing grief and anguish to most of the people who heard it. Eventually the Roman Emperor Tiberius investigated it.[452] Not everyone agreed that Pan was dead, and his death remained contested, even through the Renaissance era.[453]

When the Romans expanded their empire, they brought Pan/Faunus north to the lands occupied by the Gauls and Celts. There, they connected Pan with the Celtic horned god Cernunnos, even though there were many differences between them. The Romans also went east, and as they traveled, they established areas for Pan (and other deities) as far as India. For example, in what is now Israel, there were several shrines and temples, an established cave sanctuary, and enormous bronze masks. The city Paneas and the region of Panion were both named after him.[454] With that kind of influence, Pan may have been celebrated by people in the Roman Empire for several centuries.

Of course, the Christians rose to power, and all of that changed. They used Pan's likeness and qualities in their formulation of the devil. They may have also used traits of other "uncivilized" gods, such as Bacchus, or underworld gods, like Pluto, but the prime influence was clearly Pan.[455] He was everything the church feared, especially because he could entice people away from obeying the church's many rules. The changes in Pan's mythology were complicated, and it's unknown how the people from that time adjusted to them. Some historians believe Pan played a prominent role in magick and rituals in whatever form he took—goat-man or devil—across the many continents.[456] Sadly, there's little to no evidence to support that theory in the European Dark Ages.

In the Renaissance era, some people wrote about Pan, including Francis Bacon. It's highly likely that Pan influenced Shakespeare's character Puck in *A Midsummer Night's Dream*. But it wasn't until the Witch hunts were over and the fear they engendered was at least partially quelled that more than a handful of people publicly expressed interest in Pan again. Romantic poets such as Shelley, Keats, Wordsworth, and Byron waxed on about him. Coincidentally, this was also the era in which the word *nymphomania* was coined,

---

452. Luck, *Arcana Mundi*, 257–58.

453. Luck, *Arcana Mundi*, 327.

454. Blumberg, "Researchers Uncover Ancient Mask of Pagan God Pan in Northern Israel."

455. Luck, *Arcana Mundi*, 37.

456. Luck, *Arcana Mundi*, 57.

which combines the words *nymph* and *mania*, two associations of Pan.[457] Victorian writers continued the Pan adoration trend, and eventually he became the most written-about god in English literature.[458]

Later, the ceremonial magician and occultist Aleister Crowley wrote lovingly about Pan. Gerald Gardner, the founder of Wicca, was clearly inspired by Pan when he wrote that the God of the Witches was a phallic god with horns, among other qualities.[459] It's also certain that Pan's re-mythologizing into the devil inspired Robert Cochrane's Horned God, or Witchfather, in Traditional Witchcraft. All these writers and their works greatly influenced their generations and the ones to come.

Pan is one of the most popular Greek deities among modern Witches and Pagans. He is invoked in sabbat rituals, especially at Beltane. Some call upon him in Midsummer/ Litha rituals to evoke the folly of the Shakespearean play. Pan assists with spells for love, lust, and musical talent. He retains his stewardship and protection of the land in magick for environmental issues and activism. He is also still used in curses to cause fear and panic in one's enemies. Pan is sometimes invoked in the Witchcraft practice of rewilding the psyche. And last but certainly not least, Pan helps set the mood for a great party.

PERSONAL INSIGHTS WITH PAN
by Pam Pandemonium

When many Witches today think about the great god Pan, sex immediately comes to mind, but that has never been why I hold him so dear. Pan is my conduit to the natural world—he's the god I experience when I'm out in the woods. My personal journey with Pan has always been empowering and magickal and not focused on phalluses or rapey satyrs.

I didn't meet Pan in the pages of a mythology book or in a Witch circle. I met Pan through a syndicated Canadian cartoon. I don't recall the name of the show, but I distinctly remember Pan being a part of it. As a child, I'd often wander away from home into the woods, and when I was in those woods surrounded by trees, I felt him there.

The connection that started as a child has continued into my adult life. I still feel him when I'm away from the civilized world and surrounded by nature. My experiences with Pan are freeing. He allows me to embrace wildness. My rituals in the outdoors with Pan

457. Online Etymology Dictionary, "nymphomania," accessed June 2022, https://www.etymonline.com/word/nymphomania.

458. Hutton, *The Triumph of the Moon*, 45.

459. Mankey, *The Horned God of the Witches*, 3.

aren't conventional—they're the experiences of joy and freedom and running skyclad through the woods with the goat-footed god.

For me, Pan is "all." He helps me embrace wildness so I can return to civilization. My experiences with him provide grounding so I can function in the day-to-day of the mundane. We all have a wild part of our ourselves, and it becomes problematic if we don't acknowledge it. Feeling the wildness of Pan puts me back into a grounded human headspace.

When I'm with Pan, I feel transformed. He has an energy that envelops me and makes me feel free to be whatever I wish to be. We don't speak to one another in the conventional sense, but we can feel each other's energies and react to them. He knows what I'm thinking and experiencing, and I know the same with him.

As half-man and half-goat, Pan is uniquely positioned between the worlds of human and animal. When I'm working with animals, it's the power of Pan that helps me forge a connection with them. I often play with my neighbor's goats when they are kids to help socialize them. In those moments, Pan is with me (and the goats!) helping woman and beast to understand each other.

Primordial liminality is the best way I can describe working with Pan. By tending to the wild and my wild self with Pan, I find myself better able to appreciate civilization. Pan helps me connect with something greater than myself and my day-to-day experience, and by doing so, he brings harmony into my life.

Pam Pandemonium lives in the wilds of Michigan, where she works with animals.

PERSONAL INSIGHTS WITH PAN
by David Ravencraft

WORKING WITH PAN AS A MODERN HEALTHCARE PROFESSIONAL

My relationship with Pan is not conventional. Instead of in the woods or in a ritual circle, I mostly invoke Pan while I'm driving on the California freeway in the middle of the night on my way to my nursing job. While driving, I enter a sort of meditative state and interact with him. There on the freeway I ask him for a stress-free shift and a manageable assignment. It can be a bit choppy talking to a deity while driving in a car, as there are stoplights and bad drivers to navigate, but most of the time it feels as if Pan protects me from those distractions and obstacles. There are nights when my interactions with Pan don't go perfectly, but I find that if I remember to talk to him before work, my shifts always turn out much better than they otherwise would have.

A nurse has to juggle a wide variety of tasks and responsibilities. We could be helping a patient onto a bed pan one moment and then have to contend with a life-or-death emergency the next. I was drawn to Pan because of his primal liminal-ness and bravado. He exists between two worlds and doesn't care what anyone thinks of him. These qualities are what I seek to cultivate in myself, as a natural introvert. Pan helps me be the extrovert I need to be and gives me the confidence I need to accomplish my goals, both on the job and in life.

I am part Mexican, and in the Spanish language *pan* means "bread." So as an offering, I give Pan the best modern incarnation of a bread dish that there is: pizza! Any type or toppings will do—just give him a slice of what you enjoy having. On the night shift, Coca-Cola is my one occasional indulgence. There are nights when I just need a little extra caffeine, and that's what I sip. Because it plays a large role during my most difficult nights, a can of it sits on my altar to Pan as an offering. As a not-completely-out-of-the-closet Witch, I find that an aluminum can doesn't attract any attention at home on top of my dresser. But I know what the can is for and who it is for, and when I walk past my hidden altar, I share a wink and a smile with the god who has given me so much.

David Ravencraft is a registered nurse and practicing Witch who is an initiate of both the Cabot Kent Hermetic Temple and the Temple of Witchcraft. He lives in Northern California's Silicon Valley.

PERSONAL INSIGHTS WITH PAN
by Nik Holton

There was a series of nature trails at a local park near my house that I liked to visit. Most of my visits occurred in the evening when the Louisiana heat was just slightly less oppressive. While I walked, I would talk to the gods, the moon, the universe. I would speak just random thoughts or occasionally a prayer.

As I came around a turn in the track that brought me close to one of those giant, sprawling oak trees, a voice came from the shadows under its branches. A light but clearly male voice casually said, "Nice night for a walk."

Immediately, I ran through dozens of scenarios for protecting myself, checked for well-lit places to run to if necessary, and tried to recall all of the self-defense training I knew. But then, the young man to whom the voice belonged stepped into the pool of light cast by the streetlamp.

I think about this moment so often, and the experience is as clear to me today as it was over thirty years ago. He was gorgeous, movie star handsome, with curly brown hair and a neatly trimmed goatee. He was dressed in khaki shorts and a short-sleeve white linen shirt. He smiled at me with a grin that seemed so familiar and warm that my fear just evaporated, though coherent thought and use of language also left me.

Suddenly we were walking side by side on the moonlit jogging path. We were talking casually about the weather. I remember little of the conversation. It was polite conversation to ease the strangeness of taking a moonlit stroll with a complete stranger.

We strolled casually through the humid summer evening. When the conversation lulled, we walked in silence. More than once, our swinging hands would brush each other's as we walked. Each time it felt like I had brushed my hand against an exposed electrical wire, though he showed no sign of feeling the same.

After a brief time, we came to a part of the path with no lights, and huge oaks blocked most of the light from the nearby houses. He slowed his pace and so did I. We stopped in the middle of the path. The scent from the nearby flowering bushes was intense, as was the bright moonlight that was the only illumination.

Without a word, he took my hand and turned me to face him. He smiled at me. At once, I knew that this was no ordinary man. My heartbeat quickened. He leaned in close, and I looked into his eyes. They were a color of the deepest green I had ever seen.

He spoke softly, "You are a good one."

"A good one, what?" I asked, confused.

He did not answer. I have come to learn that he rarely gives away answers in a simple manner. Instead, he wrapped his arms around me in a gentle but strong embrace. I stood still for just a moment, surprised but only slightly. Then I wrapped my arms around him and immediately noticed two very interesting features.

The first was his scent. I cannot convey in words the deliciousness of his scent. It was sweet and musky, and it brought to mind foreign markets and spices. It was not overbearing at all, but it was intoxicating.

The second feature took some time for my brain to figure out. As my arms wrapped around his back, it felt as though he had something under his short-sleeve button-down shirt. It felt at first like padding, thick but soft. As the embrace continued, my brain was able to catch up with all the details I had only partly glimpsed in the shadowy night. This guy was not just hairy, he was furry! With this piece of the puzzle in place, I gasped.

With a knowing smile, he pulled back and asked, "Are you all right?" It was a question not about my well-being or state of mind but about my understanding of what was happening.

Without a moment of hesitation, I replied with, "I am awesome!" sounding like an excited schoolboy who just got introduced to a god. He smiled wide and said, "I agree."

The hug lasted seconds or millennia, I could not tell you which. It ended with no words. He stepped back from me and looked me over. He nodded and looked back toward the place where we had met. He took a breath, like he was preparing to make a speech, then he sighed just a little and said, "Thank you."

Without further words or glances back, he walked back along the path, from one puddle of light to the next. In the glow of the closest streetlight, his gait seemed slower. He passed into shadow and then appeared again in the second pool of light on the path. Again, he seemed to be walking even more slowly. He stepped out of the second circle of light and into the shadow of the park at night. I waited to see him step into the third pool of light, but he never did.

I have walked that path hundreds of times since that night, always hoping that I would meet the wild god again. I never did … not there, anyway.

Nik Holton is an eclectic pagan with a degree in philosophy focusing on metaphysics and world religions. He lives in the Great Smoky Mountains in Asheville, NC, where he refinishes and repurposes furniture and creates altars from recycled furniture.

MAGICK WITH PAN
by Jason Mankey

A PERSONAL SEXUAL RITUAL

Connecting with the more benign aspects of Pan is as easy as going for a walk in the woods, but what if you are looking to tap into some of Pan's more sexual energy? As the god of shepherds, Pan is credited with inventing masturbation, an activity that can help us grow closer to the lusty goat-god. (Shepherds spent a lot of time alone in the ancient world, without any fellow human beings. What else were they supposed to do out there all by their lonesome?)

Pan's sexual energy can be a bit overwhelming when you experience it for the first time. Starting alone can prepare you for what to expect with a partner. This ritual calls for wine, but any liquid can be used as long as it's something you personally enjoy. Set up your ritual space as you see fit to set the mood. You can also burn a candle and light incense for ambience.

Materials

- Something to represent Pan, such as a statue of the god or an acorn
- Time and privacy (unless your partner wants to join in or watch)
- Whatever you need while pleasuring yourself
- A chalice of wine or other liquid of choice

Place the object representing Pan where you can easily see it. Ideally you'll want the representation of Pan to be straight in front of you, so it's always in your line of sight. It's okay to dim the lights, but keep things bright enough so you can view him. Place the chalice of wine near your representation of Pan.

Disrobe or at least lose enough clothing to get completely comfortable. In most ancient art, Pan appears either nude or with very little clothing on, so showing up in your birthday suit is a great way to honor the god! Start by invoking Pan and inviting him to be present at your ritual:

Arcadian Pan, god of lust and desire, I ask you to join me in my rite so that I might grow closer to your ways. Share with me your energies of joy and delight! Help me to feel wild and free and to cast out of my mind any guilt or shame. All rites of love and pleasure are among the rituals of great Pan. God of shepherds and panic, I invoke thee! Bring me ever closer to understanding and growing with thee. Io Pan!

Pick up the wine and present it to Pan:

Touch this wine, O Pan! I offer it to you both as a gift and as a way of receiving your blessings. May it transform me into a being of pleasure capable of experiencing your mysteries. Io Pan!

Raise your chalice in honor of Pan and take a small sip.

After you've set the chalice down, anoint your genitals, breasts, and lips with the wine. You want to bless each of these four body parts with a bit of wine, so dip your fingers back into the wine after touching each one. As you anoint your body, say these words:

Giver and receiver of pleasure, to know you, Arcadian Pan, (touch genitals)
So that I might know your mysteries, (touch left breast)

So that I might know myself, (touch right breast)
So that I can say and praise your name, great Pan! (touch lips)

With your body now anointed, get comfortable! Sit or lie down as you prefer. Explore your body before touching your genitals. Run your hands up and down your sides, or do whatever feels good to you. As you touch your body, reflect on how sacred it is. Our bodies are marvels, capable of both giving and receiving pleasure! Even more important, take a moment to remind yourself that you are beautiful both inside and out.

We are taught by society that beauty has certain standards, often eroding our personal confidence. That's all absolute nonsense, and Pan is proof of that! He was born with the legs and horns of a goat and never let that shatter his belief in himself. There were nymphs that ran from his rough embrace, but many more that ran into it. Pan shared his sacred grottoes with a variety of nymphs, beings attracted to the Arcadian god despite his unique appearance.

Begin pleasuring yourself as you see fit. There's no reason to rush anything. Take delight in the sensations you are feeling. Remember that every stroke and caress will bring you ever closer to Pan! You are free to think whatever thoughts you wish, but take some time here to reflect on Pan running through the fields, embracing his freedom from society's judgments. Sexual pleasure is something to revel in and not something to feel guilty about. Push aside your cares and worries and reflect only on pleasure and Pan.

As you near orgasm, begin looking at the statue or representation of Pan. As you look, feel the god's energy around you. Feel his approval and satisfaction that you are partaking in his mysteries. When you reach orgasm, grunt, groan, and most importantly, invoke the name of the god with a hearty "Io Pan!" At that moment, you should feel especially close to him.

After climaxing, you may want to clean up, but there's no hurry. If you've performed this activity in the middle of the day, this is the perfect time for a nap! A bit of afternoon slumber is the perfect way to continue communing with Pan, a god of naps. Who knows? He might join you in your dream space. (If you do plan to nap, blow out the candle if you lit one.)

When you are ready to leave your ritual space, blow out the candle, put on some clothes (if you have to), and grab your chalice of wine. Head outdoors, find a bush or tree, and pour your remaining wine out as a libation to great Pan. As you pour the wine, thank him for being at your rite and share your intention to grow ever closer to him.

GREAT MOTHER
by Astrea Taylor

The Great Mother, Mother of the Gods, and Ancestral Mother are all names of a Great Goddess celebrated throughout ancient Greece. She is credited with giving birth to all gods and humans, protecting cities, and turning away bad weather.[460] The exact personage of the Great Mother was not thought to be important, and many ancient writers intentionally blended them together by name and reference.[461] One of the Homeric hymns to the Mother of the Gods even goes as far as to say "all the goddesses together." She was called "black earth," which suggests Gaia. There are references to her being Rhea, the daughter of Gaia and mother of many of the Olympians. Other references indicate she is Demeter, the daughter of Rhea and granddaughter of Gaia. Another goddess associated with this archetype is Cybele, who originated in Phrygia and Anatolia in pre-Greek cultures. Hera was also included.

The Great Goddess is represented alternately as a woman sitting on a throne, as the plowed earth, and as a rip in the earth. She also had a cave in which wooden images of all the other gods were kept.[462] She was celebrated in the wilderness with ecstatic dancing and music, specifically drums, flutes, and castanets, played loudly and boisterously. She also loved animal sounds, which may have been created by participants. From the artwork on an Athenian vase from the fifth century BCE, it appears that dancers may have held snakes or worn snake decorations in their hair.[463] Entire communities participated in the festivals.

---

460. Bowden, *Mystery Cults of the Ancient World*, 86.

461. Bowden, *Mystery Cults of the Ancient World*, 85.

462. Burkert, *Greek Religion*, 90.

463. Bowden, *Mystery Cults of the Ancient World*, 90.

One account says girls sang to the Mother and Pan at night, and others state that young men dressed in armor to dance. Temples to the Great Mother were often constructed in wild places, but some were found in cities. She even had a temple at the center of the Agora in Athens called the Metroon.[464]

The Great Mother's attendants were called the Corybantes, who danced with abandon in mostly private rituals. They were said to act deranged, but it was also said that they had the cure for madness. Her priests wore long, flowing gowns and hats that looked remarkably like the Pope's hat.[465]

Rome adopted the Great Mother as Magna Mater in the third century BCE when a sacred stone representing the mother was brought there. She was given a sanctuary on Vatican Hill with dedicated eunuch priests.[466] Her festival was the Megalesia, which was celebrated for a week in early April.[467] Many Roman emperors, senators, and other high-ranking citizens took part in her cleansing rituals, which involved being showered in bull blood, even into the late 300s in the Common Era when Christianity was far more dominant.[468]

The worship of the Great Mother lasted longer than that of most of the other Pagan gods. Her sanctuary on Vatican Hill became the home of the Catholic Church, known as Vatican City. Mary, the mother of Jesus, shares many similarities with the Great Mother. Eventually the church rededicated the Great Mother's shrines and sanctuaries all across the Mediterranean to Mary.[469] However, the Great Mother did not go away. She remained and welcomed Mary into her collection of holy, venerated mothers. If you remove Mary's exterior dressings, you'll find that she's like a babushka doll, with goddesses from Rome, Greece, Phrygia, and other ancient unknown mother goddesses going back to the dawn of human consciousness, which keep going all the way to her core. Some believe the Great Mother merely donned the clothing of Mary to remain in the world and give people hope and love when they needed it.

The Great Goddess can be called upon for nearly anything. She is a wonderful deity for all the solar sabbats, as she represents the earth that changes. Witches turn to her for magick dealing with all kinds of topics, especially mothering, aging, fertility, changes, protection, abundance, blessings, health, as well as dealing with feminine and/or marginalized populations.

---

464. Bowden, *Mystery Cults of the Ancient World*, 88.

465. Bowden, *Mystery Cults of the Ancient World*, 96.

466. Bowden, *Mystery Cults of the Ancient World*, 93–95. Similarly, the goddess Cybele was one of the goddesses called the Great Mother, and she was associated with Attis, the god who severed his own manhood.

467. Laing, *Survivals of Roman Religion*, 124.

468. Bowden, *Mystery Cults of the Ancient World*, 198–200.

469. Laing, *Survivals of Roman Religion*, 123.

GAIA
by Astrea Taylor

Gaia is both the earth and the Titan goddess of the earth. She is a staunch protectress of the wild and her progeny. She may be more clever and indomitable than all the gods combined—no one except Gaia could have created the first knife and given it to Cronos so he could sever Ouranos's genitals.[470] Later, she gave Rhea the stone for Cronos to swallow instead of Zeus, and she helped hide Zeus from Cronos. When Zeus overthrew the Titans, he divided up the realms between himself and his two brothers, Poseidon and Hades. However, none of them dared to claim the earth. Although it was said that all of them ruled the earth, it's clear that Gaia was the true sovereign there, and no god could ever claim her.

Gaia gave birth to many creatures and deities, both with and without gods. She extended the powers of the earth to the goddesses who came from her through her maternal lineage (Rhea, Demeter, and Persephone), even as they grew into more and more human aspects of her so they could interact with humanity. Gaia is a master of divination—she intuited that Ouranos's children would supplant him, and she also knew that Cronos's children would have the same fate. She was the original owner of the Temple at Delphi, considered the center of the world. An enormous stone there was considered her navel long before there were stories of Zeus throwing it to find the center of the earth. Both the gods and mortals swore by her. Her rituals were ecstatic and possibly even orgiastic, with drumming and dancing. She even possessed people as the goddesses Rhea

---

470. Downing, *The Goddess*, 149.

and Cybele.[471] Her Roman names were Tellus Mater and Terra Mater, which translate as "Mother Earth."

One of the coolest things that contemporary science has revealed is that the earth is indeed alive. Every spoonful of soil is teeming with living microorganisms. They interact with the atmosphere and rain or water to trigger complex chemical reactions that help plants grow. In turn, plants symbiotically feed the microbes from the starchy matter they produce near the roots. Another scientific discovery is that it appears that soil microbes contribute positively to individual human digestive systems as well to give us energy and sustain our health.[472] This could be interpreted as if we're partially composed of Gaia, and every time we consume healthful food, her microbes support our health. Some Witches even believe this connection relates to our sense of intuition, which is commonly felt in the gut. This harkens back to the Greek belief that the first human bodies were created from Gaia, and Athena (divine air and intuition) breathed life into them.

Gaia is a popular goddess among modern Witches who feel called to help the earth as we progress into an era of climate change and toxic contaminants. She is an amazing resource for magick for all kinds of fertility and green Witchery. She also promotes psychological health whenever we work with her to get in touch with our inner wildness. Her patience and perseverance are magickal aspects we can draw from as well. Her depths hide so many secrets, and she can recycle anything, given enough time.

PERSONAL INSIGHTS WITH GAIA-TELLUS
by Anastasha Verde

Gaia-Tellus has been present in my life for as long I can remember. Like many Generation-X Pagans and Witches, I spent countless hours as a child outside by myself in the woods and local wild places, where I found solace and connection. In these spaces I learned to recognize my green, furred, feathered, and scaled siblings as family.

But it was only when I found my mother coven, Circle of Light, in the 1980s that I met Gaia-Tellus as the mighty mother goddess. Ultimately, my experiences in the wild and in the Craft led me to become a botanist and ecologist. The work that I do professionally and spiritually arises from my devotion to Gaia-Tellus and the deep sense of urgency I feel con-

---

471. Downing, *The Goddess*, 153.

472. Blum, Zechmeister-Boltenstern, and Keiblinger, "Does Soil Contribute to the Human Gut Microbiome?"

cerning life in the Anthropocene. It is at this intersection that I experience the many faces of Gaia-Tellus.

While Gaia-Tellus is typically invoked as the Mother of All, she is also recognized as the ferocity of wild beasts and the controller of disastrous events involving the earth and weather. It was, and is, important to be in right relationship with her. There are many paths to achieving a right relationship with her, from participating in environmental and land work to the typical spiritual and magickal work. But we can also experience communion with the Mighty Mother of the Gods in unexpected ways. Sometimes she reminds us that while she is indeed the Mother of All, she is also ferocious and she is the tomb that we find at the end of our days.

The following experience with Gaia-Tellus occurred during a guided meditation to experience dissolution of the self and transcendence. The meditation began as many do, with the relaxation of the body and the mind. As it progressed, I fell into a deep state of consciousness. About half an hour into the meditation, it led me into the solar system as a means of expanding consciousness. My mind opened and my consciousness started to expand into space. I moved beyond the limits of my mind as "I" dissolved.

As my consciousness expanded, I felt an intense pull back down to the earth. It was as if I was being told that I should not be expanding and dissolving into space but rather expanding and dissolving into the earth. I fell to *terra firma*. After I landed, Gaia's presence filled the area around me. As is often the case with primordial deities, she did not take on any form. Her presence began to fill me. I felt life moving through me, snaking through my body, through every pore of my being. My body was pulsing. After some time, my body began to turn in on itself in a grotesque process of recycling. I was being turned inside out, over and over. This was the cycle of life and death playing out in my body. I was not afraid but instead overcome with a sense of union with her. It was a profound and earthy experience with Gaia-Tellus, one that was a reminder of who she is: Mighty Mother of All, she who creates, destroys, and recycles.

As a botanist and magickal herbalist, I invoke Gaia-Tellus before I work with plants spiritually and magickally. I was inspired by the Roman botanist and herbalist Antonius Musa, who wrote the *Precatio terrae*, the Prayer or Litany to Tellus, around 13 BCE. In it, he praised Tellus and requested her assistance with his herbal work. For my own botanical communion and spellwork, I ask Gaia-Tellus to assist in making the path to my green siblings clear and to open the channels of communication. The following is a short prayer or petition that you can say before your plant work, whether it be gardening, medicinal herbalism, or magickal/spiritual work. It was inspired by the *Precatio terrae*, and it can be personalized for your own work. During this prayer, touch the ground.

> *Gaia-Tellus,*
> *Mighty Mother of the Gods,*
> *You who cause all to grow and mature,*
> *From you all things arise and unto you all will return.*
> *Beloved by all. Great Provider.*
> *With love, I ask for your assistance with this work.*
> *Remove the green shroud.*
> *Make way the path to my green siblings.*
> *May our spirits be united in purpose.*
> *Please accept this simple offering made with love in my heart.*

Then make your offerings. I offer any combination of incense, bread or flour, salt, fruits, flowers, and honey water to Gaia-Tellus. I pour the libations onto the earth and leave food offerings outside. Sometimes I bury the food offerings.

> *Anastasha Verde is a botanist, priestess of Gaia-Tellus, and co-high priestess of the Children of Gaia Coven within the Cassandra tradition. She has been a Pagan and Witch for over thirty-five years.*

MAGICK WITH GAIA
by Astrea Taylor

GROUNDING

Every Witch and magickal practitioner should know how to ground their energy. It's one of the most basic skills to alleviate spacey energy and refocus the spirit into the body. However, grounding doesn't come easily for everyone. Some people struggle to feel a connection with the earth and their body. This practice encourages a new way to think of grounding. It uses Gaia in her raw form for a tactile experience. You may need to use a hand spade if you can't connect with the earth due to plants being there. Try to find soil that you know hasn't come into contact with pesticides or herbicides. Do this practice outside if possible. If not, use a bowl or pot to carry the earth indoors (though potting soil isn't appropriate because of how much it has been processed).

Materials
• Earth (either outside or in a bowl or pot indoors)
• A hand spade (optional)

Sit down with the earth in front of you. Place your hands just over the earth so they're hovering over it without touching it. Close your eyes and try to feel the energy of the living earth. It may feel like a slight tingling or a swarm of activity. Say hello to Gaia.

Allow your hands to come into contact with the earth. Imagine Gaia is touching you as much as you are touching her. Let your palms and fingertips feel the microbes' activity and life. Their energy may feel like a presence or spirit with some kind of weight. With your mind's eye, see the energy the microbes produce as a colorful, glowing light.

Next, turn your focus to the microbes inside of your gut. Imagine that you can see them inside of you, doing marvelous work to help your body thrive. The energy they produce gives off a golden glow at your navel. Get in touch with it and allow yourself to relax into this peaceful golden energy. Connect with your body by moving each body part or imagining yourself touching them, starting by filling out your toes. Travel up to activate your ankles, calves, knees, thighs, rear end, torso, belly, rib cage, chest, heart, biceps, elbows, forearms, wrists, hands, fingers, back, shoulders, throat, chin, face, scalp, and crown.

Expand your mental vision to include the energy of the earth in your hands. You might notice how your gut appears to be a mirror to the energy in the soil. If you wish, you can absorb energy from the soil by imagining you're breathing it in.

When you feel grounded, thank Gaia for her infinite wisdom and guidance. Finish by washing your hands with soap and water. You can use this technique whenever grounding is desired.

Popular
Greek
Gods

It's no surprise that the Olympians and their peers are frequent visitors to both the rituals and the spellwork of modern Witches. But there were thousands of deities in ancient Greece, and many of those are actively involved in Witchcraft spaces today. We thought it was important to spotlight a few of those figures in this book, and to share a few personal revelations too.

Because the stories of the gods are continually ongoing, it's possible that deities such as Eris are more popular today than they were 2,500 years ago! The definitions of just who is and is not a deity are also subject to change. While the Gorgon Medusa is not characterized as a deity in most mythology books, a quick search online will paint a different picture of her. She is most certainly seen as a goddess by many in our community, as is the sorceress Circe.

Because of how Medusa and Circe are revered in the here and now, and because this is a book for Witches practicing today, we've chosen to include them in this section of the book. In addition to those deities, you'll also find information about other goddesses and gods who are popular today. It's weird to write about deities as being "popular," but it's important to us to write about the figures who resonate most with Witches today.

SELENE
by Astrea Taylor

Selene was the goddess of the moon who drove a chariot across the sky, as well as the moon herself. She was such a powerful goddess that among some magickal practitioners she was called "The Goddess" and even "Mistress of the Whole World."[473, 474] The ancient Greeks associated Selene with magick and Witches.[475] Simaetha, the fictional Witch in Theocritus's poetry, calls upon her more than any other deity—she calls Selene "Queen."[476] Selene was sometimes called "three-faced" to denote her changing aspects, from waxing crescent to full to waning crescent. These three aspects are clarified in the Greek Magical Papyri, which says she is the source of life, the fullness of living, and the end of life.[477] The last phase of life may have been more commonly associated with Selene, as the Greeks believed she watched over graves and protected them from harm, sometimes in the company of Witches.[478] There are some ancient Greek references to Selene having horns. This may have been a reference to how the crescent moon looked like a bull's horns to the Greeks, and it also could have referenced an older deity worship associated with bulls in the area.

---

473. Betz, *The Greek Magical Papyri in Translation*, 5 (PGM 142–95), 139 (PGM VII. 756–94).
474. Faraone and Obbink, *Magika Hiera*, 192.
475. Luck, *Arcana Mundi*, 57.
476. Stratton and Kalleres, *Daughters of Hecate*, 49.
477. Stratton and Kalleres, *Daughters of Hecate*, 168–69.
478. Edmonds, *Drawing Down the Moon*, 21.

Selene and the sun god Helios had a sanctuary in Thalamae with an oracle who came to people in their dreams. That sanctuary also had a sacred spring with sweet water. Selene is strongly associated with Hekate, the goddess of Witchcraft and liminality, who similarly has three heads.

Artemis and Hekate were commonly invoked, along with Selene, in nocturnal Witchcraft. Selene is called upon in the Greek Magical Papyri for all kinds of purposes. She assists with magick for love, slandering opponents, protection from harm, general purposes, and breaking spells.[479] Greek Witches sometimes prostrated themselves before her to amplify their spells.[480]

Some modern lunar Witches work with Selene, especially for manifestation with the lunar cycle. Children in particular seem to love her. Some magickal children are obsessed with finding her in the sky, and do so several times a night. Selene evokes a primal sense of wonder and magick for many people, and she can help to create a mindset that is conducive to magick.

MAGICK WITH SELENE
by Astrea Taylor

DRAWING DOWN THE MOON

Some modern magickal practitioners such as Wiccan-Witches draw down the moon to allow the Goddess to inhabit the body of a priestess. However, this practice appears to be different from that of the ancient Greeks, who used the same terminology.[481] While the moon was Selene, there is no evidence suggesting that they drew the goddess Selene into themselves. Instead, it appears they drew the energy of the moon into themselves, either to capture its essence or to channel that power into their magick. It was mostly a magickal practice of Thessalian girls and women. In the fourth century BCE, a playwright wrote

---

479. Faraone and Obbink, *Magika Hiera*, 195–202.

480. Betz, *The Greek Magical Papyri in Translation*, 28–29 (PGM III. 410–23).

481. Mankey, *Transformative Witchcraft*, 39. For a robust explanation of the more modern practice of drawing down the moon, read this book.

that every Thessalian girl knew how to bring down the moon with her incantations.[482] However, texts suggest some men could do it as well.[483]

Writers living in early Greek times believed that this practice was useful for all kinds of magickal and alchemical purposes. Some Witches used the moon's essence in their love spells or binding lust spells. Others drew the moon down to harvest moonlit herbs, which had more lunar power at that time. Yet other people drew down the moon to gather moisture from the dew of plants, which could be used in all kinds of magick. This was known as "moon foam," and it was said to be foamier than normal dew.[484]

The ancient Greek ritual of drawing down the moon was not recorded, but snippets of the practice are scattered throughout ancient texts. We can piece those fragments together to achieve a semblance of what they did. One text indicated that it included the practice of seeing the moon reflected on the surface of water or a mirror. Other sources say the Witches chanted, sang incantations, and/or spun a disk on a rope to make a whirring noise. According to a drawing that was reportedly copied from a Greek vase from 200 BCE, a sword and staff may have been involved.[485]

There is at least one reference to this ritual happening at midnight, and from another source, it appears the moon didn't have to be full—a waxing moon was also acceptable.[486] It is best performed outside or on the roof of a building. If that's not possible, it could also be done from inside a structure while looking at the moon through a window. Before the ritual, cleanse yourself with burning herbs. Mugwort (*Artemisia vulgaris*) would be appropriate, but any herb will do. Wear loose clothing and be barefoot.

Materials
• A full or waxing moon
• A glass of water
• A sword or staff (optional)

---

482. Edmonds, *Drawing Down the Moon*, 20. Several writers in the late Greek/early Roman era believed the moon did not want to take part in the rites, and the Witches who did it were old, ugly, and/or evil. This is representative of a general shift in mindset away from magickal practices and toward the denigration of women and Witches.

483. Edmonds, *Drawing Down the Moon*, 21.

484. Edmonds, *Drawing Down the Moon*, 22–23.

485. Mankey, *Transformative Witchcraft*, 237.

486. Edmonds, *Drawing Down the Moon*, 21.

Just before midnight, take a glass of water outside. Stand under the milky white light of the moon. Hold the glass of water so the moon's reflection shines in it. Connect with the earth (Gaia) by imagining you can feel her touch upon your bare feet. Take a deep breath and lengthen your spine toward the sky and the moon. Stare at Selene and let your gaze grow soft. If the sky is cloudy, focus on the brightest part of the sky and ask the clouds there to burn away until your magick is done. Breathe in the refreshing, cool moonlight. Set down the glass of water. Raise your sword or staff to the sky. If you're not using them, raise your arms to the sky. Use the tool and your fingers to gently pull on her moonbeams. If it feels right, sing a slow song to Selene or chant her name. Let your voice draw her light closer and closer to you. Continue, with deep, drawing breaths, until you feel her silvery essence dance within you.

When you are filled with moonlight, you can do whatever you wish. You might want to do other magick, or you may desire to recharge your ongoing magickal workings by sending her energy to the end goals. Her energy can be used to remove barriers standing in the way of your magick by imagining the light blasting the blocks away. You could ask Selene to heal your emotions and remove the impurities from your water-body. Any magick you wish to do is possible.

When you're ready to be finished, begin to exhale Selene out of your body and use the sword, staff, or your fingers to push her back into the sky. Don't remove her completely—you can keep a little bit of her magick within you.[487] Give thanks to Selene and pour half of the water onto the ground. Drink the rest of the water. Touch the ground and reconnect with Gaia and your body. Ground with Gaia as long as you need to before venturing back.

---

487. I attribute this tip to a workshop taught by Laura Tempest Zakroff at the 2019 Earth Warriors festival.

HELIOS
by Jason Mankey

Helios is the Greek god of the sun and was called Sol by the Romans. In both languages, his name translates as "sun." In his hymn to Helios, Homer describes the god as having "bright rays flash from him," and he mentions that the god's beautiful robe "glows on his skin."[488] Helios made his daily journey across the sky in a chariot drawn by the winged horses Aethon, Phlegon, Eous, and Pyrois, whose names mean "blazing," "burning," "belonging to the dawn," and "fiery one," respectively.

The Greeks (and later the Romans) believed that the world was a large island surrounded by a nearly endless ocean or river, which was personified by the god Oceanus. Helios was believed to drive his chariot across this river during the daytime and then sail back across it at night in a golden bowl, often accompanied by a goblet of wine. In some sources, Helios was said to make his home on a distant island far from humankind, where the god lived with his wife, Perse, a water nymph and daughter of the Titans Oceanus and Tethys.

In the ancient world, Helios was most associated with the island of Rhodes. The Colossus of Rhodes, one of the original Seven Wonders of the World, alleged to be over a hundred feet tall, was a statue of Helios. The sea nymph Rhode, namesake and protector of the island, was one of Helios's lovers and in some accounts his wife. Whatever the nature of the relationship between the sea goddess and the sun, the connection between Helios and the island of Rhodes was strong. Outside of Rhodes, Helios made frequent appearances in art and literature, but he had few active shrines or followings.

---

488. Homer, *The Homeric Hymns*, translated by Jules Cashford, 143.

In addition to being the god of the sun, Helios was also the god "who sees over everything and hears everything."[489] Helios's power to see and hear everything was near-omnipotent and even applied to his fellow gods. In the Homeric hymn to Demeter, Helios is described as the "watcher of gods and men," having witnessed the abduction of Persephone by Hades.[490]

Because of his ability to see and hear everything, Helios was also the god of oaths, and his name often appeared on treaties, spells in the Greek Magical Papyri, and other legal documents in the ancient world. (Helios's ability to see everything apparently didn't apply to his own home, as Odysseus managed to steal some of the god's cattle in the *Odyssey*.) Helios's power as an observer and taker of oaths links him to other sun deities in the ancient world. Worship of the sun, and acknowledgment of the sun as all-seeing, can be found in Celtic, Hindu, Persian, and Germanic Pagan traditions.[491]

In Ovid's *Metamorphoses*, Helios is given credit for creating most living things on the earth with the goddess Gaia. In the aftermath of a cataclysmic flood, the poet writes, "When moisture unites with heat, life is conceived; all things come from this union.... So when earth...felt the warm fire of sunlight, she conceived...all the creatures."[492] Such lines remind me of the Great Rite in Wiccan-Witchcraft, a rite that celebrates the magick of two forces joining to create something new.

Helios has further links to magick and Witchcraft. In the Greek Magical Papyri, Helios is invoked (sometimes with Selene) in a spell to make the spellcaster invisible, in a spell to receive an omen, in a love spell, and in the making of a charm to restrain anger and gain victory.[493] Helios is also the father of the goddess, sorceress, and Witch Circe. Circe's mother and Helios's wife, Perse, was also closely connected to Witchcraft and magick.

Though Helios is a common figure in both art and literature, many of his attributes were later absorbed by the god Apollo. Apollo's epithet Phoebus (which means "bright") was originally used to describe Helios.[494] Though Apollo never directly took the reins of Helios's chariot, by the fifth century BCE Helios's role in Greek religion began to diminish.[495] (It's a testament to the elasticity of the Olympians and ancient Greek culture that

---

489. Burkert, *Greek Religion*, 336.

490. West, *Indo-European Poetry and Myth*, 198.

491. West, *Indo-European Poetry and Myth*, 196–97.

492. Ovid, *Metamorphoses*, 16.

493. Betz, *The Greek Magical Papyri in Translation*, 68 (PGM IV. 1596–715).

494. Tony Allan, *Titans and Olympians*, 82.

495. Burkert, *Greek Religion*, 149.

Apollo could become a sun god with Helios piloting his chariot.) By the time of the Roman Empire, the synthesis of the two gods was so complete that Apollo was even depicted with Helios's brightness coming from his head!

Despite Helios's conflation with Apollo, the sun god remains a well-known deity, and his image and attributes often appear any time a generic sun god is invoked. Though many Witches focus on the moon and not the sun in their practice, it's still the length of time that Helios stays in the sky that dictates the sabbats on the Wheel of the Year. As a deity with origins far from Greece among the Indo-European peoples, Helios has been an object of devotion for thousands of years.

EOS
by Jason Mankey

Eos, the goddess of dawn, was not often the object of religious devotion in ancient Greece, but she is one of the most referenced deities in Homer's *Iliad* and *Odyssey*. In these poems, when a new day begins, Homer references the "rose-fingered dawn," invoking Eos, whose name literally means "dawn." Astride her chariot led by the horses Shiner and Bright, Eos eases us each morning into a new day, preparing the way for her brother and fellow Titan, Helios.

The early morning light isn't the only gift of Eos. Her tears are the morning dew, shed for her lost love Orion, the hunter. There are several versions of Orion's death, but in one tale, the youth was abducted by Eos, which angered the gods of Olympus. To punish Eos for her hubris, Artemis shot Orion upon Eos's chariot, killing him. Today, Orion the constellation is better known than Orion the legendary hunter, and it's not hard to imagine Eos chasing her lost love across the morning sky, with Orion fading the closer Eos gets.

Eos is most often depicted with wings on her back, and it's said she is lovely to look at. Her beauty persuaded Ares to take her to his bed, but she suffered greatly for the tryst. Upon catching Ares and Eos together, Aphrodite cursed Eos to fall in love only with mortals. One of those lovers was Tithonus, a prince of Troy who was granted the gift of immortality by Zeus at Eos's request. Sadly, though, immortality is not all that's needed to live a life equivalent to that of a god. The gift of eternal youth is required as well. Eventually, the body of Tithonus began to break down, and Eos either locked him in a bedroom to escape his complaining or turned him into a cicada or a grasshopper.

In art, Eos is depicted as having an unquenchable thirst for young men, possibly as a result of Aphrodite's curse, but it might also just be her preference. What's most interesting about such depictions is that Eos is clearly the aggressor. She's the one placing her hands on her potential lovers, and she remains fully clothed in such scenes, while her physical companions are often nude and depicted with looks of surprise on their faces. Some scholars have theorized that these depictions served as a warning against expressive female sexuality,[496] but others see her as a sex-positive goddess.

These days, Eos is probably best known in Witch circles for possibly being related to the Anglo-Saxon goddess Eostre, the source of the word Easter. No one is certain exactly what Eostre was the goddess of. Eos means "dawn" in Greek, and its origins are Indo-European, meaning "glowing" or "flame." This links Eos to the Lithuanian goddess Ausra and the Vedic (Hindu) goddess Ushas, both goddesses of the dawn.[497] Both springtime and the return of warm days might be described as "glowing." This might also be an apt description of a sex-positive goddess who greets us at the start of each new day.

---

496. Grover, "The Long and Decorated Literary History of the MILF."
497. West, *Indo-European Poetry and Myth*, 219–20.

NYX
by Astrea Taylor

In ancient Greece, Nyx was both night and the winged goddess of night, ancient magick, and Witchcraft. Even Zeus was intimidated by her due to her age and strength. She was vast, dark, mysterious, and pervasive, like a starry ocean drifting in the sky above. Nyx touched all things, and her darkness was a greater force than any amount of light people could ever create. She is the first daughter of the universe, born of Chaos. Every night she revealed her children, the stars, and their agricultural secrets. Farmers knew that when they saw the rise of the Pleiades constellation on the eastern horizon at dusk, it was time to reap, and when it sank below the horizon shortly before dawn for the first time, it was time to plow and plant. Likewise, other stars marked the time to prune vines, thrash grains, harvest grapes, dock ships, and so forth.

Nyx's children include Destruction, Misery, Strife, Doom, and Death. Many ancient people were fearful of night and its mysteries. However, Nyx is also the mother of Dreams, Ether, Day, Sleep, and the gentle nymphs of evening. The goddesses of fate are also her children. Nyx witnesses every chthonic ritual, and as such, she's associated with mysteries, the underworld land of spirits, and primordial forces. While Nyx is not named in the Greek Magical Papyri, much of the magick in these texts instructs the practitioner to perform magickal activities or speak magickal words at nighttime.

Modern Witches work with Nyx for Witchcraft power, psychological magick, trance, divination of their life path, scrying, and much more. She is sometimes associated with the Star Goddess in the Feri tradition.

PERSONAL INSIGHTS WITH NYX
by Astrea Taylor

In the introduction to this book, I wrote about how Artemis lit up my mind with ecstasy and trance, but it might have been Nyx as well. She was there, in the dusky skies on the other side of the window. Perhaps she was even guiding my fingers to find the right pages. Ever since I can remember, I've loved nighttime. It is when my personal power is greatest, and ironically when I am most awake. I was a night owl even as a child, staying up late and reading books after everyone else had gone to sleep. Some of my most magickal experiences have happened in the night, especially the ones that were turning points in my spiritual development. There's also something about nighttime that seems perfect for witching.

When I first started connecting with Nyx, I associated her with breath, trance, magick, and a different pace of life. It was also clear to me that her power was available for use. Just as daytime has its photons, which can be used in magickal work, nighttime has a unique and powerful energy as well. It's when the earth exhales, and for most of us, the right hemisphere of the brain is more active, whether in dreams or in trance.

Nyx is a powerful Witchcraft ally. She enhances all kinds of magick cast in the night. She appreciates dance and music, especially the singing of spells. She has the power to possess, but it's often a light touch, more like an intoxication than another being in your body. Her presence feels raw, alive, expansive, vibrant, and primal. I drink deeply of her essence whenever I can, and with each night-soaked breath, I receive her power, wisdom, and instruction. If your practice with her is not constant, she doesn't mind. She is eternally patient. She'll wait while you rearrange your priorities and come to her again and again. Nyx interprets the slightest interaction with her as an invitation to intercede on your behalf. One smile at the skies or a twirl at midnight is enough for her to shower blessings upon you.

Of course, Nyx appreciates devotion, too. She loves dark-colored offerings, such as chocolate, coffee, wine, and myrrh incense. She adores flowers that bloom in the night, such as evening primrose and moonflowers. An altar to her could feature black or dusk-blue candles, obsidian and black tourmaline, and images of stars.

MAGICK WITH NYX
by Astrea Taylor

SHADOW WORK RITUAL

Every night, Nyx embraces everything, both the good and the bad. She loves all her children, even the ones who may seem scary. Knowing this can inspire us to practice shadow work regularly and have compassion for all parts of ourselves. This shadow work exercise can teach us a lot about the power we have hidden from ourselves. It uses the affectionate name Mother Night, which is what I call Nyx from time to time.

Materials
- 3 candles (chime/taper) in holders
- Matches
- Your book of shadows
- A pen

At night, when you can be alone and unbothered for about thirty minutes, turn off all electronic lights and light your candles. Face away from them, so you face your shadow but still have enough light to see your book of shadows. Say:

Mother Night, show me that which I fear.

Write down your fears in a list on the left side of the page. Skip every other line, and leave the right half of the page blank. Write whatever comes to mind, no matter how unlikely or silly it might seem. Maybe you'll write something like "I'm afraid I'll die if my best friend dies," "I'm afraid of breaking up with Sam," or "I'm afraid of going to the doctor for an evaluation." Pour your fears onto the page until you can't think of any more or you've filled the page, whichever comes first.

When you're done, gaze at your fears with soft eyes. Feel their energy within you. Place your hand over your heart and feel compassion for yourself. Sometimes our fears highlight what we can do to prepare for a worst-case scenario, but apart from that, fears are not very helpful. Can you see how these fears are keeping you in a limited state of being?

When you've felt all your fears, turn to face the candles and say:

Mother Night, show me my strengths.

In the right-hand column, write down the opposite of each fear. For example, the previous statement "I'm afraid I'll die if my best friend dies" could become "I won't die if my best friend dies. It might be hard, but I will survive."

"I'm afraid of breaking up with Sam" could now be "I'm afraid of staying with Sam. I'm afraid Sam and I don't love each other enough, and I'll never get a chance to love again if we break up."

"I'm afraid of going to the doctor for an evaluation" could become "I'm not afraid of going to the doctor for an evaluation. Knowing about a potential medical condition will only improve my ability to move forward." Continue until you're finished.

Do you notice a trend in your fears? Maybe your fears escalate to death or the end of the world. If so, you're dealing with irrationalities. Maybe your fears are about how you're afraid of owning your own power. This indicates there is a path for growth that you may be resisting. Try to see how, in the past, you gave your power to your fears. How much did they control your thoughts, emotions, and actions? Take a few deep breaths.

Look at your page with both the strengths and fears, the light and shadows. Say:

I embrace the unknown, just as Mother Night embraces everything, every night.

Blow out one of the candles.

Repeat the statement with the remaining two candles. In the darkness, give yourself a hug and feel the embrace of Nyx as night saturates the air all around you. Know that you are much greater than your fears because you are also your strengths. You are expansive and primal, just like Nyx, and like her, you will rise again to embrace all there is.

MNEMOSYNE
by Astrea Taylor

Mnemosyne, the Titan goddess of remembrance and memory, was thought of as a subterranean deity with complete recall of all events since the beginning of time. She's the mother of the Muses. Members of the Orphic tradition were buried with instructions etched into gold tablets instructing the deceased to look for Mnemosyne when they arrived in Hades. The tablet told the deceased to look for the lake of Mnemosyne and to not drink from the fountain of Lethe, because they would forget their life and who they were. If the guardians of Mnemosyne's lake allowed the souls of the deceased to drink from it, the deceased would retain their memories and be at peace while living among the eternal beings.[498]

Mnemosyne can be called upon in magick for mental health, concentration, healing the mind from trauma, and all sorts of mental concerns.

MAGICK WITH MNEMOSYNE
by Astrea Taylor

REMEMBRANCE POTION

This potion uses an adaptation of the instructions that were etched into the gold tablets, as well as rosemary, an herb associated with memory. It can help with memory, whether it's for a test or remembering your past or your past lives. This potion can also be gifted to your ancestors or your beloved dead. It can be poured as a libation or placed on your altar to them.

---

498. Bernabé and San Cristóbal, *Instructions for the Netherworld*, 9–11.

Materials

- A sprig of fresh rosemary about two inches long or ½ tablespoon dried rosemary
- A mug
- Boiling water
- Your wand
- A pen
- Some paper or your book of shadows
- An altar of your beloved dead (optional)

Place the rosemary in the mug and pour boiling water over it. Write down your intention, such as "I desire to remember my past lives" or "I wish to give this potion to my beloved dead so they will remember me." When you are done writing, tap your wand against the mug and say:

Guardians of the lake and Mnemosyne, I am a child of the earth and the starry heavens. Please quench my thirst and grant this water to be the fresh water from the lake of Mnemosyne.

Recite your intention.

With your wand, direct the steam to either cover your face or drift toward the altar of your beloved dead. Take slow, deep breaths to enter a trance mindset. After at least five minutes, if it's cool enough, either drink the potion or place the mug on the altar. Meditate and write down any memories or visions that come to you. When you are done with the potion, pour it out as a libation to Mnemosyne.

ERIS
by Jason Mankey

In Greek mythology, Eris is best known for beginning the chain of events that led to the Trojan War. When she was left off the guest list for the wedding of Peleus (a mortal king and the father of the warrior Achilles) and the river nymph Thetis, Eris decided to disrupt the festivities by dropping a golden apple into the festivities inscribed with "To the Fairest." An argument then broke out between Hera, Aphrodite, and Athena over just who should own the apple.

Eventually Paris, the prince of Troy, was selected by Zeus to arbitrate the dispute, with the prince picking Aphrodite after the goddess of love and beauty promised him the hand of the most beautiful woman in the world, Helen, in marriage. Unfortunately for everyone involved, Helen was already married. Paris whisked Helen out of Greece into Troy, which sparked the Trojan War, but none of it would have happened without Eris and her Golden Apple of Discord.

Eris is the goddess of chaos and discord, and when provoked or forgotten, she brings that energy into the lives of mortals. When she is invited to the party, Eris is generally a responsible houseguest. Does she bring some chaotic energy with her? Of course. But it's more of a wild and crazy type of energy, and not the kind of presence that results in conflict.

I write about Eris and her energies from firsthand experience. Many years ago, my friends and I held a rather flirtatious and wine-soaked ritual in honor of Dionysus and Aphrodite. We forgot to invite Eris, and the end result was a lot of hurt feelings and bad hangovers. Six months later, we repeated the same ritual but invited Eris, and had a party for the ages. Eris is going to show up to your party regardless, so it's much better to have her there as a welcome guest.

Depending on the story, Eris is either the daughter of Nyx or the daughter of Zeus and Hera. In mythology, Hera sometimes asks Eris to punish mortals who have angered her. Eris's daughter was the goddess Strife, a figure even more unwelcome than her mother. The presence of Eris was rarely sought by the ancient Greeks, and they built no temples to her.

Despite her unpopularity in the ancient world, Eris and her Roman counterpart, Discordia, are immensely popular in magickal spaces. In 1963, the book called the *Principia Discordia* actively encouraged the worship of Eris and promoted the idea that our own reality is chaos. (Depending on whom you ask, the ideas in the *Principia Discordia* should either be taken seriously or are meant to be a parody of religion.) In my own coven, a flubbed word or knocked-over candle often prompts a hearty "Hail Eris!" since such mistakes suggest her presence. It's always better to acknowledge her than ignore her.

The counterpart of Eris was the goddess Harmonia (Concordia in Roman myth), who promoted harmony and agreement. Seeing their natures as two sides of the same coin suggests that they might be sisters, but Harmonia's parents are generally listed as Ares and Aphrodite. Unlike the other gods, Harmonia married a mortal man, Cadmus, the first king of the city-state Thebes. Harmonia later gave birth to Semele, who in many tales is the mother of Dionysus.

PERSONAL INSIGHTS WITH ERIS
by Thumper Marjorie Splitfoot Forge

I was standing in my bathroom struggling to get a cold-and-sinus pill out of its foil packaging and wondering which deity I should write about. Athena maybe? Dionysos? Or what about Eris? And right on cue, the pill popped free from its restraint, arced impressively through the air, and landed in the toilet with a pointed plop. "Eris it is," I thought.

That's just how Eris communicates with her devotees, though. Other Witches are like, "A shimmering luna moth landed gently on my shoulder while I was meditating by a willow tree at dusk, and I knew it was Selene, making me aware of her presence." And I'm over here like, "Eris waited until I was almost out of gas and then hid my debit card until I realized I had a date wrong on my calendar. But hey [finger guns], great moth."

Eris is often portrayed as the villain of the Trojan War myth, but in truth, the actual bad hat was Zeus: there was a prophecy that if Thetis married an immortal, their son would be more powerful than Zeus, so he arranged the marriage to protect his sovereignty. Thetis wasn't given a choice in the matter.

And here's the thing. When we try to force restrictive order on a healthy, disorderly system (like, say, a goddess's free will), the inevitable result is more disorder. Eris didn't ruin the wedding for kicks; she was doing what she does best, which is to short-circuit the unnatural order imposed by an oppressive authority.

Remember how, in the Matrix trilogy, the Architect's job was to make the virtual world and the Oracle's job was to unmake it? *Bam!* The Oracle was Eris.

Today, Eris is ultimately a goddess of social justice, and we can honor (and capitalize on) that aspect with a bit of Witchcraft.

MAGICK WITH ERIS
by Thumper Marjorie Splitfoot Forge

ERIS KALLISTI POWDER

Kallisti means "to the prettiest one."[499] It was what Eris wrote on the golden apple that sowed so much discord among the Greek gods that it started the Trojan War. You will know when this magick powder is needed. A shotgun wedding would be ideal, but really, any scenario in which civil liberties are threatened would make a suitable target—an anti-abortion rally, the courtroom of a dirty judge, a corrupt conference, etc. Whatever the case, show up unannounced and surreptitiously sprinkle your Kallisti Powder where it will be stepped on or kicked around. Bail before any punches get thrown, then treat yourself to a hot dog, which, according to modern legend, Eris herself enjoyed after her work was done.

I know some readers will think, "But what about karma? Or the Threefold Law?" Believe me, I understand the concern. But to that I say this: as Witches, sometimes we are the karma. Sometimes we are tasked with the responsibility to bring about consequences. Sometimes we've got to act as the Five-Fingered Hand of Eris and create some disorder of our own to make sure we're all truly free. So let's get on with the unmaking already.

---

499. Schweller, *Maxwell's Demon and the Golden Apple.*

Materials

- Black mustard seeds (to disrupt activities)
- Patchouli leaves (to draw attention)
- Poppy seeds (to sow confusion)
- Red pepper flakes (to cause trouble)
- A mortar and pestle or a Magic Bullet blender (to grind the herbs)
- Gold glitter
- A spill-proof container
- Your athame

Grind the herbs together, then add a heaping portion of the final and most crucial ingredient: gold glitter. Seriously, add as much gold glitter as you want. Add more than you think you need, and then add a little more. Stir the components until evenly blended.

When the powder is ready, pour it into a spill-proof container and place it in front of a suitable image of Eris (for example, a statue of her, a golden apple, or an autographed photograph of Tammy Wynette). Place the tip of your ritual blade in the powder. You can use your own words to invoke Wynette or borrow the following invocation, cribbed from Discordian ritualist Prince Prance:[500]

> *Great Goddess Discordia, Holy Mother Eris, Joy of the Universe, Laughter of Space, Grant us Life, Light, Love and Liberty and make the bloody magick work!*

Once the Kallisti Powder is charged, seal the container and store it until needed.

Thumper Marjorie Splitfoot Forge is a Gardnerian High Priest, an initiate of the Minoan Brotherhood, an Episkopos of the Dorothy Clutterbuck Memorial Cabal of Laverna Discordia, a recovering alcoholic, and a notary public from Houston, Texas. You can find them online at misfitmarjorie.com and patheos.com/blogs/fivefoldlaw.

---

500. Hill and Thornley, *Principia Discordia.*

ARIADNE
by Jason Mankey

Ariadne is best known in mythology for assisting the Greek hero Theseus on the island of Crete. In that particular tale, Theseus is sent to Crete as a tribute from the city of Athens, where he must face the flesh-eating half-man, half-bull Minotaur who lives in a maze designed by the genius Daedalus. Despite being the daughter of King Minos, Ariadne falls in love with Theseus and gives him a ball of yarn to help him escape the labyrinth. Theseus then takes Ariadne with him when he flees Crete, though according to the most commonly told version of the Ariadne-Theseus myth, he abandons her on the island of Naxos and sails back to Athens without her.

If the story of Ariadne had ended with her abandonment, we would probably not be writing about her in this book, but something extraordinary happened on the island of Naxos: the god Dionysus descended from Olympus and made Ariadne his wife (and a goddess). There are other versions of Ariadne's myth after her abandonment. In one of them she sailed to mainland Greece with a prince of Dionysus, and in another she hanged herself (and on the island of Cyprus there is a spot where she is said to be buried).[501]

Due to Ariadne's prominent role in the tale of Theseus and the Minotaur, many assume that she was a goddess on the island of Crete who was "downgraded" to a mortal in later mythology. That might well be the case, though it's impossible to prove definitively. What we do know is that Ariadne was worshipped prominently on a number of Greek islands and was honored as the wife of Dionysus throughout the Hellenic world.[502]

---

501. Giesecke, *Classical Mythology A to Z*, 141.
502. Otto, *Dionysus: Myth and Cult*, 181.

As a goddess born on an island, Ariadne is intimately associated with the sea, so much so that in many places her cult crossed over with that of the sea-born Aphrodite. In parts of Cyprus, Ariadne was worshipped as Ariadne-Aphrodite, and on the island of Delos, Ariadne was hailed as a priestess of Aphrodite.[503] The strongest connection between the two goddesses can be found in the name Ariadne, which is a variant of the word *ariagne*, which means "most holy."[504] Ariagne was also a common title for Aphrodite on the island of Delos.[505]

Ariadne's cult was one of paradox. Many of her rituals were the joyous affairs one would expect from a goddess associated with both Dionysus and Aphrodite, but many were also filled with "sorrow and lamentation."[506] On the island of Argos, a tomb dedicated to Ariadne served as a spot for worshippers to leave offerings for the goddess. The version of Ariadne honored there was thought to be a goddess associated with death.[507] This would also connect Ariadne to Persephone.

While we honor Ariadne as a real and independent goddess in our home (How could we not? My wife's name, Ari, can be found in Ariadne!), her myth is very much connected to her husband, Dionysus. Ariadne illustrates the power of Dionysus to save mortals from the nothingness of death. Just like Ariadne, we can become something greater than beings of flesh when we worship Dionysus. The sorrow found in the worship of Ariadne represents the pain we all must go through before arriving at a new state of existence.

Among Modern Witches, the mortal Ariadne is often thought of as a Witch. As a goddess, Ariadne is often associated with thread and is great to call upon when working with cords or doing knot magick.

PERSONAL INSIGHTS WITH ARIADNE
by Roxanne Rhoads

My life has never been easy, but I've often found my way through circumstances I never thought I'd be able to navigate. Whenever I've hit a wall in my path, I've found a way through it, over it, under it, or around it—like magic. I credit that to Ariadne. I can't even count how many times she's left me a string to follow or a lighted path to show me the

---

503. Otto, *Dionysus: Myth and Cult*, 182–83.

504. Otto, *Dionysus: Myth and Cult*, 183.

505. Otto, *Dionysus: Myth and Cult*, 183.

506. Otto, *Dionysus: Myth and Cult*, 188.

507. Kerényi, *Dionysos*, 103.

way. I feel like she's been with me most of my life, but it wasn't until I was sixteen that her name came to me while studying Greek mythology in school. I suddenly felt a resounding click. I finally had a name for the voice that whispered to me in the darkness, a name for the push I felt when I needed to go in a certain direction.

Since then, I have been devoted to Ariadne. I read all the Greek stories about her, but I *knew* there was so much more to her than her strange choices in men—being abandoned by Theseus and being a party girl married to Dionysus—though I could totally relate. The years of my late teens and early twenties consisted of poor choices in men and drunken partying. Ariadne had my back through it all and eventually guided me out of the disaster those choices created.

Ariadne has been a continual guiding light and source of comfort in troubled times. She has helped me get through the darkness so many times, giving me hope and leading me back to the light. I don't know if many Witches or Pagans have a relationship with her. It's not a name I see appear very often when deities are discussed. In Greek mythology, she's often referred to as a minor character, but new findings in both archaeology and mythology are now showcasing her status as a goddess, which she has always been to me.

To honor her, I named my daughter Arianna, a derivative of Ariadne, although my daughter has always had a kinship with the Goddess of the Underworld and has said for years that I should have named her Persephone. Imagine our surprise when I came across an article on ancient origins that tie them together, even claiming that "Ariadne is a predecessor of Persephone."[508] Different versions of the same story, the same goddess, both symbols of duality with tales featuring descent, search, and ascent. Trade *labyrinth* for *underworld* and you see clearly that the Greeks rewrote earlier Minoan tales to fit their patriarchal ideology.

Her earlier version is described more in-depth: "To the Minoans, Ariadne was a powerful goddess in her own right who traveled to the Underworld and was, among other things, a conductor of souls and a guide for shamanic activity. Her Labyrinth is the path to your Inner Self and the Underworld."[509]

The more I dig, the more Ariadne's origins and history come to light, and the more I believe Ariadne and Persephone merged into the same goddess. I now know definitively that I named my daughter perfectly. I even recently discovered that World Labyrinth Day is the first Saturday in May. My daughter's birthday is May 2.

---

508. Winters, "The Descent of Ariadne."
509. Perry, "Ariadne Was Just a Girl and Other Urban Legends of Antiquity."

When I set up my altar to Ariadne, I include an image of a labyrinth, string, snakes, roses and lilies, and a cake stand to use for offerings, because Minoans had special offering stands that raised them above the altar surface. I also love to put strands of fairy lights in wine bottles and use these on my altar. Ariadne seems to approve. Offerings often consist of honey and wine and, now that I discovered how Ariadne and Persephone are connected, pomegranates.

When I find myself in need of Ariadne's guidance, this is what I ask:

Ariadne, please show me the way.
I am so lost, guide me on this path today.
My heart is heavy, my mind is dark.
Ariadne, please light a spark
Inside this maze of my soul.
Show me a path that makes me whole.
Ariadne, offer me a thread
To guide me out of the darkness inside my head.
Thank you, Ariadne, for guiding me.
As I will so mote it be.

Roxanne Rhoads is an author, artist, book publicist, and all-around crafty Witch.
Her books include Haunted Flint *and* Pumpkins and Party Themes.

PHANES
by Jason Mankey

Phanes (also known as Protogonos) is a major figure in the Orphic mystery tradition. Phanes emerged from an egg as "gloriously beautiful," as both female and male, with wings upon their back.[510] The Orphics believed that before Phanes, the universe was mostly chaos, but their birth brought life to the cosmos, from the tiniest snail to the mightiest god. In some instances, Phanes is believed to be the "first god" and the result of primordial forces such as light (Aether) and Chaos coming together.[511] In other versions of the story, Cronos (Time) creates the world egg, and in others it's Nyx (Night) who could be Phanes's wife, sister, or daughter, depending on the storyteller. (Myth can be complicated.)

Phanes, along with figures such as Cronus, Aether, Chaos, and Nyx, are best thought of as primordial gods. In most cosmologies, they are radically different from the knowable deities of Mount Olympus. Instead of actively intervening in the affairs of humankind, they are the backdrop upon which those affairs take place. The primordial gods were most often seen as personifications of the forces that shaped the world. All the primordial powers that birthed the universe were important, but to the Orphics, it was Phanes who gave shape to the world, either alone or due to coupling with Nyx.[512]

Phanes shined with a brightness that was too intense for the human eye. Their form was visible only to Nyx. The power of Phanes as a being was so extraordinary that it

---

510. Wroe, *Orpheus: The Song of Life*, 47.

511. Wroe, *Orpheus: The Song of Life*, 47–48. Wroe's book on Orpheus, which contains a few pages on Phanes, glows and reads like poetry.

512. Tony Allan, *Titans and Olympians*, 23.

filled the entire universe. *Phanes* in Greek comes from the word *phanein*, which relates to brightly lit torches and shining stars.[513] *Protogonus*, the other name for Phanes, simply means "first born." Both names capture the deity's cosmic nature.[514]

The hermaphroditic Phanes is appealing to many in Witchcraft because it breaks down the rigid male-female binary historically associated with Wiccan Witchcraft. In Orphic myth, Phanes created the material universe either through coupling with themselves or by joining with Nyx. The union of Nyx and Phanes, as primordial forces, was like clouds of stardust colliding in the deep darkness of space.

As a primordial deity, Phanes could be interpreted in a number of ways. In the Orphic hymns, Phanes is called Lord Priapus, Priapus being of course the well-endowed (and often hermaphroditic) son of Dionysus. There are several ways to interpret the connection to Priapus. In Greek myth, the semen of the gods sometimes created life all on its own without the need of an egg. It's likely that the Orphic mysteries began outside of Greece, most likely in Egypt, and in Egyptian mythology Atum creates the universe through masturbation in some accounts.[515]

Phanes has also been linked to Eros, the god of love and traditionally the child of Aphrodite. As Eros, Phanes retained their hermaphroditic nature and wings but gained three extra heads. Phanes as Eros is likely due to the influence of the Neoplatonists, who believed that love is one of the oldest forces in the universe and the source of wisdom and beauty.[516]

---

513. Wroe, *Orpheus: The Song of Life*, 47–48.

514. Dunn, *The Orphic Hymns*, 51.

515. Dunn, *The Orphic Hymns*, 51.

516. Wroe, *Orpheus: The Song of Life*, 111.

IRIS
by Astrea Taylor

Like Hermes, the goddess Iris is a messenger of the gods who has the rare ability to travel through Olympus, the mortal world, and the underworld. She is a virgin goddess who is depicted as either a rainbow or a winged goddess. Iris is the daughter of two Titans: Thaumas, the god of the sea, and Electra, an oceanid nymph. As such, she's an ancient force that was integrated into the Greek pantheon for her helpful abilities, specifically as a messenger of Zeus or Hera.

Little is known about Iris, but a few myths mention her. She played an important part in the Eleusinian mysteries by facilitating communication between Zeus and Demeter to negotiate the return of Persephone. Iris also brought Zeus a golden pitcher filled with the river Styx whenever he wanted to test whether someone had lied. It was impossible for any god to lie to Zeus when poured a libation from the waters of the Styx.[517] Iris outshines Hermes as the prominent messenger of the gods in the *Iliad*, though this trend is reversed in the *Odyssey*.[518] Iris also assists Leto in giving birth to Apollo and Artemis, in some myths by procuring a new island from Poseidon for the delivery to take place.

Iris isn't mentioned in the Greek Magical Papyri, and no records can be found of working with her for magickal purposes in historical times. She is commonly associated with the tarot card Temperance, which depicts a winged deity standing in the liminal place between earth and a river, pouring water from one glass to another. The image sometimes

---

517. Hesiod, *Theogony*, in *Anthology of Classical Myth* by Trzaskoma, Smith, and Brunet, 153–54.

518. Seltman, *The Twelve Olympians*, 66.

has a rainbow in the background or irises on the shoreline, both of which are literal depictions of Iris. Modern Witches work with her in their magick for messages, divination, inspiration, creativity, self-care, LGBTQIA+ issues, and activism. Iris can facilitate monumental life changes that may seem impossible were it not for her brilliant and colorful assistance.

PERSONAL INSIGHTS WITH IRIS
by Irisanya Moon

When I met Iris, I wasn't looking for her. I was only looking for an answer. I thought I was a mere being who hadn't proved herself enough to be deemed worthy, a story I'd held my whole life. But Iris found me. She reached out to me. She dropped from the sky and said, "Yes, take that step you're afraid to take. Do the thing you're meant to do." Perhaps it was the beauty of the biggest rainbow I'd ever seen, and the belief that I was truly meant to see it. That it was for me. I listened.

I named Iris through a quick Internet search, on a sparse web page that doesn't exist anymore, not knowing she was signaling to me that I was about to begin a path of service if only I trusted—for once in my life. And I did.

Iris comes to me in the quiet times. She is the color in the background and the inspiration between my pauses. She arrives in guises I don't interpret until later. She comes as a balm and an answer. *Yes, do that. Yes, feel that. Yes, you.*

Iris was the rainbow in the sky as I quit a job that was killing me. The sharpening of my vision as I lost a contact lens before walking into the night with a rainbow-painted mask over my face. The colors in the air as I was making magick in the UK. The wide arc that surfaced after a storm at a Witchcamp in Texas. The rainbow that dropped from the sky above the ocean on the first birthday after my mom's death. *Do the thing. Keep doing it.*

Over time and holding her name close to my heart, our relationship has deepened. As one who can travel at will from the height of the gods to the underworld, Iris is a psychopomp, a journeyer who knows the depths of death and the possibilities of life. I know this too now.

When I am feeling lost, I sit under the sky. I write what is in my heart and give my words to Iris. I follow the rain. I place myself in the between moments of reflection and refraction. I chase rainbows these days. And they chase me.

If you are looking for Iris, you will find her. She will travel to you. Maybe not in a rainbow. Maybe not in a wild moment of unknown. You may find her in the eyes of a friend, a lover, a teacher, or an ocean. She will tell you of messages you need, of service you can offer, and of the journey of life and death.

That thing you need to say, that thing you're scared to do—write it down and place it on an altar to Iris. Drink a cup of water and make a sacred promise. She will carry it to the places it needs to go.

Irisanya Moon (she/her) is a Witch, teacher, ritualist, and author of Reclaiming Witchcraft; Aphrodite: Encountering the Goddess of Love & Beauty & Initiation; Pagan Portals—Iris: Goddess of the Rainbow and Messenger of the Gods; *and* Practically Pagan: An Alternative Guide to Health & Well-Being. *Her writing can also be found at her blog on* Patheos Pagan, Charged by the Goddess, *and in many anthologies.*

CIRCE
by Astrea Taylor

Circe is the goddess of sorcery and herbal lore. Her name is related to the Greek word *kirkoô*, which means "to encircle." She is credited with inventing spells for both empowering and malefic purposes. Circe has the ability to curse people and their work or transform them. Her magickal tools include the loom, wand, chalice, and blade. The Greeks invoked her for all kinds of magick, but especially herbalism and necromancy. She shared her knowledge of necromancy with Odysseus to aid him in his quest.

Modern Witches call upon Circe for knowledge, inspiration, power, and wisdom. With her vast knowledge of Witchcraft and magick, it's no surprise that she is invoked when creating spells and rituals. Some herbalists and Green Witches invoke her when they forage and craft magick with plants.[519] Herbalists especially are likely to flourish under her guidance.

MAGICK WITH CIRCE
by Astrea Taylor

BRAID RITUAL FOR MAGICK, POWER, AND INSIGHT

Circe is a weaver Witch—she wove on an immortal loom and even wove her hair into braids. Weaving magick combines things together along with one's will. Circe took it one step beyond the mundane by weaving while singing her intentions in a loud "spell-binding

---

519. Brannen, *Entering Hekate's Garden*, 19.

voice."[520] This ritual calls forth three of her qualities—magick, power, and insight—but they can be changed to weave together anything you desire. If you don't have cords or ribbons, you can envision the cords and weave them together in your mind.

Materials
• 3 cords (or ribbons or strings), each about 18 inches in length, in the colors silver, dark red, and violet
• A paperweight

Cleanse yourself and cast a circle of protection. Close your eyes and think about magick as a silky, silvery glowing color. Think about power and feel blood-red energy thrum within you. Invite the violet flashes of insight into your being as well. Once you've made a connection with the personal aspects of all three, lay the cords down with patience and awareness. Place the paperweight on the ends of the strands to weigh them down. Slowly and meaningfully sing:

> The silvery color of moonlight is magick, and the color of blood is ability, power. Violet I weave in between them for insights, and my will combines them all. Magickal, powerful, insightful one. Circe, enchantress, daughter of the sun. Magickal, powerful, insightful one. Weaver and singer, wise magician.

Repeat the song and braid the cords together. Allow the song to gain momentum as you go. When you're nearing completion, make the song crest in energy and then knot the two ends of the cords together. You now have a circlet of these energies at your fingertips. Wear it as a necklace or set it atop your head. Feel yourself encircled by the magick, power, and insight of Circe. You can converse with Circe at this time if you wish. When you are ready to end the ritual, give humble thanks to her and open the circle.

---

520. Homer, *The Odyssey*, 237.

MEDUSA
by Astrea Taylor

Medusa is thought to be a primordial, Neolithic bird-snake goddess connected with the forces of life, death, and regeneration.[521] The Greek historians Herodotus and Pausanias believed she was from Libya. Medusa and her two sisters were known as the Gorgons (another sister trio amid several other sister goddesses in ancient Greek myth, such as the Erinyes, the Morai, the Charities, and the Graeae). The word *gorgon* is derived from the Greek word *gorgos*, which means "terrible, fierce, and frightening."[522] It's possible the three sisters may have been moon goddesses—Orphic literature calls the moon a Gorgon's head.

The name Medusa means "queen" or "ruler," and ancient sources said she was either beautiful or monstrous.[523] In the earliest myths about her, she had wings, bold eyes, boar's tusks, and a wild, protruding tongue, though this may have described a mask worn by her priestess.[524] Medusa's hair was not thought to be made of snakes at this time, but she was associated with them. Hesiod said that she and her sisters wore belts made of intertwining, live snakes. She was sometimes depicted in art with several tiny snakes forming a ring around her head, above her hair. Curiously, in the earliest myths about Medusa, she

521. Dexter, "The Greco-Roman Medusa and Her Neolithic Roots," 472. Hesiod said Medusa was mortal, but it seems unlikely. Considering she's the daughter of the god known as the Old Man of the Sea (Phorcys) and Ceto, the goddess of sea animals and monsters of the deep, Medusa must have been a goddess as well.

522. Dexter, "The Greco-Roman Medusa and Her Neolithic Roots," 464.

523. Dexter, "The Greco-Roman Medusa and Her Neolithic Roots," 464, 466.

524. Burkert, *Greek Religion*, 173.

and Poseidon were lovers.[525] Hesiod said they lay together in a "soft meadow strewn with spring flowers."[526]

In Homer's stories and later-era texts, Medusa was referred to as a monster rather than a queen. Of course, *monster* is a word for a misunderstood goddess/woman. In myth, Perseus, a son of Zeus, set out to slay Medusa. He brought her head back to the gods, at which point Athena placed it on her shield. Medusa's severed head became known as the gorgoneion, and it protected the people who used it against harm and ill intent. Medusa's face adorned shields, armor, temples, drinking vessels, doors, ovens, and kilns. It was even used in Hades to make the souls of the dead obey.

Symbolically, placing Medusa's head on Athena's shield confirmed the connection between the two. The power of the overthrown, ancient goddess Medusa became associated with Athena, the current, dominant goddess who was more in alignment with the patriarchal structure of Zeus. The myth is also a metaphor for the new male elite severing the head from the ruling force of goddess worshippers in Libya. Because Perseus is said to have founded the city of Mycenae, it's tempting to associate Medusa with the Minoan snake goddesses from Knossos, Crete, which is just north of Libya. However, very little is known about the Minoan snake goddess apart from the snake-wielding figurines.

Medusa's myth changed, as many myths do, to demonize her as a dangerous woman. A play by Aeschylus in 430 BCE (*Prometheus Bound*) appears to be the oldest written source of her snake hair and her ability to turn people into stone. Medusa's bold, staring eyes likely alluded to the "evil eye," a protective charm used in the region which depicts an unblinking eye. It's thought that this is the inspiration for her ability to petrify people, or turn them to stone.[527]

Then, in the third century BCE, Apollodorus wrote the most complete Greek version of the Perseus-Medusa myth, which included the snake hair and her ability to petrify. Notable additions of this era included a shield so shiny that Perseus could look at her reflection in it and not turn to stone.

Centuries later, Medusa's story changed yet again when the Roman poet Ovid wrote that Medusa was a beautiful woman whom Poseidon raped in a temple of Minerva (the Roman version of Athena). He wrote that Minerva punished Medusa for this act by making her so hideous (with snake hair) that she would turn anyone to stone. Sadly, this version of the myth, with all its misogyny and victim-blaming, is the one that is most commonly known.

---

525. Seltman, *The Twelve Olympians*, 141.

526. Hesiod, *Theogony; Works and Days; Shield*, translated by Athanassakis, 18.

527. Dexter, "The Greco-Roman Medusa and Her Neolithic Roots," 465.

Recently, many people have empathized with Medusa's story of being a misunderstood goddess or woman. When they post a gorgoneion on their doors or wear it on their clothing, it's to honor Medusa as a powerful chthonic goddess whose presence is still very much with us today.

Although Perseus killed Medusa by cutting off her head in the myths, in many ways she lives on through the gorgoneion. Her face, which is similar to a Hydra (a serpentine monster that generated two heads for every one that was severed), has been replicated countless times throughout the millennia. This has made the spirit of Medusa stronger and easy to sympathize with. Magickal practices with Medusa include protection, underdog magick, and anti-patriarchy works.

MAGICK WITH MEDUSA
by Astrea Taylor

MEDUSA'S MASK (THE SMILE SPELL)

Whenever someone tells me to smile, it's always awkward. The request or demand is usually not about my well-being—it's more about the other person wanting to feel more comfortable in my presence. If they were really concerned about me, they might ask how I am or offer to talk. Instead, they're asking me to bypass whatever I have going on and put on a face that reassures them.

I actually smile a lot, but only when it comes naturally. I don't want to change who I am or what I'm feeling to fit someone else's narrative. So lately, whenever I hear this plea to change my face, I call upon Medusa. I invoke the powerful, ancient goddess who was demonized for merely being herself, and I unleash her upon them.

This spell invokes Medusa's bold eyes and animalistic teeth. You can even whip out your lolling tongue if you want. The best part about this spell is that it's so simple. It can be done at a moment's notice. It may not turn people to stone, but it will probably turn them away and stop them from ever making this request again.

Materials

• Courage

The next time someone says "smile!" and you don't feel like it, in your mind, call out:

Medusa, reveal yourself to this person!

Let your face transform into that of a gorgoneion. Feel your eyes grow bolder, reveal your gnashing teeth, and allow your tongue to act wild. With your powerful, grotesque face, stare at the person who told you to smile. If their reaction is funny, you can smile or laugh, but stay in character, with a guttural laugh and a vicious smile. Keep wearing Medusa's mask until they turn away or you're no longer in their sight line. Release Medusa's mask with gratitude and give thanks to her for lending her power to you.

Gorgoneion Protection Charm

A gorgoneion, an image of Medusa's face, can protect nearly anything. If you want to protect yourself, buy or make a necklace with one. If you want to protect your home, buy or make a wall plaque featuring a gorgoneion. This charm spell is ideally performed on the full moon, when the majority of light will reach the charm.

Materials

• A gorgoneion

Hold the gorgoneion in your hands and gaze at it. Call upon your inner primordial power and the primal energy of Medusa. Say:

Medusa, misunderstood goddess! With a loving heart, I ask for protection from harm.

Place the gorgoneion in the moonlight. After several hours, remove it from the moonlight and repeat the invocation. Put it to use and give thanks to her.

OTHER
NOTABLE
DEITIES

OTHER NOTABLE DEITIES
by Jason Mankey

There are thousands of Greek gods, and it's beyond the scope of this book to write exten-sively about all of them. This section provides a quick look at a variety of important dei-ties, highlighting their most important attributes, accomplishments, and progeny.

The Greeks believed that there were three stages of the world. The first was that of the primordial forces headlined by deities such as Uranus (sky) and Gaia (earth). The union of Uranus and Gaia gave birth to the Titans, who deposed their father, Uranus. The cycle was repeated when Zeus and his brethren challenged and defeated the Titans. We've followed the example of the ancient Greeks and divided this section according to those three time-lines—primordial forces, Titans, and finally the age of the Olympians—with each section highlighting significant deities not profiled elsewhere in this book. We've also included a few prominent Roman deities who show up in the rites and rituals of Modern Witches from time to time.

PRIMORDIAL FORCES

The gods that make up the primordial forces explain the origins of the universe. Most of them can probably best be thought of as personified abstractions. The great majority were not honored with temples or statues. The most famous story featuring these forces was from the poet Hesiod, whose *Theogony* attempts to explain the origins of the gods and the Olympians rise to power.

According to Hesiod, at the beginning there was simply the void, Chaos, followed by Gaia (earth). Gaia then gave birth to the sky, Ouranos, and from there earth and sky went on to produce the twelve original Titans, along with several monsters: the Cyclopes and the Hecatoncheires ("hundred handers"), the latter of whom had one hundred arms and fifty heads. Repulsed by his children, Ouranos placed them back inside his wife, causing her great pain. In retaliation, the Titan Cronus cut off his father's genitals and succeeded his father as ruler of the universe. (The genitals of Ouranos fell into the ocean and created Aphrodite.)

Though Ouranos was "killed" by his son, he was more than just a god. He was the sky, and he remained as such. After assisting his mother, Gaia, Cronus imprisoned the Cyclopes and Hecatoncheires in Tartarus. They would eventually join Zeus in later deposing Cronus.

With the exceptions of Gaia, Nyx, and Phanes (who are profiled elsewhere in this book), most of the primordial deities are rare visitors among Witches. However, because of their power over day-to-day events, they are powerful magickal allies.

Aether: Aether is the middle space between the air we breathe and the cosmic sky. Because of this, Aether is the primordial god of light. Erebus was thought to hide the brightness of Aether, and the day could begin only once Hemera had scattered Erebus's essence once more. Aether is called upon in magick to hear or receive invocations and give life to them.

Chaos (or Khaos): Chaos was the first entity to be found in the universe, emerging in the void between the earth and the heavens. As a goddess of the sky, she was thought to have given birth to the birds and is the mother (or grandmother) of any other primordial deity associated with the sky. In the Greek Magical Papyri, Chaos is called upon to hold demons that have been driven out of a person. She is also called upon to subdue people and forces.

Erebus (or Erebos): Erebus is the god of darkness. It was believed that his partner Nyx drew his essence upward into the sky to bring about the darkness of the night. Erebus can bestow power upon magickal practitioners.

Eros: Eros was called the fairest of the deathless gods. Son of Chaos, he was one of the original gods who helped sire the world through attraction and love. Hesiod described Eros as a "dissolver of flesh, who overcomes the reason and purpose in the breasts of all gods and all men."[528]

---

528. Hesiod, *Theogony*, lines 120–23.

Hemera: The daughter of Erebus and Nyx, Hemera scattered the essence of Erebus each morning to bring about the light of day.

Ouranos: The son of Gaia and the father of the Titans, Ouranos was the god of the sky and the embodiment of the heavens. Ouranos was the original ruler of the world until he was overthrown by his son Cronus. When Cronus cut off his father's genitals, they fell into the ocean and created the goddess Aphrodite. In Roman mythology, Ouranos is known as Caelus, and he is currently connected with the planet Uranus.

Ourea: This is the collective name for various mountain deities: every mountain was thought to have its own deity. The Ourea have no father, being born directly from Gaia herself.

Pontos: Pontos was the original god of the ocean, and the ocean itself. With his wife, Thalassa, he is responsible for all the creatures that dwell under the water.

Tartarus: Much like Gaia is both a goddess and the ground we walk upon, Tartarus is a god and the land of the dead. He was one of the first deities to emerge, along with Chaos and Gaia. Tartarus represents the worst of the afterlife. It was where Zeus sent those who challenged or disobeyed him as punishment. Because of this, Tartarus the deity is also associated with torment.

Thalassa: Thalassa was the goddess of the sea, and the sea itself. She is the mother of all fish and everything else that lives underwater.

TITANS

After the primordial forces, the Titans were the second generation of gods. Led by Cronus, the Titans overthrew their father, Ouranos, and established rule over the world with Cronus as king. The original Titans were made up of six brothers (Cronus, Oceanus, Coeus, Crius, Hyperion, and Iapetus) and six sisters (Rhea, Thea, Themis, Phoebe, Tethys, and Mnemosyne). The twelve Titans went on to have a number of children, many of whom ended up coupling with the gods of Olympus.

The most famous of the Titans is Cronus, who swallowed all his children after they were born so they would never challenge his rule. Eventually, his son Zeus, who had been spared from being swallowed due to a trick played by his mother, Rhea (Cronus swallowed a rock instead of the baby Zeus), deposed his father and established the rule of the Olympians, along with his brothers and sisters (and later his children). The defeated Titans who fought against Zeus were cast down into Tartarus to be tortured, with the exception of Atlas, who was forced to hold up the sky for all eternity.

The battle between the Titans and the Olympians became known as the Titanomachy. In mythology, the Titans Prometheus and Themis are singled out for being aligned with Zeus and fighting against their brethren. However, many of the Titans carried on with their godly duties after the triumph of Zeus. Several Titans are profiled in other parts of this book. The rest are included here.

Asteria: Most famous for being the mother of Hekate, Asteria is also the goddess of astrology and shooting stars. Asteria is sometimes known as Delos, the island birthplace of Artemis and Apollo. To avoid the amorous overtures of Zeus, Asteria turned herself into an island to hide from the son of Cronus. The island of Delos is said to be the body of Asteria.

Atlas: A second-generation Titan best known for holding up the sky, Atlas is incredibly strong though not particularly bright. The comic book hero Shazam gets his strength from the god Atlas.

Clymene: The mother of Prometheus and the goddess of fame, Clymene is the perfect goddess for the age of social media.

Coeus: One of the original twelve Titans, most famous for being the father of Asteria and Leto, Coeus is the god of intellect.

Crius: One of the original twelve Titans and one of the most enigmatic gods, Crius is the god of constellations.

Cronus (Kronus): Cronus was the youngest of the original Titans and the son of Gaia and Uranus. After overthrowing his father, Uranus, and becoming king of the gods, Cronus learned that his children would one day overthrow him. To prevent this from happening, he swallowed all his children, with the exception of Zeus, who was saved from Cronus's wrath by his mother, Rhea, who wrapped a rock in swaddling clothes, which Cronus swallowed instead. Zeus eventually rescued his brothers and sisters and then went to war with the Titans, deposing his father and becoming king of the gods. After his defeat, Cronus was imprisoned in Tartarus.

In Roman mythology, Cronus was known as Saturn, but their mythologies are very different. Saturn was a god of agriculture, the rule of law, and wealth. The Roman holiday Saturnalia (where Christmas comes from) was named in his honor. The Romans believed that after being imprisoned by his son Jupiter, Saturn escaped and established a peaceful and prosperous kingdom on the Italian Peninsula.

Dione: A goddess of prophecy, Dione is listed as Aphrodite's mother (with Zeus) in Homer's *Iliad*.

Epimetheus: The clueless brother of Prometheus and the god of afterthought, Epimetheus is the husband of Pandora, a gift from Zeus that he created to punish men.

Hyperion: The original sun god, the Titan Hyperion is also the father of Helios, Eos, and Selene. Hyperion was often identified with his son Helios and later Apollo.

Iapetus: One of the Titans to challenge the reign of Zeus, Iapetus was cast into Tartarus with his brother Cronus and their allies. Iapetus is the father of the trickster Prometheus with Clymene, daughter of Oceanus and Tethys. Iapetus is the god of mortality.

Leto: Leto is most famous for being the mother of Apollo and Artemis but may have once been more prominent among the Greeks. In certain areas of Greece, Leto was believed to be the wife of Zeus, and honored as one of the twelve Olympians in place of Hera as a mother goddess. Leto was known for punishing her enemies. When a boastful mortal bragged that she had more children than Leto, the goddess called to her children Artemis and Apollo and had all of that mortal's children killed. Leto was the daughter of the Titans and was known as Latona by the Romans.

Melisseus: The god of honey, Melisseus was a protector of Zeus as an infant.

Metis: Metis is a goddess of wisdom and cunning and is well known for being the (almost?) mother of Athena. One of the Titans and a daughter of Oceanus and Tethys, Metis was much desired by Zeus. After resisting his advances by constantly changing her shape, Metis was eventually impregnated by Zeus. After the child was conceived, Zeus was told by Gaia that any child he produced with Metis would become more powerful than he. Zeus's solution to the problem was to swallow Metis. The result is Zeus birthing the goddess Athena.

Oceanus: One of the original twelve Titans, Oceanus is the god of rivers. Oceanus was also the name of the river believed to run around the entire earth (back when people thought the earth was flat). As knowledge progressed, the river Oceanus began to be thought of as an ocean. Oceanus's male children with his sister Tethys became all the rivers of the world, with the exception of the river Styx, which was female.

Perses: Father of Hekate, Perses is the god of summer heat and droughts.

Phoebe: The Titan Phoebe is a goddess of prophecy and was an early master of Delphi before gifting the temple complex to her grandson Apollo. Phoebe was the wife of Coeus and the mother of Leto and Asteria.

Prometheus: Though Hermes is often thought of as the most prominent trickster god in the Greek pantheon, that honor really belongs to Prometheus, the god of forethought. Best known for stealing fire from the gods and giving it to humans, Prometheus also tricked Zeus into choosing fat and bones for burnt offerings, allowing humans to keep the meat for themselves.

Prometheus was eventually punished by Zeus for his transgressions by being chained to a rock and having his liver eaten daily by an eagle (it magickally grew back each night). Prometheus was eventually freed from his torture by Heracles, with the permission of Zeus. Known for his wisdom, Prometheus later advised Zeus and is sometimes credited with giving humans the gifts of agriculture and writing.

Prometheus is one of humanity's best friends among the gods, and in some myths he is credited with creating (male) humans. He also warned Pandora, the first woman, against accepting presents from Zeus, though it did little good. Invoke Prometheus for magick to better humanity, for social causes, and for inspiration.

Rhea: The mother of Zeus and the wife of Cronus, Rhea is a fertility goddess who also has associations with death. Rhea was especially important on the island of Crete and was known as Ops.

Styx: The goddess of the river that marks the boundary between the world of the living and the realm of the dead, Styx is also the mother of Victory (Nike), Force (Bia), Rivalry (Zelos), and Strength (Cratus). As a show of his favor to her, Zeus proclaimed that the river Styx was where the gods would make their oaths to one another, making Styx a goddess of truth and promises.

Tethys: One of the original Titans, Tethys is said to have over three thousand children with her husband Oceanus! Those children became the gods of the world's rivers and various water nymphs. Tethys was a goddess of potable water and protected the goddess Hera when her brother Cronus fought his war with Zeus.

Thea (or Theia): With her husband, Hyperion, Thea is the mother of Selene, Helios, and Eos. Thea is the goddess of the blue sky and the mesmerizing properties of silver and gold. Her name derives from the Greek words for sight and prophecy.

Themis: Themis is the Titan goddess of divine law and order, but she is thought to be an old earth goddess.[529] She was the second prophet of Delphi, after Gaia. She eventually became Zeus's second wife, which benefited him because marrying her allowed him to rule over all the laws. They had several children, including Justice, Peace, and the Seasons. This pairing indicates that there is a divine order to life and its cycles, and that it leans toward positive growth.

OTHER GREEK (AND A FEW ROMAN) DEITIES OFTEN HONORED BY WITCHES

Whenever two gods procreated, the offspring was another deity. Rarely were these deities as important as the Olympians or even many of the Titans, but they still served important functions, and many had impressive, dedicated religious cults in the Greek and Roman worlds. Deities also procreated with nymphs and other beings just below full godhood, resulting in more divine children. On a few special occasions, the offspring of gods and mortals became deities in their own right, most notably Dionysus and Heracles.

What follows in this section are the "lesser" gods—beings who rarely show up in mythology but are still sometimes called to in ritual and actively participate in this world. These entries are brief, and for anyone seeking more information about the deities below, we urge you to peruse the bibliography at the end of this book.

Aristaeus: The son of Apollo and a shepherdess, Aristaeus is a god of agricultural skills. If you lack a green thumb, Aristaeus is a useful god to have as an ally. Green Witches especially can find inspiration from his insights.

Asclepius: Son of Apollo, originally human and later deified, Asclepius is the god of medicine and healing. The serpent-entwined staff (or rod) of Asclepius is used by a variety of medical groups as an identifying symbol. Sanctuaries of Asclepius, used for healing the sick, were the original versions of the modern-day hospital. This god is commonly invoked in spells and magick for healing sicknesses.

---

529. Hesiod, *Theogony; Works and Days; Shield*, translated by Athanassakis, 40.

Astraea: Astraea is the goddess of justice and, according to the Romans, the constellation Virgo. Her hope for humanity and a more just world was one of her notable characteristics. Magickally, Astraea can be helpful when the scales of justice need to be balanced or you need more hope in your life.

Calypso: A minor vegetation goddess who appears in the *Iliad*, Calypso is best known for being a sorceress who held the hero Odysseus captive. Her name appears to mean "to conceal," and her home was said to be surrounded by animals and plants that were symbolic of death. Call upon Calypso in magick to keep a secret safe, keep something sacred, or protect someone.

Charon: Charon is the ferryman who brings the souls of the dead across the river Styx. The Greeks were buried with a coin in their mouths so they could pay the toll that Charon charged to cross the river. Charon can be called at Samhain by those looking to reunite with their beloved dead, as he facilitates communication and spirit journeys.

Dione: According to Homer, Dione was the mother of Aphrodite and the lover of Zeus. In the *Iliad*, she healed Aphrodite's wounds and consoled her. Given Dione's association with Zeus, it's likely that she was once a popular goddess with a thriving following, but we know very little about her today. She can be invoked in magick for maternal and ancestral healing, especially among those who work with Aphrodite.

Eosphorus (or Phosphorus): The god of the morning star (the planet Venus), Eosphorus was known as Lucifer by the Romans. Christians later confused a passage about the "day star" in the Jewish book of Isaiah and turned Lucifer into another name for their Devil. Eosphorus was sometimes called Phosphorus. He is associated with liminal magick and bringing more power and art to one's magickal practices.

Eros: Eros is the god of physical desire, but today he is just as likely to be associated with romantic love. The god Phanes was sometimes also called Eros, but the best-known Eros is the one we know today, with the bow and arrow, who was the son of Aphrodite and Ares. The Greek Eros was generally depicted as a handsome and blonde-haired youth with wings, which is vastly different from the baby-Cupid image that became popular among the Romans and later during the Renaissance. In some myths, Eros is a primordial deity who brings desire to the universe. He is often used in magick for lust and love.

Fascinus: Like the Greek god Priapus, Fascinus is a Roman god of magickal, masculine power who was often portrayed as a divine phallus. His charms protected people against the evil eye in ancient Rome. The English word *fascinate* is derived from the Latin *fascinus*, meaning "a charm, a spell, enchantment, Witchcraft."[530]

The Fates: Known as the Moirae in Greece, the goddesses known as the Fates control one's destiny. Their power was often greater than that of the gods. The Fates personified human life in the form of a thread, with each of the three Fates in charge of a certain aspect of it. Clotho spun the thread of life, Lachesis measured that thread, and Atropos cut it. Use the magick of the Fates in cord magick, such as cord-cutting, or to try to enhance your fate.

Flora: The Roman goddess of flowers, Flora is somewhat like Persephone but without the underworld aspects. She is sometimes called upon to bless Beltane celebrations.

The Furies: The Furies, also called the Erinyes or the Arae, are female underworld goddesses who carry out curses. They deliver justice and retribution.

Harmonia: The goddess of harmony and the daughter of Ares and Aphrodite, Harmonia was know as Concordia in Rome. She can be invoked in ritual to promote cooperation and agreement. Harmonia married the mortal Cadmus, who founded the city-state of Thebes.

Hebe: The ancient Greeks prized youth, and Hebe is the goddess who rules over that phase of life. She is the daughter of Zeus and Hera. When Hercules was welcomed to Olympus, he took Hebe as a wife. Trying to appear younger than you really are? Then Hebe is the goddess to call upon. She can also be called upon to renew one's sense of innocence and wonder and to preserve relationships.

Hermaphroditus: Depicted as a male god with female genitals, Hermaphroditus is the deity of androgyny and is also linked to marriage. Hermaphroditus was the child of Aphrodite and Hermes. Depending on the circumstances, Hermaphroditus may be a good deity to invoke for fairness, gender equality, or gender issues.

Hypnos (or Hypnus): Hypnos is the personification and the god of sleep. Call upon him in magick for better sleep.

Iacchus: Originally an agricultural deity, Iacchus was eventually conflated with Dionysus, who was sometimes even addressed as Iacchus. He is sometimes called upon in fertility/abundance magick.

---

530. Online Etymology Dictionary, "fascinate," accessed June 2022, https://www.etymonline.com/word/fascinate#etymonline_v_1143.

Medea: This goddess of sorcery was renowned for her Witchcraft, specifically transformation and making potions, some of them poisonous. Herbalists and followers of the poison path would benefit greatly from her influence. Medea is a priestess of Hekate, the goddess of Witchcraft, and a niece of Circe, another powerful Witch. Medea has an incredibly powerful influence on magick for power, protection, love, and revenge/curses. She is also used magickally for healing and rebirth.

Morpheus: Morpheus is the god of dreams, and more specifically to the Greeks, the god of dreams that have humans in them. Today, Morpheus is best known for appearing in Neil Gaiman's Sandman comic book series, which contains a variety of references to the Greek gods, modern magick, Witchcraft, and Paganism. Invoke Morpheus for lucid dreams if you are having nightmares or experience trouble getting to sleep.

The Muses: Sometimes also called the Pierides, due to being born in Pieria at the base of Mount Olympus, the Muses govern various spheres or art and learning. In most mythologies, they are the daughters of Zeus and the Titan Mnemosyne, the goddess of memory. Early depictions of the Muses show them as young women, each playing a musical instrument. Over time, each muse would come to rule over a specific function and carry an item signifying that function. The number of Muses varied in early Greece until Hesiod established their number as nine. They are:

- *Calliope:* Sometimes portrayed as the leader of the Muses, Calliope is the muse of epic poetry. Her name means "beautiful-voiced."[531] She is also the mother of the demigods Linus (known for his elegant speech) and Orpheus (the legendary poet and musician), with either Apollo or King Oeagrus of Thrace. Calliope is often depicted holding a writing tablet. She can assist with magick for all kinds of writing.

- *Clio:* Generally depicted holding a scroll, Clio is the muse of history. Her name means either "proclaimer" or "praiser," as the Greeks believed Clio was especially favorable to those historians who chronicled the deeds of great people or cities. She is an excellent aid in learning magickal history and traditions.

- *Erato:* Erato is the muse of lyric poetry, and more specifically, lyric poetry focused on love and emotion. She is usually represented by the lyre.

---

531. Giesecke, *Classical Mythology A to Z*, 30.

- *Euterpe:* As the muse of the flute, Euterpe is most often depicted, not surprisingly, holding a flute. Her name means "one who brings delight or pleasure." Call upon Euterpe for magick with musical instruments.

- *Melpomene:* Melpomene's name means "singer," but she is actually the muse of tragic poetry. She often holds a tragic mask in her hand when depicted in art. Melpomene can inspire magickal songwriting.

- *Polyhymnia:* With the words *poly* (many) and *hymn* in her name, Polyhymnia is obviously the muse of hymns and sacred poetry. If you chant or sing in ritual, you are utilizing the power of Polyhymnia. Perhaps the most mysterious of the Muses, Polyhymnia is often shown wearing a veil. Call upon her in a circle to invoke more power in group chants and singing.

- *Terpsichore:* Terpsichore is the muse who delights in dance. More than just the muse of dancing, she is also the muse of choral groups. She is usually depicted dancing, and sometimes holding a lyre or flute while doing so. Merely saying her name invokes a playful rhythm. Terpsichore can aid in dance magick, especially in ritual.

- *Thalia:* Thalia's name means "cheerful" or "blooming." As the muse of comedy, she often holds a comic mask. Invoke Thalia when writing plays or dramatic acts for inspiration.

- *Urania:* The "heavenly" Urania is the well-named muse of astrology, astronomy, and other sciences. When casting an astrological chart, it's advisable to call upon Urania for assistance.

The Muses can be worked with as a whole or individually when practicing their various disciplines. Because modern society is radically different from that of ancient Greece, we like to think that the domains of the Muses have expanded over the centuries to encompass other sorts of artistic expressions not practiced 2,500 years ago.

Nemesis: Nemesis is a goddess who lives up to her name: she is the goddess of retribution. If you throw around a lot of curses, you should get to know her. Nemesis was called upon in a protection spell in the Greek Magical Papyri.

Nike: Nike is the goddess of victory and often appears with wings. She is frequently pictured with Zeus and his daughter Athena. According to Hesiod, Nike and her siblings, Zelus (Emulation), Bia (Force), and Cratos (Strength), resided with Zeus on Mount Olympus.

Nymphs: Nymph is a broad name for female spirits or minor goddesses of wild places. These include *dryads*, spirits of oak trees; *naiads*, nymphs of fresh water; *oceanids* and *nereids*, spirits of the seas; *hesperides*, spirits of evening, sunset, and dusk; *lampades*, spirits of the underworld; *napaeae* and *alseids*, nymphs of groves; *hyades*, spirits who bring rain; and several others. Many scholars believe the country people of ancient Greece revered them religiously.[532] Nymphs have powers of healing and seduction as well as knowledge of nature.

Orpheus: A legendary Greek hero with magickal musical abilities, Orpheus's music was so lovely that he healed sadness in people. He was heavily associated with magick in ancient Greece, and modern musicians can work with him for musical talent and to uplift others.

Pomona: The Roman goddess of orchards and flowering trees, Pomona is now primarily associated with apples. A late fall festival in honor of Pomona and apples is sometimes (erroneously) listed as an influence on the Irish-Celtic holiday of Samhain.

Priapus: Most often thought of as the son of Aphrodite and Dionysus, Priapus was imported into Greece from Phrygia (located in modern-day Turkey). He is both a fertility god and a deity associated with luck and good fortune. Priapus is best known for being depicted with a comically large and erect phallus. He is used to avert the evil eye.

Satyrs: These creatures are the wild, raunchy companions of Dionysus who delight in dancing, drinking, sex, and making music. They lived in remote areas such as forests, mountains, and the countryside. Satyrs were sometimes portrayed with snubbed noses, horns, and the legs of a horse or goat. These animalistic body parts allude to their tendency to attempt to have sex with everything, whether it was desired or not. But they weren't solely lust-driven—the satyr Silenus helped raise Dionysus. A satyr is also known as a silenus or a faun. An experienced practitioner may call upon satyrs in celebrations with Dionysus to ensure a wildly good time, but they should use caution with their words to create a culture of consent.

Thanatos: Thanatos is the Greek god of nonviolent death, but he is perhaps best known today for being the inspiration for the Marvel Comics villain Thanos. Thanatos can be invoked in magick for a peaceful transition or for making contact with the underworld.

Triton: The son of Poseidon, Triton had a human torso and a fish tail instead of legs. Mythology is full of tritons, and *triton* might also refer to a race of divine mermen instead of one specific deity. Various tritons often had a horrifying appearance, and they

---

532. Hesiod, *Theogony; Works and Days; Shield*, translated by Athanassakis, 43.

were thought to have scales instead of skin and gills. Triton the god was thought to live at the bottom of the ocean, making him the deity of the ocean's deepest depths. He is sometimes associated with psychological magick and probing the depths of emotions.

Tyche: The goddess of chance, Tyche was also known as Fortuna among the Romans. Though we tend to think of Tyche as a beneficial goddess, she was just as likely to share bad luck as she was good luck. (In other words, do your best to stay on her good side!) Tyche's parentage varies depending on the writer. She is either one of the daughters of Zeus or the daughter of the Titans Oceanus and Tethys.

A poem dedicated to Tyche would become a part of the drawing down the moon ceremony common in Wiccan-Witchcraft. Aleister Crowley's 1907 poem *La Fortuna* is an ode to good fortune and features a lovely invocation to the goddess:

> *Hail, Tyche! From the Amalthean horn*
> *Pour forth the store of love! I lowly bend*
> *Before thee; I invoke thee at the end ...*
> *... bring me luck who am lonely and forlorn.* [533]

Crowley's poem has appeared, basically word for word, in numerous Witchcraft books since the 1970s. Sadly for Tyche, the most common change to the poem is the substitution of Aradia for the goddess of luck.

The (Four) Winds: Instead of calling elementals, quarters, or watchtowers, some Witches call to the four winds to bring in the energies of air, fire, water, and earth. We suggest doing so only if you have solid relationships with the deities who rule the winds. The four winds were all the children of Eos and Astraeus. The winds were often depicted with wings and sometimes as horses, which they also fathered.

- *Eurus:* The god of the east wind, morning breezes, and autumn, Eurus's breezes were thought to be beneficial to both grapevines and beehives.
- *Notus:* The god of the south wind and summer, Notus was also believed to bring in autumn and winter storms.
- *Zephyr:* As the god of the west wind, Zephyr was the bringer of spring and warm, pleasant breezes and was associated with vegetation.
- *Boreas:* The god of the north wind, Boreas was associated with both cold and death and was the bringer of winter.

---

533. Mankey, *Transformative Witchcraft*, 271.

Conclusion

The gods of the ancient Greeks never went away. They still surround us in the modern world. At Samhain, we call Hekate and Persephone to reunite us with our beloved dead. We feel Aphrodite's touch when our hearts beat a little faster while thinking about a deepening love. As Witches, we toil over crafting the perfect spell, reveling in the handiwork of Athena when our efforts are successful. And when we cast a magick circle with an athame or sword, we feel the result of Hephaestus's genius in our hands.

On rainy nights, the storms of Zeus rage over our heads, and on ocean shores, we feel the power of Poseidon in the crashing waves. With every sip of wine, we feel the intoxicating essence of Dionysus, and with every mistake, we are made aware of Eris's presence. Demeter weaves her spell every autumn, sharing with us the bounty of the harvest and the power of Gaia, Mother Earth. The music of Apollo enchants us, and the forests of Artemis and Pan call to us. As the wheel of our lives turns, Hera assists us when we bring new life into this world or enter a new partnership. And when our last breath has passed our lips, Hermes will greet us and lead us to Hades, the land of the dead.

No matter how one interprets the gods, they are ever-present. For some, they are anthropomorphic forces: poetic references to the power found in the natural world. For others, they are frequent visitors to magickal spaces and our partners in the spells we weave as Witches. Some see them as parts of a greater whole, while others find their individuality to be a defining characteristic. The gods of Mount Olympus have been with us in some form or another for over four thousand years now, and they are just as vital today as they were in the days of ancient Athens or the Roman Empire.

Mythology books make it appear that the story of the gods has ended, but nothing could be further from the truth. The gods have always changed and adapted, and they will continue to do so. As long as they inspire art, poetry, and devotion, their stories will be ongoing. The gods are not beings preserved in amber—they are continually evolving forces, and they are capable of change. It's important to understand the past, but it's equally important to embrace the present moment and the future.

Every book that an author undertakes is a journey. There are revelations and discoveries, and sometimes you uncover the unexpected. The knowledge gleaned while writing this book has drawn both of us (Astrea and Jason) closer to the gods we love so much. But our most cherished moments with the gods of ancient Greece have never been found in the pages of a book we read. They were uncovered as we worked and interacted with those forces so much greater than ourselves.

If you feel the call of the gods, we hope this book will assist you on your journey, but perhaps even more importantly, we hope it leads to doing magick or devotion with them. While many of the gods profiled in this book live on mighty Olympus, the gods also live on our altars and in our ritual spaces. Invoke them when you celebrate a sabbat. Call upon them when you craft a spell. And perhaps most importantly, talk to them when the circumstances call for such things.

Sometimes the gods don't choose us—we choose them, and that's okay. If you want to know a god, leave them offerings and libations, write poetry for them, and offer them praise. The gods love to be flattered, and when their names are spoken, they listen. Gifts to the gods do not have to be material things; often, a sincere heart is more than enough.

Our goal for this book was to present the gods of ancient Greece honestly and thoughtfully—to share their pasts and their origins, and also to relate how they make their influence felt in today's Witchcraft. The gods of the ancient Greeks have been cultivating new relationships with humanity for a very long time, and that will likely continue long after we're gone. As long as new bonds between humanity and deities continue to be forged, there will be new paths for all of us to walk.

Hail the Gods!
Jason Mankey
August 2021

Appendix I:
Calendar of Ancient Holidays
& Celebrations

There were most likely hundreds, if not thousands, of holidays and feast days dedicated to the gods of the Greeks (and Romans). Among the ancient Greeks, most religious holidays were limited to specific city-states, though events such as the Olympics were celebrated universally. The celebrations we know the most about from ancient Greece were those that occurred in Athens, which is why this list is heavy on holidays from that particular city-state.

We've also included a separate list documenting several Roman holidays that honor the deities featured in this book. We both believe the more holidays one can celebrate the better! Because of the Roman influence on much of the world, many of the Roman holidays on our list influenced a variety of Christian and secular holidays, most notably Christmas.

This is not an exhaustive list; it's meant as a starting point for anyone interested in celebrating specific deities and seasonal happenings involving the gods of Olympus. The dates here represent our best guess since we don't know exactly when many of these feast days were celebrated, especially the ones from ancient Greece.

Making things even more difficult as to the matter of Greek celebrations is the fact that the ancient Greeks used a lunar calendar that varied by geographic region. All the ancient Greeks used a lunar calendar, but that lunar calendar was different across Greece. Most Greek lunar calendars were in agreement that a new month started at the new moon.

The best known of the ancient Greek calendars is the Attic calendar, which was used in Athens. Despite having a lot of information about the Attic calendar, we still don't know everything about it, and because it was a lunar calendar, a thirteenth month was added to it periodically for balance (similar to, but more drastic than, our modern calendars having a leap year). To make things even more confusing, the Attic calendar was just one of several calendars that were used simultaneously in classical Athens.

Attic Calendar
Month in the Attic Calendar / Modern Equivalent

Gamelion: mid-January / mid-February

Anthesterion: mid-February / mid-March

Elaphebolion: mid-March / mid-April

Mounikhion: mid-April / mid-May

Thargelion: mid-May / mid-June

Skirophorion: mid-June / mid-July

Hekatombaion: mid-July / mid-August

Metageitnion: mid-August / mid-September

Boedromion: mid-September / mid-October

Pyanepsion: mid-October / mid-November

Maimakterion: mid-November / mid-December

Poseideon: mid-December / mid-January

* When a thirteenth month was required, it was inserted after Poseideon.

Because of the difficulty that comes with using the Attic calendar, and because this is not a book for Hellenic Reconstructionists, we've chosen to use the Gregorian (modern) calendar for the dates of the following Greek festivals and celebrations. If you are interested in using the actual ancient Greek dates, there are easily found resources for this online (though they don't all agree!). The Athenians celebrated the start of a new year near the Summer Solstice, but we've chosen to begin our list in January, with the exception of the Noumenia, which was held monthly on the day after the new moon.

Many Witches celebrate the Greek gods along with the standard Witch's Wheel of the Year, which is more than acceptable. (You don't have to celebrate any of the traditional Greek holidays if they don't interest you.) Many Greek deities fit easily upon the modern Wheel of the Year.

Samhain can be used to honor harvest deities or liminal ones such as Hekate, Hermes, and Persephone. Sun gods such as Helios were frequently invoked on the Winter Solstice, which is also a great time to celebrate deities associated with joy and/or abundance. Imbolc is a time for deities associated with cleansing or the home, such as Hestia. The Spring Equinox can be used to honor Eos and her descendent Eostre. Beltane and Midsummer are the perfect times to honor deities such as Aphrodite and Pan. The harvest celebrations of Lammas and the Autumn Equinox were tailor-made for deities such as Demeter and Dionysus. However you celebrate (or don't), be sure to pour the gods a hearty libation and be sincere in your devotions.

Major Ancient Greek Festivals/Holidays

Day after the New Moon: Noumenia—This is a Greek household celebration of the gods of the home. The Noumenia honored Hestia as well as other home gods.

End of January: Lenaia—This festival was about enjoying wine and watching comic plays. Dionysus was the presiding deity.

February 19–21: Anthesteria—This three-day celebration was dedicated to Dionysus and his wife, Ariadne. The holiday celebrated both wine and departed ancestors.

Mid-late February: Lesser Mysteries—The Lesser Mysteries, also known as Persephone's mysteries, were held in early spring on the banks of an Athenian river at a temple to Demeter. They were instructive and preparative for the Greater Mysteries, but they were not mandatory. There was purification, fasting, bathing, singing, and dancing, along with stories and plays about Persephone. It was also a time to venerate the goddess and gift her with sacrifices. The Lesser Mysteries may have also served as an opportunity to cleanse anyone who had previously spilled the blood of another person. (Murderers, even if their actions were justified, were not allowed to take part in the Greater Mysteries without purification.) Those who needed purification were presented with the "fleece of Zeus" as a form of cleansing.[534]

Mid-March: Great Dionysia (or City Dionysia)—This Athenian festival was held in honor of Dionysus in the second week of March. In addition to drinks and sacrifices to Dionysus, the Great Dionysia was also a time for watching tragic plays and other forms of entertainment.

May 24–25: Thargelia—This Athenian festival in honor of Artemis and Apollo was likely celebrated to ensure a growing season free of drought and disease.

---

534. Mylonas, *Eleusis and the Eleusinian Mysteries*, 232, 236.

June 20: Adonia—Adonia may have been celebrated near the Summer Solstice, though others believe it may have been in the spring. It commemorated the death of Aphrodite's lover Adonis. The holiday was only celebrated by women, who danced, cried, and sang together. The festival required the planting of a "garden of Adonis," usually in a broken pot. In the hot Greek sun, the seeds would sprout but then quickly die. The dead plants were then buried or taken to the sea in a mock funeral procession in honor of Adonis. The Adonia was a time to expel grief in a socially acceptable manner.

June 28: Panathenaea—The premier holiday of ancient Athens, the Panathenaea was celebrated in honor of Athena. There are conflicting dates for just when the festival was held, with some believing it was held in June on Athena's birthday and others believing it was in August. The event was also similar to the Olympic Games in that in its greater form, it was held only once every four years. A smaller celebration took place the other three years.

Late July/early August: Aphrodisia—This celebration in honor of Aphrodite typically took place over several days.

Mid-September/October: Eleusinian mysteries—Dedicated to the goddesses Demeter and Persephone (Kore), the Eleusinian mysteries were the most famous secret, initiatory tradition in the ancient world. We know very little about the mysteries, but they most likely revealed something having to do with the afterlife. The mysteries were also related to the harvest and the symbolic descent of Persephone into the underworld (or possibly her return). If you choose to honor the mysteries in some way, build them around where you live. If you live in the Southern Hemisphere, celebrate the return of Persephone. If you live in the Northern Hemisphere, celebrate her descent into the underworld.

Late October: Thesmophoria—An agricultural celebration limited to women only and celebrated in honor of Persephone and Demeter, the Thesmophoria commemorated either the late harvest or the sowing of seed in places like Athens. (In Athens, seeds were planted in the winter. The summer was too hot to be a part of the growing season.) The Thesmophoria occurred near the end of October and lasted for three days in Athens. In other areas, the festival was held earlier in the autumn.

Late October/early November: Chalceia (or Khalkeia)—This Greek holiday celebrated the arts and crafts, especially metalworking. It was held in honor of Athena and Hephaestus.

December: Rural Dionysia—This festival celebrating the birth of Dionysus featured a procession of comically large phalluses though the streets, drinking, dancing, and merriment.

Notable Roman Holidays/Festivals

Start of every month: Kalends—The Romans celebrated the start of every month as one of the kalends. The January kalends in particular was a huge influence on both Christmas and modern celebrations of Yule. More information about each of these celebrations can be found online.

February 13: Parentalia—A weeklong celebration beginning on February 13, the Parentalia was a time to celebrate one's ancestors.

February 15: Lupercalia—Lupercalia was dedicated to fertility and purification. Many modern Pagans erroneously believe that this festival was a precursor to the more modern celebration of Valentine's Day.

March 17: Liberalia—A Roman festival held on March 17, Liberalia celebrated the transition of boys into young men. It was also sacred to the god Liber Pater, who was later equated with the Roman Bacchus and his wife, Libera.

Early April: Megalesia—This festival in honor of the Roman mother goddess Magna Mater was held for a week.

June 7–15: Vestalia—This was a Roman festival in honor of Vesta, the goddess of the hearth.

June 24: Festival of Fors Fortuna—This Roman festival was celebrated on June 24 in honor of Fortuna, the goddess of good luck. Her celebration may have also doubled as a Summer Solstice celebration.

July 6–13: Ludi Apollinares—A weeklong Roman celebration from July 6–13, the Ludi Apollinares games were a time for plays, athletic contests, and dances.

July 23: Neptunalia—Not surprisingly, the Neptunalia was a Roman celebration in honor of Neptune.

August 19: Vinalia Rustica—This Roman celebration held in honor of Jupiter and Venus commemorated the start of the grape harvest. A lesser celebration, the **Vinalia Urbana**, was celebrated on April 23, most likely to celebrate the previous year's wine vintages.

August 23: Vulcanalia—This was a holiday in honor of the Roman Vulcan. Instead of being a joyous summer celebration, the Vulcanalia was a time to make sacrifices to Vulcan to protect one's home and city from the threat of fire.

September 13: Epulum Jovis—This celebration was a ritual feast in honor of the Roman god Jupiter.

October 13: Fontinalia—This was a Roman celebration of fountains and springs and the deities who reside in those spaces. It began specifically for the Roman god Fons, the god of wells.

November 1: Festival of Pomona—The Roman Festival of Pomona was a harvest festival held in honor of the orchard goddess Pomona. Celebrations of Pomona are often linked to the Irish-Celtic Samhain.

December 17–23: Saturnalia—Originally a one-day celebration, then extended to three days and finally a full week of feasting and drinking, Saturnalia might be the most influential of all the Roman holidays. For Saturnalia, Romans decorated their homes with holly and evergreen boughs and exchanged presents. It was also a holiday about inverting the social order. Saturnalia had a major influence on the Christian Christmas. If you feast, indulge in too much drink, sing carols, and find yourself being extremely generous, you are celebrating the holidays like a Roman.

Appendix II:
Classical Spell Structure
by Astrea Taylor

The Greek Magical Papyri have a relatively simple method for spells and magick with the gods. The general structure for most of them is to invoke the deity; state their attributes, epithets, or accomplishments that relate to the request (usually three); recite your detailed request; and finally recite a simplified version of the request with a movement and repeat it several times. As always, we recommend that you learn about a deity before calling upon them.

Some spells were repeated for up to seven days for maximum effect. In one survey of ancient spells, a little less than half of them (42 percent) used an offering. This could mean that offerings were not always necessary or that simply reciting their attributes and qualities was enough for them to act on your behalf.[535]

Try it for yourself. Fill in the blanks with your notes and your magickal intentions or goals.

O _____ *(deity invocation)*,
_____ *(attributes of deity)*.
_____ , _____ , _____ *(3 epithets or accomplishments that relate to the request)*.
_____ *(detailed request)*!
_____ *(simplified request with a movement—repeat several times)*!

---

535. Björkland, "Invocation and Offerings as Structural Elements in the Love Spells in *Papyri Graecae Magicae*."

Here's an example:

O Dionysus,
Liberator of mortals and bringer of ecstasy.
O raucous god of dance and intoxication, blooming one, giver of wings.
I ask you to grant me and my friends a blissful, festive, and safe night as we celebrate our
successes. Let us experience fun and euphoria!
Dionysus, let there be joy!

As the last line is said, raise your hands up toward the sky, then allow them to drop slowly to your sides. Repeat the last line of the spell with the motion several times. It is done!

APPENDIX III:
GREEK-STYLE RITUAL STRUCTURE
by Jason Mankey

Working with the Greek gods doesn't require a Greek-style ritual. The deities of Olympus have been invoked in a variety of contexts for over 2,500 years, and we believe the gods are just as comfortable in a Wiccan-style circle as they are in a traditional one. However, it can be fun and certainly different to work with the gods in a very traditional sort of format.

Ancient Greek rituals are simpler than most Wiccan-style rituals. They mostly consist of a few elements: purification(s), prayers, and offerings. It's also commonplace to recite established Greek poetry, such as the Homeric hymns. However, as a word of warning, the Homeric hymns don't always sound inspiring to modern ears. If you don't like them, don't use them. It's completely fine to use something else, such as modern poetry or prose.

The materials necessary for a Greek-style ritual are minimal. You'll need a bowl of water, salt (or a toothpick and a lighter), barley (or another grain), and offerings for the gods. Traditional offerings include liquids such as wine, olive oil, clean water, incense, and honey. Physical offerings include cereal grains, meat (particularly lamb), figs, and apples. Other fruits and vegetables native to where you live can be used here too. Offerings should either be placed in a libation or tossed into a fire (if available) after being given to the gods. When the ritual is over, the contents of the libation bowl should be deposited outside in a place that is magickal to you or one that won't be disturbed.

While it's true that animal sacrifice was practiced by the ancient Greeks, it was not routine, and it usually resulted in the eating of the cooked meat. If you're interested in such things, there are resources online outlining the process.

Outlines of Greek-style rituals vary from group to group and participant to participant. This ritual outline was inspired by Walter Burkert's in his book *Greek Religion*. Most of the activities and rituals in this book can be inserted into the middle of this outline.

GREEK-STYLE RITUALS

Procession

Hellenic ritual traditionally began with a procession toward the temple of the deity being honored. Most of us won't process to a temple, but it can still be undertaken. You can have a procession by walking into your backyard or living room or taking a walk in your neighborhood before your ritual. While walking, think about the purpose of your rite and the deity you are hoping to commune with.

Traditionally, those involved in a procession dressed up for the event, usually with flowers in their hair and garlands around their necks. Often, rituals for the ouranian (heavenly) gods started at sunrise, and those for chthonic (earthly or underworld) gods began at sundown.[536] Singing or chanting can be added to the procession. It was customary for everyone to carry the implements of the ritual during the procession, but this is not necessary.

Cleansing

Cleansing is not optional in Hellenic ritual. While the cleansing might be strictly symbolic, it's still necessary. For cleansing, you'll need a large bowl of clean water made holy. The Greeks called this lustral water. The water used to create lustral water traditionally came from the ocean or a spring, but tap water or bottled spring water is also acceptable.

There are two ways to make your water lustral. The easiest is to add a measure of salt to it while invoking the goddess Hestia. The second and more traditional way is to extinguish a flaming stick in the water while invoking Hestia. I've found that toothpicks work really well for this since they ignite easily and are readily available. Matches are not recommended because of the chemicals they contain.

After the water has been blessed, everyone should wash their hands with it. Clean towels should be placed nearby to dry the hands. After the water has been used for cleansing, it's no longer considered pure, and it should be disposed of after the ritual.

When all the participants have been purified, the space where the ritual is taking place should be purified. The ancient Greeks purified their spaces with barley, which was thrown on the altar and around the ritual space. If barley is not an option where you live, other grains would be appropriate, as would salt, though these are not traditional flourishes.

---

536. Burkert, *Greek Religion*, 200.

An Offering to Hestia

In Hellenic ritual, Hestia was always first and last. Before inviting any other deity to your rite, it is customary to give an offering to Hestia. As with all the gods called to in a Hellenic ritual, the offering should be placed in a libation bowl or thrown into a fire after the call to deity. You can say whatever you wish to Hestia, but the Homeric hymn to her is appropriate:

> *Hestia, in the high dwellings of all, both deathless gods and men who walk on earth, you have gained an everlasting abode and highest honour: glorious is your portion and your right. For without you mortals hold no banquet,—where one does not duly pour sweet wine in offering to Hestia both first and last.*[537]

Welcome the Gods

The deities of Olympus love to be flattered! The more flowery words you can say to them, the better. It's traditional to begin with a Homeric hymn, but it's not absolutely necessary. As an alternative to the Homeric hymns, you could read an Orphic hymn or a more modern piece of poetry or write your own poem or prose.

Give Offerings

After calling upon a particular deity, give them an offering. The words you say are not particularly important. You simply want to let the deity know you're giving them something of value.

> *O great (deity), to you we give this offering. Taste of our fruit and cakes and accept our libation if it pleases thee. We offer you the sacred wine (or other item) as a measure of our adoration. Hear our prayers and be with us in our rite, O mighty one!*

Place the food offering in their libation bowl, followed by the liquid offering.

Prayers to the Gods

This step is not necessary, but before beginning a rite or activity that involves asking a deity for assistance, I like to offer a prayer to them as a way of personalizing the experience a bit more. Prayers should contain flattery, but they should also represent what is truly in your heart. If you are asking for assistance from a god with a particular issue, this is a time to share that type of personal information. Prayers to the gods of Olympus are done with

---

537. Evelyn-White, *Hesiod, the Homeric Hymns, and Homerica*, 448–49.

arms and hands outstretched toward the sky with the palms facing up. If an image of the gods (such as a statue) is present to venerate, hold the arms straight out from the body with the palms of the hands facing the statue.

Activity or Ritual

After the gods have been called, given proper offerings, and spoken to, you are free to begin whatever specific rite or activity you have planned. If you have nothing specific planned, this is the point of the ritual where you could ask the gods for something specific, followed by providing them with another libation.

Gratitude and Final Offerings (Ending the Rite)

Thank the deities you have called for their presence in your rites and give them more offerings. This second set of offerings does not need to be elaborate—just barley and wine are appropriate. Say goodbye to the gods in the inverse order of how they were called, ending, of course, with Hestia, who is always first and last. There is no great moment signifying the end of the ritual. It is simply done when the gods have all been thanked and given a final set of offerings.

When you're done, pour the libations outside in a sacred spot or an out-of-the-way place. Pour out the ceremonial handwashing water in another out-of-the-way place or down the drain. Due to the unclean aspect of the used lustral water, you shouldn't dispose of it where you poured your libations, lest you contaminate the offerings.

Summary

The Greek-style ritual outline is simple: procession, cleansing, hymn/poem, offerings, prayer, rite or working, and thanks and final offerings. Hail the gods!

Acknowledgments

I (Astrea) thank everyone who helped me during this journey. The pandemic was not an easy time to write a book. At times I felt like Odysseus in Homer's *Odyssey*. There were many bright moments—Athena guided my journey with bright blessings and insights, and I had the good fortune of encountering Circe.[538] But like Odysseus, I also experienced hardships. At times I felt as if I were stuck on a remote island with no hope of leaving, or as if my metaphorical west wind had been emptied from my bag. However, I was able to prevail and bring this book home thanks to the following people.

Jason, I thank you for your perseverance, your friendship, your vast knowledge of Witchcraft, and your networking abilities to find the majority of the people who wrote the passages. It was both a pleasure and a privilege to write this book with you. This book has been a dream of ours to write for quite some time, and I'm happy we did it.

An enormous thanks to my husband, Tim. Our peaceful home and our mutually supportive relationship have fostered my creative spirit so much—five books' worth now! Your musical creativity inspires me to no end. Thank you for being so helpful. I don't know how you always find everything I misplace, but I hope you never lose that ability.

Scarlett, thanks for being my ride-or-die in so many ways and in multiple universes. You bring out the best in me, and you inspire me to continue living artfully. I also thank my network of creative/spiritual friends for all the support, including Heron, Phoenix, Laura, Tatiara, Elliot, and Willow. I also thank my friend Maevyn Stone and her mellifluous harp music that kept me writing and editing through the long hours Thanks to Llewellyn's team of friendly, smart, and savvy people, including Elysia, Andrea, and Kat. Lastly, I thank the gods and spirits who assisted in the writing of this book.

---

538. The book *Witches, Heretics & Warrior Women* by Phoenix LeFae facilitated this amazing experience.

Without all of you, this book might not exist. You not only helped me—you also helped everyone who reads this book and feels inspired to deepen their spiritual practice.

—Astrea Taylor

ⵀⵀⵀⵀⵀⵀⵀ

I (Jason) wish to thank Astrea for all the work and passion she put into this project. Astrea did much of the heavy lifting on this book, formatting my scribbles and laying out the wide variety of materials we assembled for what you now hold in your hands. Astrea, your brilliance, kindness, grace, enthusiasm, and diligence deserve to be shared with anyone who will listen. Astrea, you've become one of my closest and dearest friends in the wide world of Witchcraft, and my thank-yous will never be enough, but I'll say it one more time anyway: thank you for everything.

I have been exploring the Greek gods with my wife, Ari, for nearly a quarter of a century. Together we have poured libations to Aphrodite and Dionysus, felt the power of our returning ancestors with Persephone, and embraced our wild sides with Pan. Those experiences are among the most amazing of my entire life. Ari, thank you for being a part of this journey, my Priestess of Aphrodite.

Much thanks to the people at Llewellyn who do such an amazing job with all of these books, especially our editors Elysia Gallo and Andrea Neff. Elysia helped to shape this book and believed in it. Andrea is just sheer bloody brilliance, and she makes everything she touches better.

In the long, long ago of my high school experience, I crafted a very crude temple to the goddess Aphrodite in the hopes of attracting a girlfriend. That particular magickal experiment failed spectacularly, but my love of the gods has most certainly endured. It's incredible to me that all these years later I've coauthored a book on the gods! Life is a strange thing sometimes.

Special thanks to everyone who contributed a passage for this book. Both Astrea and I appreciate it more than we can put into words. Placing the gods of ancient Greece firmly in the Modern Witchcraft world was of great importance to us when it came to this project, and your contributions assured that we were able to do just that!

And to everyone who helps to keep the flame of the gods alive in the modern world, thank you! Whether you are a Witch, a Reconstructionist, or a Pagan, keeping the names of Hermes, Artemis, Athena, Helios, Selene, and all the rest on our tongues and in our hearts helps to power the gods we love so much.

Io Pan!
—Jason Mankey

Bibliography

There are nearly 500 citations in this book, which means this is a pretty long bibliography. It also means that if you want to know more about the Greek gods, there's plenty of material here you'll be interested in. I've written books with long bibliographies and lots of footnotes before, but this book definitely outdoes anything I've done previously. I usually dread writing passages with lots of footnotes, but I truly enjoyed the experience this time around, as every deep dive into a particular deity revealed fresh insights and understandings. This was just a terrific experience to be a part of.

All comments in the bibliography come from my keyboard, so if there's something snarky here, don't blame Astrea.

—Jason Mankey
November 2021

Adler, Margot. *Drawing Down the Moon: Witches, Druids, Goddess-Worshippers, and Other Pagans in America Today.* Boston, MA: Beacon Press, 1981.

Aeschines. *The Speeches of Aeschines.* Translated by Charles Darwin Addams. Cambridge, MA: Harvard University Press, 1919.

Agrippa, Heinrich Cornelius. *Three Books of Occult Philosophy.* Edited by Donald Tyson. 1993. Reprint, Woodbury, MN: Llewellyn, 2014.

Allan, Arlene. *Hermes.* New York: Routledge, 2018. Released in paperback in 2020 just in time! Hermes, and this book, are both a delight.

Allan, Tony. *Titans and Olympians: Greek & Roman Myth*. London: Duncan Baird Publishers, 1997. This is one of those pretty hardcover books that used to grace the racks of bargain books at Barnes & Noble back in the early 2000s. I miss those days.

Armstrong, Steven. "The Veil of Isis: The Evolution of an Archetype Hidden in Plain Sight." *Rosicrucian Digest* 1 (2010): 51–57.

Atlas Obscura. "Necromanteion of Ephyra." March 27, 2010. https://www.atlasobscura.com/places/necromanteion-of-ephyra.

Bekoff, Marc. "Your Brain and Health in Nature: Rewilding Is Good for Us." *Psychology Today*. July 23, 2015. https://www.psychologytoday.com/us/blog/animal-emotions/201507/your-brain-and-health-in-nature-rewilding-is-good-us.

Bel, Bekah Evie. "Nyx and Asteria: Day 19 of My Sacred Month." *Heart Witch* (blog). Patheos. December 9, 2017. https://www.patheos.com/blogs/hearthwitchdownunder/2017/12/nyx-asteria-day-19-sacred-month.html.

Bernabé, Alberto, and Ana Isabel Jiménez San Cristóbal. *Instructions for the Netherworld: The Orphic Gold Tablets*. Translated by Michael Chase. Boston, MA: Brill, 2008.

Betz, Hans Dieter, ed. *The Greek Magical Papyri in Translation*. Chicago, IL: University of Chicago Press, 1986.

Björkland, Heta. "Invocation and Offerings as Structural Elements in the Love Spells in *Papyri Graecae Magicae*." *Journal for Late Antique Religion and Culture* 9 (2015): 29–47.

Blakely, Julia. "Myrtle: The Provenance and Meaning of a Plant." Smithsonian Libraries and Archives: Unbound. June 28, 2018. https://blog.library.si.edu/blog/2018/06/28/myrtle-the-provenance-and-meaning-of-a-plant/.

Blakely, Sandra. *Myth, Ritual, and Metallurgy in Ancient Greece and Recent Africa*. Cambridge, MA: Cambridge University Press, 2006.

Blavatsky, H. P. *A Modern Panarion: A Collection of Fugitive Fragments from the Pen of H. P. Blavatsky*. London: Theosophical Publishing Society, 1895.

Blum, Winfried E. H., Sophie Zechmeister-Boltenstern, and Katharina M. Keiblinger. "Does Soil Contribute to the Human Gut Microbiome?" *Microorganisms* 7, no. 9 (August 23, 2019): 287. https://pubmed.ncbi.nlm.nih.gov/31450753/.

Blumberg, Antonia. "Researchers Uncover Ancient Mask of Pagan God Pan in Northern Israel." Huffington Post. Updated December 6, 2017. https://www.huffpost.com/entry/pan-mask-israel_n_6925070.

Borgeaud, Philippe. *The Cult of Pan in Ancient Greece*. Translated from the French by Kathleen Atlass and James Redfield. Chicago, IL: University of Chicago Press, 1988. One of Jason's favorite books ever, but he didn't use it for this work—Astrea did!

Bowden, Hugh. *Mystery Cults of the Ancient World*. Princeton, NJ: Princeton University Press, 2010.

Brannen, Cyndi. *Entering Hekate's Garden: The Magick, Medicine & Mystery of Plant Spirit Witchcraft*. Newburyport, MA: Weiser Books, 2020.

Broad, William J. *The Oracle: Ancient Delphi and the Science Behind Its Lost Secrets*. London: Penguin Books, 2007.

Budin, Stephanie Lynn. *Artemis*. New York: Routledge, 2016. Budin has long been one of my favorite writers when it comes to classical Greece, and in *Artemis* she knocks it out of the park. Her fearlessness when it comes to contradicting previous orthodoxy brings a smile to my face. Since this book was written for a more general audience, it's also a much easier read than her previous work on Aphrodite.

———. *The Origin of Aphrodite*. Bethesda, MD: CDL Press, 2003. Perhaps *the* tome on the origins of Aphrodite, Budin's book is a masterwork, but also a very difficult read. We didn't cite this book here, but it had a major impact on how Jason views Aphrodite and her origins.

Bulfinch, Thomas. *Bulfinch's Greek and Roman Mythology: The Age of Fable*. Dover edition. Mineola, NY: Dover, 2000.

Burke, Mike D. "Athena: The First Non-Binary." *Mike D. Burke* (blog). Medium. May 18, 2019. https://mikedavidburke.medium.com/athena-the-first-non-binary-8a293cd73e3b.

Burkert, Walter. *Ancient Mystery Cults*. Cambridge, MA: Harvard University Press, 1987.

———. *Greek Religion*. Translated by John Raffan. Cambridge, MA: Harvard University Press, 1985. Originally published in German in 1977. Burkert's opus is in just about every one of Jason's bibliographies.

Burton, Diana. "Worshipping Hades: Myth and Cult in Elis and Triphylia." *Archiv für Religionsgeschichte* 20, no. 1 (March 2018): 211–27. https://www.degruyter.com/document/doi/10.1515/arege-2018-0013/html.

Carrette, Jeremy R. *Foucault and Religion*. New York: Routledge Press, 1999.

Cartwright, Mark. "Magic in Ancient Greece." World History Encyclopedia. Last modified July 26, 2016. https://www.worldhistory.org/article/926/magic-in-ancient-greece/.

Cochrane, Robert, with Evan John Jones. *The Robert Cochrane Letters: An Insight into Modern Traditional Witchcraft.* Edited by Michael Howard. Milverton, Somerset, UK: Capall Bann, 2002.

Collins, Derek. "Theoris of Lemnos and the Criminalization of Magic in Fourth-Century Athens." *The Classical Quarterly* 51, no. 2 (2001): 477–93. https://www.jstor.org/stable/3556523.

Cosmopoulos, Michael B. *Bronze Age Eleusis and the Origins of the Eleusinian Mysteries.* New York: Cambridge University Press, 2015.

Cyrino, Monica. *Aphrodite.* New York: Routledge, 2010. This book is wonderful! Full of so much great information and super easy to read.

D'Este, Sorita. *Circle for Hekate, Volume 1: History & Mythology.* London: Avalonia, 2013.

D'Este, Sorita, and David Rankine. *Hekate: Liminal Rites.* London: Avalonia, 2009.

Deacy, Susan. *Athena.* Volume in Routledge's Gods and Heroes of the Ancient World series. London: Routledge, 2008.

Deacy, Susan, and Alexandra Villing. "Athena Past and Present: An Introduction." In *Athena in the Classical World*, edited by Susan Deacy and Alexandra Villing, 1–25. Boston, MA: Brill, 2007.

Dexter, Miriam Roberts. "The Greco-Roman Medusa and Her Neolithic Roots." In *Materiality and Identity in Pre- and Proto-Historic Europe*, edited by Senica Turcanu and Constantin-Emil Ursu, 463–82. Suceava, Romania: Karl A. Romstorfer, 2018. https://www.academia.edu/39228396/The_Greco_Roman_Medusa_and_her_Neolithic_Roots.

Donovan, Josephine. *After the Fall: The Demeter-Persephone Myth in Wharton, Cather, and Glasgow.* University Park, PA: Pennsylvania State University Press, 1989.

Dowden, Ken. *Zeus.* New York: Routledge, 2006. I was absolutely dreading having to write about Zeus, as most literature doesn't make him out to be the most inviting deity, but Dowden's book had me excited about the king of the gods! For an academic book, this was a joy to read.

Downing, Christine. *The Goddess: Mythological Images of the Feminine.* New York: Crossroad, 1981.

Dunn, Patrick. *The Orphic Hymns: A New Translation for the Occult Practitioner.* Woodbury, MN: Llewellyn, 2018. Dunn's translations are gorgeous, and his introductory notes provide some really insightful information on the Orphic hymns. If you love the Greek gods, you must buy this volume.

Edmonds, Radcliffe G., III. *Drawing Down the Moon: Magic in the Ancient Greco-Roman World.* Princeton, NJ: Princeton University Press, 2019.

Eldridge, Dori. "Divinely Feminine Chypre Perfume Made with Essential Oils." The Blossom Bar. Accessed June 2022. https://www.theblossombar.com/blog/chypre-perfume-essential-oils/.

Evelyn-White, Hugh G., trans. *Hesiod, the Homeric Hymns, and Homerica.* New York: G.P. Putnam's Sons, 1920.

Fantham, Elaine, Helene Peet Folet, Natalie Boymel Kampen, Sarah B. Pomeroy, and H. Alan Shapiro. *Women in the Classical World: Image and Text.* Section 1. New York: Oxford University Press, 1994.

Faraone, Christopher A., and Dirk Obbink, eds. *Magika Hiera: Ancient Greek Magic and Religion.* New York: Oxford University Press, 1991.

Foucault, Michel. *The History of Sexuality, Vol. 2: The Use of Pleasure.* Translated from the French by Robert Hurley. New York: Vintage Books, 1990.

Freeman, Charles. *A.D. 381: Heretics, Pagans, and the Dawn of the Monotheistic State.* Woodstock: NY: Overlook Press, 2009. This book is not cited in the text, but Jason is a big fan of it.

Fry, Stephen. *Mythos: The Greek Myths Retold.* San Francisco, CA: Chronicle Books, 2019. Every few decades, a new retelling of the Greek gods brings them to an entirely new audience.

Fuller, Hailey Marie. "From Daimon to Demon: The Evolution of the Demon from Antiquity to Early Christianity." MA thesis, University of Nevada, Las Vegas, 2013. http://dx.doi.org/10.34917/4478241.

Gager, John G., ed. *Curse Tablets and Binding Spells from the Ancient World.* New York: Oxford University Press, 1992.

Gaiman, Neil. *The Sandman.* Comic book series. 8 issues. New York: DC Comics, 1989–96.

Gardner, Gerald B. *Witchcraft Today.* 1954. Reprint, Lakemont, GA: Copple House Books, 1984. Gardner's books have greatly influenced Modern Witchcraft, but they are not easy reads. If you do want to read one of Gardner's books, this is probably the easiest one.

Garland, Robert. *Daily Life of the Ancient Greeks.* 2nd ed. Indianapolis, IN: Hackett, 2008.

Gately, Iain. *Drink: A Cultural History of Alcohol.* New York: Gotham Books, 2008. This is perhaps my favorite survey of alcohol, and the stuff on Liber/Dionysus is especially terrific.

Giesecke, Annette. *Classical Mythology A to Z: An Encyclopedia of Gods and Goddesses, Heroes and Heroines, Nymphs, Spirits, Monsters, and Places.* New York: Black Dog & Leventhal, 2020. Giesecke's encyclopedia wins the award for longest title in our bibliography, but it's also great! Highly readable and up-to-date, this book should be in your library if you love Greek and Roman myth.

Godwin, Joscelyn. *The Pagan Dream of the Renaissance.* York Beach, ME: Red Wheel/Weiser, 2005.

Graf, Fritz. *Apollo.* New York: Routledge, 2009. This is one of the more difficult reads in Routledge's Gods and Heroes of the Ancient World series, but it's full of great information nonetheless.

———. *Magic in the Ancient World.* Translated by Franklin Philip. Cambridge, MA: Harvard University Press, 1997.

Graves, Robert. *The Greek Myths.* Baltimore, MD: Penguin Books, 1955.

Grayle, Jack. "Hekatean Devotion and Magic in the Hellenic Age." Class lectures at Woolston-Steen Theological Seminary in Index, WA, 2018.

Graziosi, Barbara. *The Gods of Olympus: A History.* New York: Metropolitan Books, 2014.

Grover, Eliott. "The Long and Decorated Literary History of the MILF." InsideHook. May 8, 2020. https://www.insidehook.com/article/arts-entertainment/literary-history-milf-mrs-robinson-stiflers-mom-wife-bath.

Hadjicostis, Menelaos. "More Than a Scent: Cypress Promoting Its Perfume Past." Phys.org. May 12, 2019. https://phys.org/news/2019-05-scent-cyprus-perfume.html.

Hamilton, Edith. *Mythology: Timeless Tales of Gods and Heroes.* New York: Mentor Books, 1940. After Bullfinch, Hamilton's retelling of Greek mythology has had the biggest impact over the last 150 years.

Hansen, Claire. "The World's Oldest Cities." U.S. News & World Report. November 21, 2018. https://www.usnews.com/news/cities/slideshows/10-of-the-oldest-cities-in-the-world.

Harris, J. Rendel. "Athena, Sophia and the Logos." *Bulletin of the John Rylands Library* 7, no. 1 (July 1922): 56–72.

Hellenic Republic, Ministry of Culture and Sports. "The Acropolis Restoration Project." Accessed June 2022. https://www.culture.gov.gr/en/service/SitePages/view.aspx?iID=2580.

Henderson, Raechel. *The Scent of Lemon & Rosemary: Working Domestic Magic with Hestia.* Woodbury, MN: Llewellyn, 2021.

Hesiod. *Theogony & Works and Days.* Translated by M. L. West. Oxford, UK: Oxford University Press, 1988. Reading Hesiod is a pretty easy undertaking. *Theogony* is less than thirty pages long in most translations, and it packs a lot of information into its short size.

———. *Theogony; Works and Days; Shield.* Translation, introduction, and notes by Apostolos N. Athanassakis. 2nd ed. Baltimore, MD: Johns Hopkins University Press, 2004.

Hill, Gregory, and Kerry Thornley. *Principia Discordia; or, How I Found Goddess and What I Did to Her When I Found Her: The Magnum Opiate of Malaclypse the Younger, Wherein Is Explained Absolutely Everything Worth Knowing about Absolutely Anything.* Olympia, WA: Last Word Press and Books, 2015.

History.com. "The Bible." History.com. Updated April 23, 2019. https://www.history.com/topics/religion/bible.

Homer. *The Homeric Hymns.* Translated by Jules Cashford. London: Penguin Books, 2003.

———. *The Iliad of Homer.* Translated by Richard Lattimore. Chicago, IL: University of Chicago Press, 1961. Jason has this particular edition because he found a used copy for five dollars at a college bookstore many years ago. Jason also used the Richard Fagles translation from 1990 in this book (New York: Viking, 1990).

———. *The Odyssey.* Translated by Robert Fagles. New York: Penguin Books, 1996.

Hornthal, Erica. "Dance/Movement Therapy: Using Movement to Heal Mind, Body, and Soul." Dance Informa. Accessed June 2022. https://www.danceinforma.com/2018/03/06/dance-movement-therapy-using-movement-to-heal-mind-body-and-soul/.

Hughes, Bettany. *Venus & Aphrodite: History of a Goddess.* London: Weidenfeld & Nicolson, 2019.

Hutton, Ronald. *The Triumph of the Moon: A History of Modern Pagan Witchcraft.* New York: Oxford University Press, 1999. A second edition of this book with additional material was published in 2019.

Johnston, Sarah Iles. *Restless Dead: Encounters Between the Living and the Dead in Ancient Greece.* Berkeley, CA: University of California, 1999.

Kerényi, Carl. *Dionysos: Archetypal Image of Indestructible Life.* Translated from the German by Ralph Manheim. Princeton, NJ: Princeton University Press, 1976.

———. *Zeus and Hera: Archetypal Image of Father, Husband, and Wife.* Translated by Christopher Holme. Princeton, NJ: Princeton University Press, 1975. Originally published in

German in 1972. You'll notice how Kerényi doesn't list Hera as a mother. I think she'd probably approve of that.

Kirsch, Jonathan. *God Against the Gods: The History of the War Between Monotheism and Polytheism.* New York: Viking Compass, 2004.

Klimova, Blanka, Martin Valis, and Kami Kuca. "Dancing as an Intervention Tool for People with Dementia: A Mini-Review Dancing and Dementia." *Current Alzheimer Research* 14, no. 12 (2017): 1264–69. doi: 10.2174/1567205014666170713161422.

Laing, Gordon J. *Survivals of Roman Religion.* New York: Cooper Square, 1963.

Leadbeater, C. W. *Freemasonry and Its Ancient Mystic Rites.* New York: Gramercy Books, 1998.

LeFae, Phoenix. *Witches, Heretics & Warrior Women.* Woodbury, MN: Llewellyn, 2022. Despite what some people online seem to think, most writers, especially Witchcraft writers, don't make much money on our scribblings, but we do sometimes get access to books before they are released, as was the case with this terrific volume.

Lefkowitz, Mary R. *Women in Greek Myth.* 2nd ed. Baltimore, MD: Johns Hopkins University Press, 2007.

Leland, Charles Godfrey. *Aradia, or the Gospel of the Witches.* Custer, WA: Phoenix, 1996. *Aradia* was originally published in 1899 and has been a Witchcraft classic ever since!

León, Vicki. *The Joy of Sexus: Lust, Love, & Longing in the Ancient World.* Bloomsbury, NJ: Bloomsbury Publishing, 2013.

Long, Charlotte R. *The Twelve Gods of Greece and Rome.* Leiden, Germany: E. J. Brill, 1987.

Luck, Georg, trans. *Arcana Mundi: Magic and the Occult in the Greek and Roman Worlds: A Collection of Ancient Texts.* Translated, annotated, and introduced by Georg Luck. 2nd ed. Baltimore, MD: Johns Hopkins University Press, 2006.

Mackin, Ellie. "Girls Playing Persephone (in Marriage and Death)." *Mnemosyne* 71, no. 2 (2018): 209–28. doi: https://doi.org/10.1163/1568525X-12342276.

Mankey, Jason. *The Horned God of the Witches.* Woodbury, MN: Llewellyn, 2021. In this book Jason writes extensively about Pan in the ancient world, plus Pan's rebirth over the last 200 years. Jason thinks this is the best book ever on the Horned God, but he's a bit biased.

———. *Transformative Witchcraft: The Greater Mysteries.* Woodbury, MN: Llewellyn, 2019. It's pretty cool that I get to edit a bibliography that has me in it as a source!

Matyszak, Philip. *Ancient Magic: A Practitioner's Guide to the Supernatural in Greece and Rome*. New York: Thames & Hudson, 2019.

Miller, Erston V. "The Story of Ethylene." *The Scientific Monthly* 65, no. 4 (October 1947): 335–42. http://www.jstor.org/stable/19231.

Miller, Madeline. *Circe: A Novel*. New York: Little, Brown, 2018. Reading Miller's beautiful prose is about as close as any of us in the English-speaking world will ever get to experiencing Homer. Miller's writing reads like lyric poetry. Captivating. Also be sure to check out Miller's *The Song of Achilles* (published by Ecco in 2012).

Mitchell-Boyask, Robin. *Aeschylus: Eumenides*. New York: Bloomsbury, 2013.

Moon, Irisanya. *Aphrodite: Encountering the Goddess of Love & Beauty & Initiation*. Winchester, UK: Moon Books, 2020.

———. *Pagan Portals—Iris: Goddess of the Rainbow and Messenger of the Gods*. Winchester, UK: Moon Books, 2021.

Mylonas, George E. *Eleusis and the Eleusinian Mysteries*. Princeton, NJ: Princeton University Press, 1961.

National Geographic. "Delphic Oracle's Lips May Have Been Loosened by Gas Vapors." August 13, 2001. https://www.nationalgeographic.com/science/article/greece-delphi-oracle-gas-vapors-science.

O'Connor, George. *The Olympians*. New York: First Second Books, 2010–22. The Olympians is a series of twelve graphic novels ostensibly for young adults, though not much is held back. The art is gorgeous, but most importantly O'Connor modernizes the gods while keeping them recognizable. I was sold the first time Hermes referred to Zeus as "Pops."

Olympic Games. "Tokyo 2020: The Torch." Accessed June 2022. https://olympics.com/en/olympic-games/tokyo-2020/torch-relay.

Otto, Walter F. *Dionysus: Myth and Cult*. Translated with an introduction by Robert B. Palmer. Bloomington, IN: Indiana University Press, 1965. Perhaps the best chapter in Otto's little book on Dionysus is the one dedicated to Ariadne.

Ovid. *Metamorphoses*. Translated by Rolfe Humphries. Bloomington, IN: Indiana University Press, 1955.

Owl, Russ (@russ_owl). "Was thinking that I really need the train to come quickly and then saw that someone has installed a little cardboard shrine to Mercury, god of transit (?) in my subway station," with two photos. Twitter, October 14, 2020, 1:21 p.m. https://twitter.com/russ_owl/status/1316444003315978240.

Park, Arum. "Parthenogenesis in Hesiod's *Theogony*." *Preternature: Critical and Historical Studies on the Preternatural* 3, no. 2 (September 2014): 261–83. https://doi.org/10.5325/preternature.3.2.0261.

Penglase, Charles. *Greek Myths and Mesopotamia: Parallels and Influence in the Homeric Hymns and Hesiod.* New York: Routledge, 1994.

Perry, Laura. "Ariadne Was Just a Girl and Other Urban Legends of Antiquity." WitchesAndPagans.com. January 21, 2015. https://witchesandpagans.com/pagan-paths-blogs/the-minoan-path/ariadne-was-just-a-girl-and-other-urban-legends-of-antiquity.html.

Plato. *Plato in Twelve Volumes: Vol. 12.* Translated by Harold North Fowler. Cambridge, MA: Harvard University Press, 1921.

Plutarch. *Plutarch, Moralia, Volume XII.* Translated by Harold Cherniss and William C. Hembold. Cambridge, MA: Harvard University Press, 1957.

Pomeroy, Sarah B. *Goddesses, Whores, Wives, and Slaves: Women in Classical Antiquity.* New York: Schocken Books, 1995.

Pomeroy, Sarah B., Stanley M. Burstein, Walter Donlan, and Jennifer Tolbert Roberts. *A Brief History of Ancient Greece: Politics, Society, and Culture.* 2nd ed. New York: Oxford University Press, 2009.

Regino of Prüm. "A Warning to Bishops, the Canon Episcopi." In *Witchcraft in Europe: 400–1700*, edited by Alan Charles Kors and Edward Peters, 60–62. 2nd ed. Philadelphia, PA: University of Pennsylvania Press, 2001.

Rinella, Michael A. *Pharmakon: Plato, Drug Culture, and Identity in Ancient Athens.* Lanham, MD: Lexington Books, 2010.

RoadsideAmerica.com. "Parthenon and Statue of Athena." Accessed June 2022. https://www.roadsideamerica.com/story/14603.

Ruck, Carl A. P. *Sacred Mushrooms of the Goddess and the Secrets of Eleusis.* Berkeley, CA: Ronin, 2006.

Sabin, Frances E. *Classical Myths That Live Today.* Chicago, IL: S. Burdett, 1958.

Samorini, Giorgio. "The Oldest Archeological Data Evidencing the Relationship of *Homo sapiens* with Psychoactive Plants: A Worldwide Overview." *Journal of Psychedelic Studies* 3, no. 2 (2019): 63–80. https://doi.org/10.1556/2054.2019.008.

Sappho. *The Poetry of Sappho.* Translated by Jim Powell. New York: Oxford University Press, 2007.

Schweller, Randall L. *Maxwell's Demon and the Golden Apple: Global Discord in the New Millennium.* Baltimore, MD: Johns Hopkins University Press, 2014.

Seltman, Charles Theodore. *The Twelve Olympians.* Apollo edition. New York: Thomas Y. Crowell, 1962. This is an old book, and much scholarship has been accomplished since its publication. Because of its age, we avoided citing it when its contents appeared to be in conflict with other sources.

Seznec, Jean. *The Survival of the Pagan Gods: The Mythological Tradition and Its Place in Renaissance Humanism and Art.* Princeton, NJ: Princeton University Press, 1981.

Shakespeare, William. *The Yale Shakespeare: The Complete Works.* Edited by Wilbur L. Cross and Tucker Brooke. New York: Barnes & Noble Books, 1993. This is an insanely oversized volume and is over a foot tall and weighs several pounds. It is not light reading.

Shaw, Beth. "When Trauma Gets Stuck in the Body: How Do We Heal?" Psychology Today. October 23, 2019. https://www.psychologytoday.com/us/blog/in-the-body/201910/when-trauma-gets-stuck-in-the-body.

Shearer, Ann. *Athene: Image and Energy.* London: Arkana, 1996.

Smith, William, ed. *Dictionary of Greek and Roman Biography and Mythology, Volumes I–III.* Boston, MA: Little, Brown, 1867.

Steiner, Rudolf. *The Goddess: From Natura to the Divine Sophia.* Translated by Christian von Arnim. East Sussex, UK: Sophia Books, 2001.

Stratton, Kimberley B., ed., with Dayna S. Kalleres. *Daughters of Hecate: Women and Magic in the Ancient World.* New York: Oxford University Press, 2014.

Stratton-Kent, Jake. *Geosophia: The Argo of Magic.* Vol. 2 of *Encyclopedia Goetia.* London: Scarlet Imprint, 2010.

Taunton, Gwendolyn. *The Path of Shadows: Chthonic Gods, Oneiromancy, and Necromancy in Ancient Greece.* Auckland, New Zealand: Manticore Press, 2018.

Theoi Project. "Hera." Accessed June 2022. https://www.theoi.com/Olympios/Hera.html. This website is an absolute treasure trove of information when it comes to the Greek gods.

Time Magazine. "Art: Blood and Roses." September 15, 1947. http://content.time.com/time/subscriber/article/0,33009,793831,00.html.

Trzaskoma, Stephen M., R. Scott Smith, and Stephen Brunet, trans. and eds. *Anthology of Classical Myth: Primary Sources in Translation.* Indianapolis, IN: Hackett, 2004.

Tzorakis, George. *Knossos: A New Guide to the Palace of Knossos*. Athens, Greece: Hesperos Editions, 2008.

Vernant, Jean-Pierre. *Myth and Thought Among the Greeks*. London: Zone Books, 2006.

Weigle, Marta. *Spiders & Spinsters: Women and Mythology*. Albuquerque, NM: University of New Mexico Press, 1982.

West, M. L. *Indo-European Poetry and Myth*. Oxford, UK: Oxford University Press, 2008. Not an easy read, but worth a thorough study if you are interested in the gods of the Indo-Europeans and their descendants.

Whitmarsh, Tim, trans. "Read Sappho's 'New' Poem." The Guardian. January 30, 2014. https://www.theguardian.com/books/2014/jan/30/read-sappho-new-unknown -poem-papyrus-classical.

Winters, Riley. "The Descent of Ariadne: Minoan Queen of the Dead to Mistress of the Labyrinth?" Ancient Origins. Updated January 9, 2018. https://www.ancient-origins .net/myths-legends-europe/descent-ariadne-minoan-queen-dead-mistress-labyrinth -009407.

Wroe, Ann. *Orpheus: The Song of Life*. New York: Overlook Press, 2011.

Yeomans, Sarah. "Borrowing from the Neighbors: Pagan Imagery in Christian Art." Biblical Archaeology Society. February 2, 2020. https://www.biblicalarchaeology.org /daily/ancient-cultures/ancient-near-eastern-world/borrowing-from-the-neighbors/.

Index

Z

To Write to the Authors

If you wish to contact the author or would like more information about this book, please write to the author in care of Llewellyn Worldwide Ltd. and we will forward your request. Both the author and publisher appreciate hearing from you and learning of your enjoyment of this book and how it has helped you. Llewellyn Worldwide Ltd. cannot guarantee that every letter written to the author can be answered, but all will be forwarded. Please write to:

Jason Mankey and Astrea Taylor
℅ Llewellyn Worldwide
2143 Wooddale Drive
Woodbury, MN 55125-2989

Please enclose a self-addressed stamped envelope for reply,
or $1.00 to cover costs. If outside the U.S.A., enclose
an international postal reply coupon.

Many of Llewellyn's authors have websites with additional information and resources.

For more information, please visit our website at http://www.llewellyn.com